McCoy Mem. Baptist Church
134 St. Clair Avenue
Elkhart, IN. 46516
Ph: (219) 294-1131

W9-CEQ-700

Hannah's Daughters

Bette M. Ross

Fleming H. Revell Company
Old Tappan, New Jersey

Library of Congress Cataloging in Publication Data

Ross, Bette M.
    Hannah's daughters

    I. Title.
PS3568.O842H3   1986   813'.54   85-14642
ISBN 0-8007-1452-0

Contents

Genealogy

FLOURINOT HARMONIE m. MARIE THERESE in Le Havre, France, in 1727
  They had two children, GENEVIEVE (GENNIE) and PHILLIPPE—
  FLOURINOT and the son, PHILLIPPE, d. 1743

The widow, MARIE THERESE HARMONIE, m. HENRI ZELLAIRE in German-
  town, Pa., 1745
The daughter, GENNIE HARMONIE, m. GOODMAN AMOS, also in Germantown,
  in 1745
  They had a son, BENJAMIN, b. and d. 1747
  GOODMAN AMOS d. 1747

GENNIE HARMONIE m. THOMAS ROEBUCK, 1748, in a homestead in the
  Northwest Territory
  And they had four children: WILLIAM, ROSALIND, MARGUERITE, MARIE
  THERESE
The son, WILLIAM, m. FAITH, of Boston, and returned to the Territory
  And their six children were: HANNAH and HARMON, twins; PHILIPPE;
  MATTHEW; THOMAS; and JOEY
The son HARMON ROEBUCK m. ISABELLA MARIA LISA Y HENRY, 1804, in Saint
  Louis
The daughter, HANNAH ROEBUCK, m. TECUMSEH, 1811, in Fort Detroit
  They had a son, DANIEL
  TECUMSEH d. 1813
HANNAH m. MICAH MACGOWAN, 1816, in Cincinnati
  They had two children, ALISSA and MOLLY

LA DEMOISELLE, last great war chief of the Miami, m. a wife
  Their eldest daughter, BLACK HOOF, became hereditary chief of the Miami
BLACK HOOF m. LITTLE TURTLE, war chief of the Shawnee
  Their son, TECUMSEH, m. HANNAH ROEBUCK, 1811
  TECUMSEH d. 1813

BY Bette M. Ross:
Song of Deborah
Gennie: The Huguenot Woman
The Thirteenth Disciple
Our Special Child
Journey of No Return
Hannah's Daughters

Part I

Alissa

1

They made a beautiful couple at the rail of the brig *New Horizons,* his arm around her, her head tilted against his. The young woman's hair was thick and honey colored, her eyes blue gray. Her traveling dress was a heavy, smooth linen, sensibly dark blue to conceal soil, offset by a silvery gray silk waist with ruffles at the throat that embraced her tanned face like a topaz set in platinum. Her fiancé's complexion had deepened to the ruddy color of nutmegs. Despite a spring heat wave, he wore the conservative black wool trousers and topcoat favored by most American lawyers in 1845. The absence of a beaver top hat was his only concession to the weather and the boisterous winds. His fingers toyed with the new engagement ring on her left hand.

"Happy?"

"I wish it could last forever."

"You do not."

Alissa laughed. "You're right. I don't. When do we get off this reeking ship?"

Stephen burst into a deep, knowing laugh. "When we left Boston you told me you could sail forever!"

"Yes, but not *forever* forever." She twisted to see his face, her glance teasing. "And then, after all, it was a floating department store. I knew we would be trading our lovely goods, but for cattle hides and buckets of grease? Whoosh!" She waved away hordes of imaginary flies and not wholly imaginary odors.

Mexico owned only three trading ships on the Pacific rim yet did not officially approve of foreign traders. Before their ship, or any from the United States and other foreign lands, had been permitted to trade at Alta California ports, they had had to put in at Monterey, the capital of the California department, and pay duties.

The *New Horizons* had been detained at the capital for several weeks. While Stephen chafed to be underway and selling goods, the couple had been entertained aboard a China clipper and a Russian whaler whose captains similarly awaited inspection of their cargoes and the toting of duties.

A week ago they left Monterey, sailing southward toward San Diego. They found the coastline of Alta California a chain of endlessly fascinating scenes, from the cool fog-shrouded forests south of Monterey through long barren stretches of desolate gray sand to the tropical lushness of Santa Barbara. Now, half a day north of San Diego, the passing shore once again provided entertainment.

"Look, Alissa, the top of the bluff! Those stacks of dried hides."

"Is it a game?" Delightedly Alissa watched as two Indians lugged a huge reddish brown object as thin as a plate and eight feet across to the brink of a sandstone bluff and sailed it out on the wind.

"No, not a game. They have no better way to get the hides from the mission down to that ship."

"Then those are our hides."

"No, the ones we'll pick up in San Diego are finish tanned. These will be ready for us next trip."

"For us or someone else."

"Not for anyone else. I intend to have sole rights to those hides before we leave San Diego."

The intensity of his voice surprised her, but she said nothing. After all, that Stephen was ambitious for the future of Roebuck Trading was one of the things that had attracted her from the first time they met, the young lawyer with aspirations to be an important businessman and the daughter of Micah MacGowan and Hannah Roebuck MacGowan.

The sun was nearly overhead, exposing the other ship, the cliffs, the people, in perfect detail. The shouts ashore drifted to them dreamlike, softened by the thrash of waves. Alissa felt Stephen's presence next to her like a magnet. She cast a smoky, sidelong glance at him, admiring the dark hair that curled like a cap around his face and neck, the deep brown eyes, the determined set of his mouth, and wishing they were already married.

Stephen smiled as if he could read her perfectly. He took her hand and drew her arm around his waist. "Wait until you see the rancho, sweetheart. A Mexican wedding is a glorious affair. I promised Ramon—"

"We would be married there," she finished. "Why?"

"Why?"

"We could have just as easily have been married in Boston or Saint Louis. In a church. With both our families in attendance."

"I thought we agreed this would be more romantic," Stephen protested. "And—also—let the Californians know we admire their customs."

"Stephen! You're not serious?"

"Why not? The Bandini-Warners are an important family in California. We'll be living among them, doing business—"

"But isn't this carrying it a little too far? Next you will be telling me that we've had our honeymoon before the wedding."

Stephen's head slunk a little toward his shoulders.

"You didn't! You *did* think that!"

"I promise you, sweetheart, as soon as we are married, after we sell the cargo and get the consignments from Boston—"

"After we sell the cargo!"

"Alissa, we've been over this," Stephen said patiently. "It's good business sense. Why do you think your uncle hired me?"

"Honestly, Stephen, the way your mind works," Alissa sulked.

"Mr. Davis?" A bandy-legged man rolled down the narrow deck toward them. "Begging pardon, sir, the captain says will you want to go ashore here? Padre at San Juan always welcomes company."

Stephen and Alissa stepped apart, exchanging a look.

When the mate received no answer, he added helpfully, "Cap'n says we mought drop anchor off the point...."

More hides? Alissa mouthed, her body convulsing with laughter.

Stephen nodded. "That will not be necessary, bos'n. I'd rather make straight for San Diego."

"I'll tell the cap'n, sir."

Five hours later they reached the bare curve of San Diego bay, the only deep-water port between La Paz and Yerba Buena. Contentedly Alissa leaned once more against Stephen on the deck below the aftermast. She felt his deep sigh. Usually Stephen's mind was running at a fast trot. She loved the quiet times like this, when she could feel his body relax against hers.

Together they watched gulls wheeling on the air currents over the lacy curl of waves. A school of dolphins frolicked offshore, and on a cluster of pocked brown rocks she noticed sea otters cracking together clams as large as plates and placidly eating the meat.

"Stephen?"

"Mm?"

"Why doesn't the captain want to put ashore tonight?"

There was the barest pause before he answered. "We'll be more comfortable on board."

"Isn't your friend coming to meet us?"

"Yes." His arms tightened around her.

"It's Indians. Is it Indians?"

"Ramon would be here with his *vaqueros* if it were."

She gazed toward the scattering of adobe buildings and tule shacks on shore. Several hatted men moved back and forth like tiny doll figures in black trousers and white shirts. Scores of other working men appeared to be nearly naked. "Perhaps Ramon has forgotten."

"I sent a message from Monterey. . . ."

They both felt the ship creak underfoot and glanced automatically toward Baja. Although it was nearing sunset, the air from the south suddenly streamed heat in their faces. "Weather front?" asked Alissa.

"Spoken like a true sailor. It does feel like a shift, doesn't it?"

As Stephen spoke, they heard the captain bawl orders. Moments later a sailor shimmied up a rope ladder to a spar. The mainsails were set and the spanker loosened to catch the wind. Suddenly a rope snapped free, and the spanker billowed out. The ship tilted sharply with the jolt of released wind.

Alissa heard a scream. Eyes drawn to his perch high on the spar, they saw the sailor scrambling to regain his balance.

"He's falling!" Alissa cried. "He can't get his footing!"

The seaman grabbed at the outer tip of the spar. They heard the crack of wood.

"Stephen!" she shouted. "Do something!" A scream echoed in her head. His screams. Hers. Searing pain.

The waves crashed inside her head.

2

Voices nuzzled into her consciousness, a stream of voices. But sense was not to be made. Sensibility of lights and shadows. Coolness. Shade. A creak of wooden wheel, gentle movement. Alissa opened her eyes. She was looking into a dappled canopy of oak trees, moving. Her eyes drifted lower. A horse's ears bobbing. A wide black hat. A handsome masculine face. Again the voices that she could not understand. Pain surging up again. Rich and musical voices, dancing away on a crest of pain that sank her again.

"Drink this, *por favor, senorita.*"

Alissa opened her eyes at the sound of a new voice, a woman's, comforting. She was in a cool, dark place. A square of light shone whitely from one side.

"*Senora?*"

Alissa gathered her fractured senses to focus on the woman leaning over the bed, holding a glass goblet. A patrician face, oval, with magnificent dark gray eyes. The corners of her full mouth curved slightly downward. "Do not be afraid. The doctor is here to set your shoulder and your collarbone. Then you will not hurt so much. Drink this."

Where is Stephen, is he all right? The woman's expression did not change. Alissa took the drink. As she swallowed it she wondered if she had said the words or merely thought them. The powerful drug began to work almost immediately, pulling her into a dizzying void. Somewhere she felt terrible pressure on her body. She struggled and tried to cry out, to beg them to stop....

The next time Alissa awakened she was aware of ravenous hunger. She glanced around. She was in a large white room richly appointed with dark, oiled furniture with burgundy tassled cushions and velvet draperies. A six-foot red and gilt statue held a huge candle like an upright sword. Square windows on adjacent walls let in sunlight through walls that seemed to be three feet thick. Above her head, supported on square, knobbed posts, stretched a tapestry depicting Spanish hunt scenes.

She moved her hands. Only her left responded. She felt her body. Her upper torso seemed to be encased in bandages. She was filled with a sudden fright when she could not find her right arm. Then she discovered its shape bound close to her chest and felt life in that member as it responded to pressure. Experimentally she moved her legs and felt no pain. Encouraged, she lifted her head. Immediately sharp pain knifed through her chest. She gasped and fell back. *Better.* She moved her head. *Good.*

Stephen must be terribly worried about her. "Stephen?" Her voice sounded thin in her ears. She inched slowly out of bed, gasping at the pain in her ribs. The bed was on a dais a foot higher than most beds. She was wearing one of her own nightdresses, a new one meant for her trousseau. She saw no bell to summon anyone. A senseless rush of panic set her trembling. She sagged against the bed. "H-Hello!" she ventured.

A door opened noiselessly. A bright-eyed Mexican woman with a white apron tied around her middle peeked in, gave an exclamation of pleasure, and disappeared again.

Automatically Alissa lifted a shaky hand to smooth her hair.

Voices speaking rapid Spanish grew louder. A woman entered and Alissa recognized her. *"Buenos dias, Dona Alissa."* Her name sounded like *Ayeesa* in the soft Spanish syllables. The full, drooping lips lifted in a warm smile. "I am Dona Arcadia Bandini-Warner."

"You speak English."

"My husband is an American."

"Please, where is Stephen? Would you tell him I would like to see him?"

Dona Arcadia engaged her eyes with warm sympathy. "Stephen is not here," she said gently.

"But then what am I doing here? Where is he? He's not hurt, is he?"

The lady lifted a narrow white hand as if to put aside the question. "He is not hurt. I have sent Concepcion for a dressing gown. Then you must eat something."

"But—"

"Then we will talk."

A nameless fear hovered at the edge of her consciousness. He would not go off and leave her! Concepcion brought a brocaded satin dressing gown and helped Alissa put her left arm in the sleeve and gently buttoned the frog closures over her injured body. Even such slight movement brought pain knifing through her chest.

A string of words tripped from Concepcion's tongue. Her mistress laughed. "She says she has never seen hair the color of *melcocha.*" Arcadia's hands made lifting motions. "That is candy. Pulled candy made from molasses."

"Taffy. . . ."

"Yes. She also wants to tell you that you are very beautiful and that she will be happy to brush your hair and help you with your toilet." She glanced at a tray of cooling food beside the bed. "Are you fond of chocolate, Alissa? Yes? *Bueno.* Some fruit and bread and hot chocolate will be better for you than this, I think." A few more words to Concepcion and her hostess glided regally from the room.

Alissa watched her retreat with something like panic. *Come now, Alissa,* she ordered herself. *You are letting your imagination run away with you. If Stephen isn't here, he has a perfectly good reason. He always does.* But the fear, the awareness of how vulnerable she was, did not leave.

Concepcion left the room briefly, returning with a fresh tray. She spoke to Alissa in a soft, respectful voice. When she did not respond, the servant took her hand and led her to a chair next to the writing table. The tantalizing fragrance of hot chocolate reminded her of her hunger, and she reached for the cup as Concepcion nodded encouragement and picked up a hairbrush.

An hour later she followed Concepcion out of the room into a riot of colors and bird calls. A tiled outside corridor led to a large, arching doorway with a huge mustard-yellow dog sprawled across the entrance. Double oak doors were thrown wide to admit the somnolent warmth of late afternoon. As they reached the threshold, the dog obligingly rose and stretched and padded out of the way.

Dona Arcadia came forward to greet her. A comforting hand under her elbow led her to a large carved love seat plumped with cushions. A man with sandy hair streaked with gray, with a big, grizzled face and the hard, muscled form of a man who has worked hard for a lifetime, crossed polished floor tiles and thick, fringed rugs.

"I am Don Juan Julian Warner," he boomed in a deep voice. "This is my son," Juan Julian beckoned to a young man close on his heels, "Ramon Antonio."

The younger man was about Alissa's age, twenty, moustached, with the pallid skin and black hair of his Castilian mother. The olive black eyes watched her with a curious, guarded expression.

"Please call me Ramon," he said in careful English. "We do not speak English often, only when we have the good fortune to have guests."

Alissa gripped the arm of the bench. When would they tell her where Stephen was? "I appreciate your hospitality," she began formally. "I am sorry to be a burden upon you. As soon as I am able, that is, as soon as Stephen comes. . . ."

Swiftly Arcadia sat beside her. Mindful of the bandages, she embraced her in a gentle caress. *"Por dios,* my dear child. Do not think of leaving us. Do you not remember what Stephen told you before he left? You were delirious for two days, perhaps you do not remember."

Alissa shook her head.

"He had to go back to his ship" said Juan Julian. "No sense bringing cargo all the way from Boston and letting some bounder get in ahead of you. The best prices go to the first with the goods, don't you know."

He went without me. Without marrying me. He left me alone. How could he?

Seeing her desolate expression, the family seemed at a loss for words.

As if from a distance, Alissa realized the vast separation between them. These strangers, foreign language speaking, with foreign customs, Roman Catholics; and because their son and her betrothed had once struck up a friendship, they were trying to draw her in by a family bridge across the void she was now feeling.

"He did not want to leave you, but you were still too ill to travel," Arcadia said. "We asked Stephen to leave you here with us while you mended. I hope you will not be too unhappy."

With her fingers Alissa sought comfort in the shape of her betrothal ring.

Arcadia followed the gesture. "I hope we may still celebrate your wedding at the rancho, when Stephen returns. Our daughter, Mariana, will be wed next month."

Alissa nodded. She rubbed her temple. "What happened to us? I remember—all I remember is someone pushing me. And shouting. A lot of shouting."

Juan Julian said, "A mate lost his footing in the rigging. The captain said just at that time a *santa ana* seized the ship and tipped it sharply about. The unfortunate man grabbed a spar, but it did not bear his weight. He fell on you like a seaman's duffle. Lucky you were not killed."

"Is the man all right?"

"Fared better than you," declared Juan Julian. "Well enough to sail when the *New Horizons* left."

They sailed off without her. Even the thought hurt.

"We brought you here in a *carreta,* a cart," said Ramon.

"I think I remember your face," said Alissa.

Ramon smiled. "I rode beside you the whole time. You were looking up at me."

Alissa leaned back and closed her eyes. She felt as weak as a babe. She heard Ramon's voice: "He shouldn't have—," and then his mother's, cutting in smoothly: "We prayed for you daily and lit candles in the chapel."

Juan Julian spoke in low tones to his wife. She said, "I will take you back to your room now, *Donita* Alissa." Alissa nodded gratefully.

As Alissa lay back on the pillows, she surprised a stare of intense speculation on Dona Arcadia's face. "What is it?"

"Ramon was so happy to see Stephen again. The two became as close as brothers on your *amante's* last trip to California. We were so happy to receive the letter from Monterey telling us of your coming marriage. . . ."

"Please go on, Dona Arcadia, I am not too tired to talk."

Arcadia smiled and stroked her hair. "It is nothing that cannot wait. We will do all we can to help you recover. Our house is yours."

She left, and Alissa was alone again. Alone. She ached to feel Stephen's arms around her. She felt tears coming. She had not cried since she was a child. She began to pray and felt the familiar comfort of her Lord making her problems his own. Without realizing it she drifted into sleep.

3

"*Buenos dias, Alissa.*"

Alissa jumped. She had been sitting lost in thought under a white flowering oleander that had been trained into a small tree. "Oh. Good morning, Ramon. *Buenos dias.*" Stiffly she made room on the rough-hewn bench, tucking her voluminous skirts down with her left hand.

Her trunks had been brought from the ship, and she had managed with Concepcion's help to don her steel corset, her crinoline petticoat, then the corded calico, and her white embroidered muslin petticoat. Over this her dark blue skirt, consisting of a full ten yards of fabric, was secured at her slim waist. From the waist up, Alissa had to be content with a makeshift shawl of white dimity over her bandages, tucked in the band of her skirt, and atop this a soft plaid shawl of English wool, in shades of blue, gray, and raspberry. Concepcion's nimble fingers had dressed her hair madonna fashion, drawing it into a large chignon at the back of her neck. It was held in place by a blue net resembling fisherman knots, and she wore the pearl earrings Stephen had given her at their betrothal.

Ramon's eyes swept her with appreciation. "You look very beautiful this morning." He propped a boot toe on the opposite end of the bench and leaned his arms negligently over his knee. The tight black broadcloth trousers flared out from the knee into a bell shape at the top of his boots. A row of silver conchos decorated the last six inches below the knee.

"It is good to see you out here in the patio." Under the carefully groomed moustache, his mouth seemed set in a permanently benign expression. His quick gaze held hers for a moment, then wandered idly around the walled garden. Three sides of the patio led to rooms of the house. A tiled walk, roofed with rounded red tiles, enabled people to pass from one door to another, protected from the elements. Glistening fronds of a pepper tree drooped lazily against the fourth wall, completing the privacy of the enclosure. His glance returned to her.

"It is pretty here, *no?* My grandfather wanted this garden to be like the one in the home he left in Seville. Even to the goldfish pond."

"Pretty, yes. When did he come to Mexico?"

"As a very young man. Later he became an officer in the army of Mexico, in the revolution. When Mexico won her independence, my grandfather was given a grant of land here in Alta California." He laughed. "Most Mexicans of culture never come up here to California. It is too far from civilization."

"But you were born here."

"Yes. Then after my grandfather died, my mother inherited the rancho."

"I thought your father—"

"Oh, no. He is a naturalized citizen. He sailed before the mast in his uncle's whaler, then became a supercargo for Boston traders, just like Stephen."

Alissa smiled. "Juan Julian is an unusual name for an American."

"Do you like it?" Ramon seemed pleased when she nodded. "He chose it himself. To marry mother he adopted our Catholic faith. When he was baptized, he also changed his name because it was easier to do business that way."

Alissa laughed, a trace of rue in her voice. "That also sounds like Stephen."

"Yes." He added flippantly, "But that is the kind of man you like, no? One who is all business."

She stared at him.

"*Lo siento mucho.* Sorry," he mumbled.

Alissa cast about for a way to change the subject. A breeze stirred the spiky leaves of the oleander and rippled through Ramon's full white shirt. Suddenly she remembered something. "Who is Santa Ana?"

"Presidente Santa Anna?"

"Oh certainly not him! The one who was on the ship when the accident happened."

"Oh *that* santa ana. That is a wind, a hot, dry wind that comes without warning from the desert. When the hills are dry, the old women pray that the santa anas will not come."

"Why is that?"

"They bring fire." He paused. His air of good-natured banter dissipated, and he seemed to be weighing something in his mind. At last he said, "I was so happy to see Stephen again. I said to myself, *He is a* Californio *in his soul.* But maybe not so much, with the business, eh?"

His eyes watched hers with a wary expression that Alissa found disquieting. What was the matter? Was there something more about Stephen that no one had told her?

Finally, as if he had reached a decision, Ramon slid gracefully beside her and took her hand. "Alissa, you may tell me that I have no right to question you. Stephen is not here, so it is my right to act as your next of kin, your—elder brother."

Mystified, she was still aware of his discomfort. He was, after all, as young as she. "Very well."

"It is our custom to care for any woman who is without the protection of her own men."

"Stephen told me."

"And so I must ask you," Ramon's tone was a mixture of challenge and defensiveness. "Who is Daniel?"

Alissa withdrew her hand and stared at him. Suddenly she understood why he, and Dona Arcadia, too, had sometimes seemed restrained toward her. "Did I talk about Daniel when I was ill?"

"You did," he said with careful dignity.

Their eyes locked in a challenging duel. Anger bloomed in her breast. How dare he?

They both looked up as Concepcion came down the bricked path toward them. Her black skirts and petticoats created a billowy sway as she walked, an elegance that belied her bare feet.

She spoke with Ramon with an ease that showed liking and trust. If he was impatient with the interruption, he did not allow his servant to feel it. Courteously he translated for Alissa. "Padre Zalvidea has come to visit. Do you feel well enough to join us?"

"I shall be delighted," she said with equal formality. Ramon helped her to her feet.

By the time they reached the hall, Ramon was once again the lively host in his father's absence. "I would bet my best horse that the padre made the trip just to talk to you. He has a great hunger for news beyond our borders."

As Ramon had guessed, the friar had traveled the ten leagues from San Juan Capistrano Mission to the Warner rancho primarily to meet Alissa. He was a tall, ascetic figure in a black, cowled robe, with a tonsure of gray hair. His fingers were extraordinarily long and slender. His first question startled her. Having no command of English, his questions were filtered through Ramon. "Did you bring any books with you?"

"Why, no. What sort of books?" Alissa was thinking books might be an item of trade for future voyages.

Zalvidea laughed with a surprising resonance from one so spare. "Any books, my child. Latin, French, Spanish—when I was in the colegio at Zacateca we were required to do great quantities of reading, no chore for one who loves books. Ramon, here, cares nothing for books."

Ramon translated and added with a laugh, "I care about the rancho. I can tell you to a bushel how many *arrobas* of wheat we will produce this year. And how much wine and how many thousands of hides. Our records may not rival yours, padre, but we know our land."

Alissa's ears pricked up when Zalvidea mentioned that the mission books recorded not only all the produce of their vast holdings, but also births, baptisms, and deaths of all the Indians who had lived at his mission since its founding.

"May I visit your mission when I am able to ride again?"

The friar allowed a smile of pleasure when Ramon interpreted. He asked Ramon a question, adding a few more words that caused a seep of color on her young host's face.

Alissa thought better of asking what the padre had said.

Dinner that night became a celebration in honor of Alissa's first night up. Mariana, Ramon's spirited younger sister, was home from her visit to the rancho of her husband to be. Talk of her wedding plans flew about the dinner table, interjected with remarks hopeful of a future wedding for Alissa and Stephen.

Finally Ramon cut it off, "*Basta!* Enough. What is the sense of making plans without the groom?"

Juan Julian, at the head of the table, lifted his brows thoughtfully. Then he said, "My son is right. We have filled our good friar's ears with enough weddings for one night."

Dona Arcadia translated the gist of conversation to Alissa, but after the servants had cleared the table of all but the crystal decanters and glassware, stories flowed like good drink, with much hearty laughter, so rapidly that Alissa found her smile fixed with increasing strain as she tried to connect the unfamiliar customs with her own background. The afternoon and evening with Padre Zalvidea and the Bandini-Warner family had drained her more than she realized. Thoughts of Stephen engulfed her like a physical ache. The stiff corset encasing her body prevented her from taking a deep breath. Her right shoulder throbbed persistently. She surprised Ramon's glance resting on her.

Her discomfort communicated itself to him, and he was up and at her side almost within the same breath.

She took his arm for the short stroll to her room. "Why have you not married, Ramon? Mariana must be at least two years younger than you."

"I have never met anyone I chose to marry."

She smiled in the balmy, orange-scented night. "You will." They stopped at her door. He offered her another dram of the drug she had taken while ill, but she declined, certain that sleep would be no problem.

"You are still very pale. Alissa . . . ," Ramon took her hand. "I asked you something this afternoon, in the patio. I will sleep better tonight myself if you will answer me."

"I will answer you because I know that you love Stephen as a brother, not because you have any right to question me," she said. "You asked me who Daniel is. Daniel is my brother. My half brother. He left home when he was fourteen. He might be in California. I promised my mother I would look for him without ceasing."

"Your brother!" Joy leaped into his voice. "Oh, that is good. Good. I thought that you and Stephen had quarreled about this Daniel, and that is why he left y—" All at once he smashed a fist against the doorjamb. "I am sorry! I am a donkey!"

"You were going to say he left me."

"No. . . ."

"Yes. He left me. And if it had been you, you would not have left an injured woman, if you loved her." She could not keep the tears out of her voice.

Ramon tried to take her in his arms.

"Oh, no," she said. "I could not bear it."

He stepped back. "We will do all we can to help you find your brother." He raised her hand to his lips. "I will send Concepcion to help you now, eh?" He kept her hand in his until she pulled away.

"Yes. Thank you."

Once in bed, she fell into an exhausted sleep. She was back in Saint Louis. Something was wrong. She heard her mother crying. She was crying for Alissa and Stephen. No. No. Stephen hadn't even come to work for Uncle Harmon yet, for Roebuck Trading Company. Mother was crying because Daniel was gone. Alissa's eyes snapped open.

She lay in the huge bed, her eyes dark, not seeing the tapestry overhead, reflecting the images that still filled her mind. Twelve years ago. She had been only eight years old, but she remembered her brother. Daniel had been fourteen the summer he left. He was as tall as a man, strong enough to catch her when she jumped out of the top branches of the cherry tree. She thought he was the handsomest brother anybody ever had, with coarse black hair and piercing, pewter gray eyes.

"I am the son of Tecumseh!" she remembered him shouting at their father one indelible Sunday afternoon after church. "I am not your *boy* any longer." Alissa had crowded in a corner of the verandah, hoping her father wouldn't see her and order her to find some chores to do.

The spare frame of Micah MacGowan grew rigid with anger. He still wore his preaching suit, as Daniel and Alissa called it. His red hair had thinned and faded with the years, but his temper had become more acerbic.

MacGowan's voice gentled with the weariness of repeating an argument that had gone on as long as Alissa could remember. "You are my son. I reared you, and I love you."

"I love you, too," was Daniel's usual grudging reply. Today he said, "I'm leaving anyway, Pa." Alissa's childish stomach did a flip-flop at her brother's bold words.

MacGowan lowered himself to the top step. He stared out over the farm where Alissa had been born. "Who was it today, Son? A lad at school? Some ignorant fool in town calling you a half-breed?"

Daniel sat on the steps next to him. "That doesn't bother me anymore, Pa. I just—I just," he pounded his knee silently with a rangy, coiled fist, "I just got to go. My father's people—*my people*—call me by a different name. They say I belong to them."

"Where will you go?" The words came out tight. Alissa knew somehow that her brother's words were hurting her father about as much as a body could bear.

"There is a trader heading out to Mexico, who wants a guide."

"You've never been that far west. How can you guide someone else?"

"You know me, Pa." For the first time that afternoon an edge of affection crept into Daniel's voice. "I never been lost in my life. And he wants me because I speak a heap of dialects, and some Spanish, thanks to Aunt Isabella. . . . There's Shawnee living down that way, too, I hear."

Micah nodded. "So that's it. You don't know whether to be an Indian or a white, do you, Son?"

"I guess not. But I love God, Pa. You taught me that."

Micah dropped an arm across his son's shoulders. "What are you going to tell your mother when she gets back?" The head shot up swiftly. "You weren't thinking of going without—"

"I wouldn't do that, Pa."

As Alissa had watched from her corner, her father had hugged Daniel and said a blessing. Daniel left the next morning, and none of them had seen him since.

Twelve years ago. Daniel was six years older than she. Daniel was twenty-six this year. She still loved her brother. What would he look like, as a man? Did he have a wife and children, grandchildren for Hannah and Micah? Had he gone back to the Shawnee way? Alissa moved her left hand under the quilt, until it rested over her heart, and began to pray for Daniel. Tomorrow. Tomorrow she would begin to look for her brother.

4

Ramon had been out with his vaqueros all morning. At midday he came striding through the patio, hot and sweaty, wavy black hair plastered to his forehead, and found Alissa feeling slightly sorry for herself because in the weeks since her injury she had heard not a word from Stephen.

Ramon's sudden appearance flustered her. "How large is your farm?" she asked when he apologized for his appearance. He had been out since dawn rounding up a few more horses.

"Rancho."

"Rancho."

"It is easier to show you than to tell you. Can you ride a horse?"

Alissa was taken aback. The bandages were off, her steel corset offered all the support needed for her cracked ribs, and it was true that she was feeling more comfortable each day. "I'd laugh, but it hurts when I do. . . . I can ride, but perhaps I should wait."

"No," said Ramon.

"No?"

"Three weeks is plenty of time for cracked ribs to mend. You will not injure yourself. I have a very gentle animal. He will carry you like a feather on the wind, at no more than a walk."

"A very gentle animal you just caught?"

This time Ramon chuckled. "Your spirit is mending nicely, Dona Alissa. No, this one we have had since yesterday."

"Might we ride to the mission?" she asked suddenly.

"Of course!" Ramon's voice rang with pleasure. "Tomorrow. We will have a *merienda,* a picnic! We will make a day of it." He stared at her full skirt. "That will never do. Ask my mother to find you a riding dress."

When Ramon said *picnic,* Alissa had no idea how much was involved. The rest of the day servants moved in a flurry under the direction of Dona Arcadia, Concepcion, and their Indian cook, whom they called, for reasons Alissa could not fathom, Ben Gee. Food baskets were set out to be packed, blankets rolled, and vaqueros sent off to nearby haciendas to invite the neighbors.

That afternoon, drawn by the exotic aromas filling the air, Alissa wandered toward the kitchen behind the house to watch the preparations. Ben Gee was a small, dark man of indeterminate age whom Warner had hired away from the mission kitchens with Zalvidea's resigned blessing. Mission cooks were highly prized, since they were the only Indians with any skill at all in preparing Mexican delicacies. Ben Gee ran the Bandini-Warners' main kitchen and a smaller one for servants and vaqueros with a combination of efficiency and temper.

When Alissa reached the kitchen, servants were busy making mountains of tamales by filling tender green corn husks with layers of corn meal and meat sauce, occasionally stopping to stir iron pots of spicy beef chili. Their hands moving too fast for Alissa to follow, two others shaped and slapped tortillas on a hot, dry griddle, turning them with quick fingers and piling them with soft slapping sounds in a tule basket. Her mouth fairly watered.

"You like?" said Ben Gee, pointing at the tamales and tortillas.

"Oh, yes!" she said, and then grinned as she realized she was talking extra loud, as if a loud voice would make English words more understandable to him.

Within seconds Ben Gee had scooped hot beef into the center of a soft tortilla and handed it to her.

The delectable aroma filled her with hunger. She folded the hot tortilla around the meat and bit into it. "Mm. Good," she mumbled with her mouth full. She was curious about Ben Gee. "Have you lived here long? Live long time here?"

He nodded. "I speak good English. I cook for Don Juan Julian when he still John Warner."

"Ben Gee, did you ever know a young man who was called Daniel? He is half Indian. Shawnee."

"Not many Shawnee in Mexico. Apache, yes. Yumas." In an aside he issued a direction to the women making the tamales.

She shook her head. "Half Shawnee, half American. My brother."

"Your brother, so," he nodded. "I remember only one Shawnee, long time, four-five year. Not called Daniel."

"Tell me about him," she urged. What if she should actually find Daniel? "What did he look like? What color were his eyes?"

Ben Gee shrugged an apology. "Who remembers eyes? Not have corn-husk hair like you, *es verdad.* Che-Muc-Tah is Shawnee, that is all. Big man. Good man." He peered up at her. "Got to get food cooked now. You like *merienda.* Good food. Yum-yum."

She had to laugh at the childish American expression on his lips. At that moment Mariana rounded the corner of the cookhouse, laden with a pile of neatly folded black and white clothing.

Mariana paused. She glanced briefly at the cook then back at Alissa. *"Venga usted, por favor.* Come with me, please."

Ben Gee's eyes followed the retreating figures of Mariana and the American *dona.* His gaze softened with the never-forgotten memory of his single meeting with the Shawnee, Che-Muc-Tah.

"You must take back your lands," Che-Muc-Tah had urged.

"You do not understand, Che-Muc-Tah," Ben Gee had said patiently. "We will never fight to conquer land. I will fight to revenge myself on my enemy, but not to take land. Land does not belong to me."

"Since the time of the Coyote you traveled freely and lived any place you desired."

"I do not remember."

"It was true, once. Now you work for this man who says he owns your land. Your sisters and brothers living at the mission must work for a priest until they die. They do this because he tells them God wills it. Do you believe that?"

"You speak with the tongue of a Coyote yourself," Ben Gee complimented him, at the same time evading the question. But Ben Gee had done nothing, and one day he heard that Che-Muc-Tah had left the valley and was seen no more.

Ben Gee sniffed his stew appreciatively, picked up his ladle and plunged it once more into the cauldron of hot beef.

Alissa followed Ramon's sister back to her own room. Mariana barged in ahead and turned to greet her with a pleased expression. *"Aqui. Para usted."* The meaning was clear as Mariana thrust the bundle of clothing at her.

"For me? For the ride?" A smile broke over Alissa's face. "You're so much smaller than I."

Mariana said a few more words, and Alissa slipped off her clothing and allowed Mariana to help her into the unfamiliar costume. It consisted of a white waist, then a short jacket that did not meet at the front, similar to a man's jacket. The skirt was full, of a heavy, durable black broadcloth, but split in the middle. Alissa exclaimed in dismay as she became entangled in the unwanted seam as she tried to pull it over her head. Mariana giggled and showed her how to step into it. The practicality of a split skirt for riding was immediately apparent. Alissa felt like a wanton in the outrageous outfit, but Mariana's giggles were infectious, and soon she was laughing, too.

The next morning, as was customary, Alissa took her morning coffee, bread, and fruit in her bedroom. Eagerly she made her toilette and put on her new riding costume. When she emerged from her room, Ramon was waiting in the patio.

"Good morning!" His good-humored face looked puckish in anticipation of fun.

"Good morning. Are the others here?"

"*Si.* In a moment." Ramon stared at her feet with pursed lips. "You cannot possibly ride all day in those silly things," he decided.

Alissa knew her soft kid boots were not sturdy enough for riding, but Mariana, with her tiny foot, had been unable to help her out here. "They'll be all right," she started to say.

"Let me see what we have." Ramon pretended to search among the oleander bushes and fished out a beautifully finished pair of black boots. "Aha! Sit down, please."

"Ramon, they are beautiful!" He knelt before her and removed her shoes. She pulled on the boots. He helped her to her feet, and she took a few steps. The heel was rather high and the toe quite pointed. "They feel wonderfully comfortable, Ramon. How did you find a pair to fit my big feet?"

"My secret, *nina,*" beamed Ramon. He took a last survey of her. He reached forward and tilted the brim of her black hat slightly. "*Asi,* perfect." Alissa caught a scent of sandalwood. Their eyes met for an instant; then they heard horses being brought up outside the patio gate, and Alissa glanced away. He stepped back and offered his arm.

The first "short" ride was four hours. Alissa could barely conceal her relief when Juan Julian raised his hand for a halt. It was apparently a favorite picnicking spot, for everyone immediately dismounted and began climbing a path through dry, golden rye grass, toward the top of a rise. Servants followed carrying the heavy picnic baskets and blankets for sitting under the oaks dotting the knoll.

"Our rancho covers eight leagues of land," said Ramon as they strolled near the knoll after eating.

"We are not still on your land, are we?" She was nearly as tall as he. In her black costume and soft boots, surely the most comfortable she had ever worn, she felt completely at ease.

"Yes."

"Then all the cattle herds we've passed, the sheep and the horses. . . . "

"About thirty thousand animals belong to the rancho."

"What do you do with them all?"

"Do with them?" Ramon made a comic face, watching her. "Make boots for pretty senoritas who sail in on big ships."

Alissa burst out laughing. Ramon's eyes gleamed with the success of his entertainment.

Later, when the ride was underway once more, Juan Julian loped up beside her, as agile as any native, his big face relaxed and jovial. "Good afternoon, Alissa. Enjoying yourself?"

"Oh, yes, sir."

"Nothing like it in Boston, is there?"

She shook her head, leaning forward to pat the horse's shining withers. "May I ask you a question, Don Julian?"

"Of course."

"Where do you find so many horses all just alike? Do you breed them for color?"

Juan Julian threw his head back and laughed, and Alissa feared she had asked a childish question.

"No need to breed them. Most of us capture and train our own."

"Are there that many wild horses in California?"

"Thousands. As many as the grains of sand. As many as the sea gulls." He spoke with the fervor of a man in love with his land. He glanced easily at her. "It is a matter of pride with us to cull from the horses we capture a pure color *caponera.*"

"A—"

"*Caponera.* It is a band of horses. Twenty-five identical horses. The most prized color is black. Every ranchero has a black caponera. These we train much more than the horses the vaqueros use. We keep them as mounts for family and friends."

"Ramon says you round up hundreds each year. Why do you need so many?"

Juan Julian shrugged. "They die."

"Oh, no! How—"

Ramon jogged up on his father's other side. "Pardon me, Alissa. This is where we leave you, Father."

Juan Julian nodded. "Bring the padre with you, Ramon. *Vaya con dios,* you two."

"We will bring him," Ramon promised. "We will see you this evening." He and Alissa pulled out of the party as Juan Julian and the rest veered off toward a small ranch owned by the Bandini family, where they would pass the night before returning inland.

As soon as they were alone, Ramon turned serious. "Mariana tells me you were talking with Ben Gee."

"Yes. I thought he might have heard something about a young Shawnee—"

"Ben Gee sometimes says strange things."

"Like what, Ramon?"

Ramon chewed on the inside of his cheek, causing his trim moustache to wiggle.

"Is it something bad? You would not have him on the rancho if it were bad."

"I think he gets confused sometimes. Ben Gee was brought up at a mission up north. He had run away and was hiding on a wharf trying to steal food when my father found him. He brought him south on his ship and gave him to Padre Zalvidea. Now, once in a while, Ben Gee swears Padre Zalvidea sets bear traps in his orange orchard to catch Indians who rob his fruit."

"But that's terrible! Could it be true?"

"You have met him. Do you think it is true?"

"No," she admitted. "Might he be confusing it with the mission where he grew up?"

Ramon frowned. "Yes," he said reluctantly. "Yes, it could be true. Such things do happen in the north."

5

Alissa and Ramon rode on in companionable silence. As the afternoon waned, a fresh breeze sprang up off the ocean. Soon the Pacific was visible, a bright, shining band of blue appearing and disappearing between the hills. Alissa spied a white, gleaming dome looming on the horizon, taller than anything she had seen since leaving Boston. The sun was in her eyes, making it appear that part of the dome was gone. She cupped her hand to the brim of her hat.

"Unbelievable, isn't it?" said Ramon. "My mother remembers when it was whole."

"Am I seeing aright? Part of a dome? It is so huge! What is it?"

"It was the original church of San Juan Capistrano Mission. The mission Indians built it. It took them twelve years. Six years later there was a mighty earthquake, and the church collapsed. That was in 1812, before my time."

"But then where is Mariana to be married?"

"Oh, Mariana is not being married here. In the hills near our rancho is a smaller chapel, an *asistencia*. It has no permanent padre anymore, but it is very beautiful. Padre Zalvidea will discharge his holy duties there."

As they wound around a ravine they came unexpectedly upon the padre himself, his sandaled feet planted far apart, the ample sleeves of his black robe tied back. Under a wide-brimmed straw hat, he was tackling the rich humus with a shovel. Nearby lay several twiglike trees with bound roots. As soon as he spied the riders he stopped work.

"Buenos dias, Padre," Ramon said.

"Welcome, Ramon Antonio," said Zalvidea eagerly. "You are looking well, Dona Alissa. This life must agree with you. Have you completely recovered?"

Ramon translated, and she said, "Yes, nearly, thank you, Padre."

The men spoke in rapid Spanish a few minutes. Alissa caught the words *Bandini rancheria* and saw Zalvidea's face light up. Ramon must be telling him about the invitation to dine at the Bandini's.

Ramon courteously reverted to his dual role of translator and her host. He asked Zalvidea, "What are you doing out this far from the mission?"

"Planting peach trees so that the broncos will have some fruit."

Ramon added for Alissa, "Broncos are Indians who used to live at the mission but have run away. Since they were once baptized, Padre Zalvidea is responsible for their souls." He grasped the shovel and helped the padre finish planting his saplings.

When it was done, they started for the mission, Ramon leading the two horses as they walked.

Zalvidea turned to Alissa. "Ramon says you wish to look at the records of Indians who have lived here."

She paused for Ramon to translate, then nodded. "Especially the Shawnee nation."

"Shawnee? I do not remember any Shawnee. Is there one particular soul you are seeking?"

"Yes. His name is Daniel."

Zalvidea stopped and gave her a look of surprise. "Daniel?"

"That is his Christian name."

"Baptized then?"

"Yes, by my father. My father is a Protestant pastor. Daniel is my half brother. Our family thinks he might have crossed the wilderness to California. His father was killed when Daniel was just a baby. Then his mother married my father."

Zalvidea scrutinized her so closely that she had to hold her breath to keep from bursting into a giggle. "Is your mother Shawnee also?" the padre said kindly.

"No," she laughed.

They were entering a grove of stiff manzanita bushes, and Zalvidea pulled his robes close to keep from getting snagged. He forged ahead for several strides, his head down, using his digging shovel as a staff. He stopped and peered back at her. "I have heard of a Shawnee outlaw up north around Sacramento. He hates the missions. He leads the broncos in raids against our brethren. He says it is wrong, what we have done, when all that we have done is to bring the word of God to his heathen brothers. Satan has given him much power for evil." Zalvidea crossed himself.

Alissa shook her head firmly. "That could not be Daniel. Daniel is a Christian. We lived on the frontier of the United States, Padre. My father welcomed any man of God, whether he was Catholic or Protestant or a Hebrew. Daniel would not hate any mission dedicated to God." After the barest pause she added, "What is this Indian's name?"

"Che-Muc-Tah."

"Che-Muc-Tah!"

Suddenly a young Indian rushed out of the bushes before the padre. He was stocky and broad of face, with darker skin than the Shawnee and a shock of black hair. He was wearing only a loincloth.

The youth began shouting at Zalvidea, brandishing a wooden lance. Ramon grasped her arm, thrusting the horses' reins in her hands and pulling her behind him all in one motion. He sprang up beside the padre. Now the youth seemed to be pleading with Zalvidea. Ignoring the lance, Zalvidea raised his shovel and brought it down on the head of the Indian. The Indian shrieked and dropped the lance. He covered his head with both hands. Howling, he ran off like a whipped dog.

Alissa stared after him in shock.

"They are like children!" Padre Zalvidea's mouth pursed in displeasure. He would not say another word, but stolidly continued the hike toward the mission.

Ramon and Alissa exchanged glances and followed the old man like chastened children themselves. Alissa noticed fields of green, ripening wheat. Soon they passed women tending rows of vigorously healthy vegetables. By the time they reached the mission the padre was behaving as if nothing had happened. Inside the walled square, women were weaving cloth, grinding acorns, content as far as she could see. Alissa was completely mystified.

One young woman she noticed, pretty and shy, about the age of her own sister, Molly, got gracefully to her feet. Her skin was lighter than most of the others, her features more European. Her cotton tunic ended just above the ankles. With an air of expectation the girl tracked their progress across the broad open square of packed earth. Alissa caught her eye and smiled. The girl smiled shyly back. Children ran to and fro, playing, little breechcloths flapping over their bare buttocks as they ran. Very few of the workers were men.

Ramon took her elbow. "Ten years ago, the padre had a thousand men of the Luisenos in his flock."

Alissa was amazed. "How did he feed them all?"

Ramon gestured at the working women. "You've seen the fields. There are also apple orchards, peaches, oranges, figs. The Indians do it all. In those days, the mission brand was on ten thousand head of cattle. Every year they killed a quarter of those for the tallow and hides."

"Stephen told me there was a lot of money to be made."

"Your Stephen would know," Ramon said cryptically. "It is not as much now as in past years."

"It's like a separate kingdom," said Alissa, "the missions owning all this."

"The church."

"The church?"

"The Roman Catholic Church," Ramon said patiently. "They sent the padres in to Christianize the Indians, civilize them in their Spanish ways. When they had been baptized and educated, the Indians were to inherit their property as full citizens."

"Then it belongs to them now."

"Do not be ridiculous, Alissa," Ramon scoffed. "Of course it doesn't. How can you imagine these wretches capable of managing all this?"

"Then who—?"

"Our government."

Alissa was confused. She dimly remembered that Spain had ceded California to Mexico some twenty years ago. But Ramon obviously did not want more questions. If the Indians—the Luisenos in this part of the country—were promised their inheritance of land, why had it been denied them? Strange. If Daniel had ever been to this country, what must he have thought?

The young girl she had noticed earlier approached toward them. Now she appeared to Alissa to be more frightened than shy, with difficulty gathering enough courage to speak to the priest. She put an arm out in an entreating gesture.

Zalvidea halted abruptly. Alissa watched his face. The begging tone in the girl's voice was unmistakable. The priest's face remained firm. His words grew sharp with chastisement. The girl straightened. Her expression changed from entreating to rebellious. Zalvidea dismissed her shortly.

Ramon looked discomfited. She caught his eye, and he shook his head slightly.

Afterward Zalvidea again behaved as if nothing had happened. He took Alissa and Ramon into the room where his records were kept, a pitifully meager enclosure more like a prison cell than anything else she could imagine, with typically thick walls, only one window, and a door adjoining a similar room. These constituted Zalvidea's living quarters. Even today, a hot day, the room was chilly and damp.

Zalvidea left them to their search. As Ramon hoisted from a shelf the first of two huge, heavy volumes covered in scarred black cowhide, Alissa stopped him. "Wait."

"What is it?"

"Ramon, I know I am a stranger here and your customs are different, but what is going on? Are these poor people slaves?"

"Of course they are not slaves!"

"Then why does he treat them so badly? I think it's terrible. How can you just stand there and not do anything?"

"Are you talking about the girl and her lover?"

"Her lover!"

"The Indian in the grove. He ran away last month. Now the girl wants to go, too," Ramon said offhandedly.

"Well, why can't she?"

Instead of answering, Ramon said, "Padre Zalvidea is willing to marry them if they go on living at the mission, where he can take care of them."

He began to turn the thick parchment pages.

"What will happen to him, the young man?" she persisted.

"He has joined those living in the mountains." He glanced at her troubled face. "Look, Alissa, everything is fine as long as the Indians stay where they belong, at the mission. The ones living in the mountains do not live by our rules. They take whatever they want and camp where they please. They have developed an unpleasant taste for horseflesh. . . ."

"You mean they *eat* horses?"

"*Con mucho gusto.* Now, do you want to see these books after we have come all this way, or don't you?"

"Yes, but I still don't think it's right. They are people, too!"

"And you are a foreigner," Ramon said pointedly.

By the look on Ramon's face, he was becoming exasperated with her. Very well. She would let it go for now. But she wouldn't forget.

She bent her head to look at the open ledger. In columns of spidery writing in Spanish was a careful accounting by year of all the planting and harvesting at the mission, all the births and deaths, baptisms and weddings, and numbers and tribes of the Indian flock. None of the Indians registered in the last dozen years had been of the Shawnee nation.

An hour later Ramon closed the final ledger. She cast a discouraged look at him. He covered her hand with his. "I am sorry, Alissa. And I am sorry I spoke sharply to you. It is just that you do not yet understand everything." He cocked his ear.

"What is it?" she asked.

"Horsemen." They walked into the bright sunshine as a dozen men galloped across the square, raising dust in the faces of the children and working women, bearing down on Ramon and Alissa. Not until they were scant feet away did they rein in their horses.

They were as unkempt and evil looking a group of men as Alissa had ever seen. Some carried rifles jammed into saddle holsters. The looks they threw her way frightened her, and she stepped behind Ramon.

"*Cholos,*" Ramon said under his breath. "Do not show fear."

Without dismounting or displaying any of the civility Alissa had come to associate with Californians, their spokesman rattled off a series of demands at Ramon. She picked up the name *Zalvidea*.

Before Ramon could answer, the padre came out of the door of his living quarters. He slipped his hands in the sleeves of his robe and faced them with his mouth set in a hard line.

A torrent of words met him, delivered with insolence by one of the horsemen and followed by a piece of paper thrown on the ground before him. It was Ramon who picked it up.

The padre said something, and Ramon began reading. It was a short list. "They want fifty horses, ten cows, twenty *arrobas* of wheat, and half of the vegetables and fruit stored at the mission," he informed Alissa in an aside.

Robbers! Alissa glanced at Zalvidea, waiting for him to chastise them in the name of Christ, as he had done the Indian boy.

Zalvidea made a little futile gesture. Obviously the *cholos* were not asking, they were taking, and not for the first time. The *commandante* barked orders. Men wheeled their horses off in all directions. One soldier stopped by the black horses of Ramon and Alissa. Ramon strode over and spoke sharply to him, at the same time stripping his whip from the slipknot at the saddle. The soldier backed off, palms up, his eyes on the whip.

Half an hour later they were gone, a faint thundering sound and dust clouds rising from the disappearing herd of animals.

Zalvidea gazed at them bleakly. "Our Lord places much need for patience on our hearts," he said. He glanced at Alissa, speaking to Ramon.

"He said to tell you not to look so stricken. Nothing stays the same. In this way our Lord teaches forebearance. The same thing is happening at all the missions. They are expected to support not only themselves but to provide horses, wheat, and beef to local officials of the government."

"But those men did not look like government soldiers."

Ramon said scornfully, "They are convicts. They were emptied out of Mexican prisons in Jalisco and brought north by the new governor to be his bodyguard. They are not paid. They have been told to live off the countryside. They know that a mission is undefended."

"It is a loan," said Zalvidea. "But nothing is ever repaid."

The anger Alissa felt earlier at Zalvidea's treatment of the Indian youth and the girl vanished in the face of this immense outrage. She could not help feeling compassion for him. Living alone, unprotected save for a few soldiers assigned to the mission, who neither read nor wrote, without the priestly comfort of other brothers in the faith, expected to recruit, administer, teach, train, feed, clothe, and oversee hundreds of Indians year after year, persuading them to work to support themselves and the church, the priest's chosen work seemed impossible. Could this truly be what Christ wanted?

As they left the mission, accompanied by Zalvidea, the mood of gaiety with which they had begun the day had grown infected by a cloud of evil. Even Ramon's face reflected it.

"When we landed at San Diego," Alissa said, "Stephen said we would not put ashore until the next morning. I thought he was afraid of an Indian raid."

Ramon shook his head. "He has met the *cholos* before. They robbed him and nearly killed him one night in Santa Barbara. My father and I and several of our friends were in Santa Barbara for a celebration. We were able to stop it."

"He never—"

"Then I should not have mentioned it. Forgive me. Padre," turning back to the man riding behind them, " I think we must organize some protection for you. It is useless to appeal to Governor Micheltorena."

"The last time the *cholos* came, they stole three of my girls, and still he did nothing. For myself I do not fear," said Zalvidea. "For my children, I do. They must be protected."

"When we reach the Bandini rancho, we must talk to the others."

"If you think it will help, my son."

"If we do not stop them now, it will not be long until they try a raid on one of the ranchos."

Alissa listened to the patient, anxious tones of the padre. Who would believe this man had a few short hours ago beaten an Indian over the head with a shovel—and then later stood up brave and defenseless against a gang of ruffians? And what of the Shawnee, Che-Muc-Tah? Had the padre called him evil out of anger or in truth? The Indian Ben Gee did not think he was—

"Alissa! You're letting your horse wander!"

"Sorry, Ramon." Diligently she spurred the horse and caught up with the men.

6

Dona Mariana Warner rode perched in front of her father on a huge jet stallion in the traditional wedding procession. Her black dress gleamed in the golden morning, symbolically representing the sorrow she felt at leaving her father's house. The skirt billowed over the pommel and down both sides of the horse, below which her ankle-length kid boots peeped like doll shoes. A matching lace *mantilla* framed her radiant face with mystery.

Following Mariana and Don Juan Julian rode Dona Arcadia, resplendent in black satin, long coils of pearls about her neck. Ramon rode at her side, also in black, a slim replica of his father—narrow hipped in black trousers, with a broad-shouldered, waist-length jacket bordered with silver and black braid, ruffled white shirt, and a low-crowned, broad hat.

Ramon glanced back at Alissa with a reassuring smile. His second glance lingered appreciatively on her new gown. The bodice exposed the curve of creamy shoulders and the swell of bosom. Alissa wore the black silk because it had the only skirt full enough to properly accommodate a sidesaddle. She recalled the days in Saint Louis when she was being fitted for her trousseau and had envisioned wearing this gown at an elegant ball in some equally elegant ballroom. Now here she was, wearing her silk ball gown on a horseback ride through wild countryside, on her way to a wedding!

If only Stephen had made it back before the celebration! She did not know if he were even receiving the letters she wrote to Yerba Buena via the traders.

They had been up since dawn, preparing for the bridal ride to the *asistencia* chapel two leagues from the rancho. The horses, all as black as the heart of Satan, had been exercised, washed, and curried to perfection to carry the procession. The leathers and beaten silver decorating the saddles gleamed with oil and polish. Dozens of vaqueros ranged out on either side of the family procession, several of them strumming guitars as they rode. The clear air reverberated with their ballads, sung in slightly nasal voices that seemed as carefree as the birds themselves.

How strange the customs of this religion of Ramon's family, Alissa pondered as she entered the little chapel with the other guests. It was beautiful in a primitive way. Thick adobe walls, whitewashed outside, inside were colorfully painted. Even the ceiling bore Aztec-like geometric designs of green, pink, turquoise, and white. Oils of dark, Spanish men with long, sallow faces and medieval costumes hung over the wall murals.

Used to the simple eloquence of her father's Protestantism, the wedding ritual seemed to her like a bizarre ceremony in a strange, ancient tongue. Zalvidea wore a foreign costume completely at odds with his customary homespun robe. She could see fold lines on the outer robe, suggesting that the costume spent most of its time laid safely away in some huge chest. The layered robes of heavy silk brocade were faced with cream-colored satin. Broad bands of gold braid formed a gigantic cross over the front of the gown. Heavy gold chains encrusted with jewels from shoulder to shoulder, enough to weigh down a slighter man, flashed in the light of a hundred candles.

Even Zalvidea's voice was changed. She listened to the singsong chants roll off his tongue. Now Felipe and Mariana knelt before him on a plain uncushioned altar bench, responding in the same tongue. At one point he put something in their mouths.

Then there were more chants. Around her, the Bandini-Warner family were making the sign of the cross on their breasts, alternately standing, sitting, or kneeling. Alissa remained seated firmly on the backless bench, marveling that the worship of her God had grown in so many different directions. How did it ever take this form? Did Mariana and Felipe's families ever feel free to utter a simple prayer to Jesus? She was relieved to file out once more into the sunlight.

The jubilant wedding party, its retinue swelled by Padre Zalvidea and his attendants, headed back to the rancho.

Alissa saw the smoke and smelled the delicious aroma of roasting meat even before they climbed the final arroyo to reach the rancho.

On a level field a short distance from the main house, whole sides of beef sizzled over six barbecue pits. With Ben Gee supervising, Indian women moved about, basting the beef with bunches of flayed reeds dipped in pottery crocks of sauce. Iron cauldrons redolent with odors of chilies and tomatoes simmered nearby.

In minutes the air was ringing with fast Mexican tunes that set toes to tapping. As the horses were herded away, the musicians, two violinists and a guitarist, launched into a *jarabe,* a traditional dance for the bride and groom.

Forgotten were the piety and solemnity of the wedding vows as Mariana and her new *esposa,* Felipe Novoa, took their places in the ring of onlookers and musicians. Mariana slipped her castanets on her fingers. She glanced coyly at her husband. With a riffle of the castanets, they began to circle each other with slow, insistent steps. Minutes later, the music slyly changed tempo into a joyous and earthy *fandago.* With loud shouts, other couples from ancients to children leaped into the dance.

"Would you like to try it?" asked Ramon.

"No," Alissa laughed.

"You do not mean that." Ramon seized both her hands and pulled her toward the whirling couples.

"Yes, I do," she protested. "I will be happy to dance with you when Stephen is here."

Don Juan Julian overheard the exchange and came to her side. "Ramon! Behave yourself!" he said in a low voice.

"No wonder Stephen stays away," he muttered.

Juan Julian apologized and led her to a seat among the chaperones. Alissa could not help smiling at Ramon. He was behaving like a spoiled child who sulks when he does not get his way. He had no lack of partners, she noticed, as skillful and able as he. Dona Arcadia whirled by, Alissa gaping in admiration, trying to picture her own mother dancing with the grace and wholehearted enjoyment of Dona Arcadia.

These Californians! What stamina and exuberance! The women she knew back east would consider such skills and athletic grace unfeminine. It was *most* becoming, Alissa decided, even to the fine sheen of moisture glistening on the hot, laughing faces.

At midafternoon the dancing stopped as a stream of Indian servants passed back and forth between the cookhouse and an enormous trencher table set up near the barbecue. Ramon appeared at her side again and bowed smartly. "May I escort you to the love feast?"

"The *love feast!* Honestly!"

His round face broke into a lighthearted grin as she rose and took his arm.

Platters of barbecued beef, tamales, a small, flat cheese called "asadera," tortillas, frijoles, and a meat stew containing tripe, sweetbreads, chilies, garbanzos, and tomatoes in a spicy sauce filled the length of the table. In a seemingly endless parade, empty platters were whisked away and replaced. When there were no more guests to serve, vaqueros and servants helped themselves to the abundant food, carrying it off to eat in a shaded spot.

When they finished, Ramon and Alissa climbed the browning hillside, with several other young people, to the shade of a sprawling aliso tree. Propped against the bole of the tree, Alissa listened drowsily to their dulcet Spanish tones.

The dark, tousled head of a sleeping child was cradled in her lap. She sighed contentedly and glanced around. A multitude of sleeping children were scattered among the resting adults. Alissa had no idea whether the laps little heads occupied were those of parents or sisters or even family members. How wonderful that the children were made to feel at home on any accommodating lap.

She watched a young man with slight build and pock-marked face plod up the hill and drop at Ramon's other side. Ramon nodded amiably by way of greeting.

With scarcely a look at Alissa, the young man said in a low tone, "Ramon, amigo, I need a loan." Ramon's friends assumed she did not understand and so were free about speaking to him of personal matters.

"How much do you need?"

Alissa thought she heard the mumbled reply, *"One hundred reals."* She watched Ramon's face. His lips pursed in a soundless whistle.

"So much! Not gambling again, are you?"

The young man's head dropped. "My father will whip me if he finds out this time."

"It is no good for you," agreed Ramon. "With you it is a disease, eh?"

The youth's eyes were those of a trapped rabbit. "I won't do it again. Will you lend me the money?"

"Ah, *nino,* of course I will, but you have to stop this. You pray about it. You go see the padre, you tell him you need special prayers to help you stop, eh?"

"Yes, Ramon. I will. I promise." The youth's face became wreathed with smiles. As he climbed down the slope, Alissa fancied his gait was far freer than when he had come.

Ramon glanced at Alissa. "You understood, didn't you? I was watching you."

"Yes," she answered in his tongue. "I understand well, but I am not so good speaking."

He smiled encouragingly. "You do fine. You are very quick. It is good. . . . It's a lot of money, no?"

Alissa was surprised that he asked her. "I thought it must be."

Ramon nodded. "Now I have to figure out how to get it for him."

"You mean you don't have it?"

"I told you it was a lot of money."

"Then why did you tell him—"

"He is a friend. I can get it more easily than he."

Ramon clambered to his feet and stretched. He threw off his vest and sash and opened the full white shirt at the throat. He glanced at Alissa, then at his friends, with a look of mischief in his eye. "I think," he said, "it is time for a *coleo.*"

The cry was taken up by half a dozen young men. Two or three young women as well sprang to their feet and headed for the hacienda.

"What is that?" Alissa asked.

"Wait and see," he grinned. He leaned down and touched her cheek, then called to several vaqueros and headed in the direction of the corrals. Alissa touched her cheek in the same spot. What a complex young man he was, warm and funny and unpredictable. She eased out from under the sleeping child and went in search of Dona Arcadia, hoping to discover what was going on.

"A sport of the young," laughed Dona Arcadia when Alissa found her. Just then Juan Julian loped by, his legs encased in hide leggings with the fur left on. Arcadia spoke sharply to him in Spanish.

Juan Julian drew himself up and retorted in kind.

"Ninos, they are all *ninos,"* Arcadia sighed. "Come. We will watch from the alisos. My husband will not be outshone by his son."

The women and children stood in the shade or climbed into the generous lower branches of the huge aliso trees. Where shortly before they had been dancing, a double line of a hundred vaqueros on horseback created a chute twenty-five feet across and two hundred feet long. At the far end Alissa heard shouts and screeches.

"Hi-hi-hi, *andale!"*

A wild steer came thundering down the line. Hot on its hooves raced three horsemen. The center man leaned out of the saddle, dangerously close to the flying hooves of the wild steer. He reached for its tail. A shout then a groan rose from the spectators as he seized it but could not hold it. In a twinkling another vaquero moved into the center.

Arcadia clutched her arm. "That is Ramon!"

Ramon seized the tail, and a split second later the beast upended and sprawled in the dust. An appreciative roar rose from the crowd. The three horsemen swept through the chute, leaving the steer to stagger to its feet. A rope dropped over its head, and it was led away.

"He is too reckless!" cried Arcadia.

"He is acting like a peacock in a mating dance," said an elderly lady nearby.

Ramon streaked on through the hot tule grass and wheeled in a wide circle up the knoll. In front of the three women he leaped off, breathless, his eyes crackling with excitement.

"Since my good friend Stephen is not here, I will have to be content with congratulations from his lady."

He pulled Alissa into his arms. A lusty kiss was deposited on her lips.

She struggled and pushed him away. "How dare you? How could you have so little regard for Stephen, if not for my own honor!"

"I add my anger, Ramon," said Arcadia. "You dishonor our name. Alissa is a daughter of the family, under our protection until her young man comes back. You will apologize at once."

Ramon laughed. "Yes, Mother." He swept an exaggerated bow before Alissa. "I shall die a penitent coyote if you do not forgive me!"

"I forgive you." As he bent over her hand she added in a voice meant for his ear alone, "Can't you just be my friend?"

"Thank you," he nodded crisply. Then he whispered back in a parody of her voice, "I am trying not to, but I am falling in love with you. Now shall we kiss and make up?" He glanced up at her face. "No, eh? Not yet? Then look, I stand here with you, and we will watch the next team." He threw her another sly look. "I have just earned the one hundred reals my rash young friend needs. Betting has its good side, eh?" He laughed.

Another team appeared at the far end, the small one looking like—"Isn't it Mariana?" Alissa gasped.

"Yes. Mariana has tailed the bull since she was fifteen." Mariana had exchanged her bridal dress for a riding habit.

"And that is her husband and my foolish old one with her," added Dona Arcadia.

Another steer was turned loose in the corridor. It seemed to hesitate. Then, gathering its wits, it exploded in a frenzied run down the human chute. Recklessly the three horsemen tore after it. A shout went up. One minute Alissa was clutching her throat in fear for Mariana, the next she was seized with the wild, reckless joy that infected her companions, pounding on Ramon, yelling, and imitating the cries of the vaqueros.

She did it! On her wedding day! Oh, the glorious, reckless girl! Tearing after a bull, actually making the dangerous *coleo* herself! Alissa was so proud of her she could not stop shouting, even after Felipe, Mariana, and Juan Julian were out of danger and the bull had righted itself, bellowing at the outrage.

Stephen was forgotten. It was his loss that he was not at her side, and she refused to pine any longer.

7

In the three weeks since leaving Alissa with Ramon and his family some hundred leagues south, Stephen had been very busy. Anchoring the *New Horizons* off various coastal settlements, he was welcomed ashore with the same eagerness he felt. The freshness of the wind excited him, the newness of life in his adopted land.

He felt uncomfortable thinking about Alissa, lying injured and enduring a painful recovery. (Praise the Lord, she would recover fully!) But what could he have done had he stayed? Reasonably, nothing! Meanwhile, all about him, others were plying his trade, making the important connections, winning allies and friends.

He thought about this as he rode out one day to the rancho of Don Luis Vignes, two leagues distant from Santa Barbara, to deliver some cuttings ordered from Boston. For the past ten years Vignes had invested his time and money in planting wine-grape cuttings imported from France.

The air was hot. Despite the lack of humidity Stephen was perspiring. He loosened the starched stock. Stephen had not yet been able to bring himself to wear California style clothing, but he had to admit that the tight, Boston-tailored business suit was not comfortable worn on a horse or under a hot sun.

He located the vintner, energetic, compact, and graying, between rows of a vast vineyard planted in sandy loam of rolling tableland, so absorbed in his labor that he did not notice Stephen until he called out.

"Si, senor?" Vignes answered, straightening and squinting up at him. Deep furrows from years of working in sun and wind creased Vignes's eyes and coursed his cheeks.

The young man dismounted carefully, not born to the saddle, Vignes decided. They shook hands. Davis had a firm, dry grip and appraising eyes. Vignes was inclined to like him, reserving judgment until he revealed more of himself.

"Stephen A. Davis, Senor Vignes. I am the supercargo on a Boston trader, the *New Horizons*. I have brought you a new batch of cuttings." He indicated the second horse, halter tied to his saddle.

Vignes nodded. "That is very kind of you, Senor Davis. You could have left them at the warehouse and sent word."

Stephen flashed a grin that lit up his dark eyes. "In truth, I wanted to see your vineyard for myself. I was in port the day the French trader brought your cuttings to Boston. I am an *aficionado* of good wine."

Vignes smiled. "It is really a very small operation," he said modestly. "Would you like to see it?"

"Very much indeed!"

The smile broadened. "Many people love good wine. Not everyone would be interested in the care that must go into producing it. Come. You must be thirsty, no. First we will sample some wines which are not too bad, and then I will show you around."

Vignes led the way to a large building made of rounded fieldstones mortared together. Inside it was as cool as an eastern springhouse.

Stephen gazed around, enthralled. A fragrance distilled of aged wood casks and fruity aromas held him spellbound. "Someday I would like to try to raise grapes." He glanced at his host. "But that is years away. First I want to build up our trading company."

"You are ambitious," Vignes approved. "Are you married, Don Stephen?"

Don Stephen. The affectionate form of address among friends and acquaintances. He basked in the warmth of the casual address. "Not yet, sir." Briefly he told Vignes about Alissa.

It wasn't until the following morning that Stephen left the hospitality of the vintner, laden with goodwill, bottles of wine to speed Alissa's recovery and for Vignes's good friends the Bandini-Warners, and a promise to consider allowing him to make an exclusive market in Vignes's wines.

Stephen was a modest enough man to realize that it had not been the strength of his own personality that had prompted such generosity. No . . . , it was something in the spirit of the old man himself. Something he had also recognized in Ramon and his family. It occurred to him that Don Luis Vignes had ceased his labors when Davis arrived, a stranger, and devoted the next twenty-four hours to him. For Don Luis, evidently, time and money did not mean the same thing. Well. He would have to think about that. Later. For the moment his thoughts raced eagerly ahead to Santa Barbara and the reloading of his ship for the next port.

Entering Santa Barbara from the northeast, Stephen appreciated anew the beauty of the settlement. Nestled in a shallow crescent along the coast, it received enough fog to green everything that grew and enough sunshine to bathe the flowers in color. *Alissa would like this place,* he decided. He wondered if enough Americans could ever be persuaded to come to this isolated port to make it a real town.

Like a cloud on the Elysian landscape, Stephen recalled an ugly incident last year on his first trip to the Pacific. A lone trader, he had gotten lost a league or two inland and suddenly found himself surrounded by ragged, surly beasts who called themselves soldiers. A party of Californians from the south happened along the road, sparing him from being robbed of his goods or worse. His Spanish was poor then, but he had understood that the ruffians were men of the governor's private army.

His saviors, the Bandini-Warner clan, forty strong, enroute to Santa Barbara to attend a ball, had taken him under their wing. It was in this manner he became acquainted with the famed hospitality of the rancheros and came to know Ramon. He wondered if by this time Alissa had grown to respect the Bandini-Warners as much as he.

As he drew nearer to Santa Barbara, Davis noticed a lone traveler, approaching the village on the northward trail, one that led, he believed, all the way to the ports of Monterey and Yerba Buena. The traveler was obviously a gentleman, well tailored and at home on his horse. He considered waiting for him. It might be pleasant to have dinner at the local inn with a fellow traveler. But Stephen felt the pressure of time on his thrifty nature and denied himself the privilege. After all, he chided himself, there was enough daylight left to visit the padre at Santa Barbara mission and discuss the next shipment of hides. He could dine anytime. And in the morning he wanted to make an early start for San Diego. The thought of holding Alissa in his arms quickened his pulse and his pace. *Business before pleasure,* he had to remind himself.

"Good morning! May I share your table?"

Stephen rose to his feet, dabbing at his lips with the linen napkin. The speaker was a handsome man with sharply defined features, who appeared to be in his mid-thirties, with reddish gold hair curling in on each temple. From the forest green frock coat and gold satin vest to the skintight riding breeches, the man looked like a fashion plate.

"Certainly, sir." Stephen waved his hand at the facing seat of the small table in the dining room of the inn. After introductions Stephen remarked, "Didn't I see you riding in just before sunset yesterday?"

"Yes! I though you might be the gentleman ahead of me. Don Luis Vignes lives out in those hills. Were you visiting him, possibly?"

"Indeed I was! You know Don Luis?" Happy to meet a fellow American, Stephen was less reserved than usual. At the end of an ample and leisurely breakfast he felt comfortably established with his new friend.

"You know, I've been admiring the cut of your clothes," said Lansford Hastings. "Who is your tailor, if I might inquire?"

"Thank you! I'm afraid he is back in Boston."

"Where you are from, by your accent."

"Originally. Now I work for a trading company in Saint Louis, Missouri.

Supercargo." Stephen launched into a wholehearted tale of his involvement with Roebuck Trading and Alissa's unfortunate accident. "But now I intend," he concluded, "to establish a branch of my company in California."

"Indeed!"

Stephen brushed off the implied compliment. "But you, Hastings. You are not much older than I, yet the things you've done! You've served in the military, been a scout, a wagon leader, a friend of important people back in America—do you know the American consul here in California? I've yet to meet him."

"Thomas Larkin? I know of him, of course. As a matter of fact, I shall be meeting with him myself next week. Our government is quite concerned over—well—" Hastings smiled. "Nothing to interest you."

Stephen leaned forward in rapt attention.

Hastings glanced around the dining room and lowered his voice. "Our government is most eager to persuade large numbers of Americans to emigrate to California as quickly as possible. I have a modest part in that effort. Currently I am writing a book that will serve as a guide for future overland parties."

"Why overland? Why not by sea? Roebuck Trading could add passenger lines—"

"You are that large, are you?" Hastings said quickly. "Hm. Not practical here, though, Davis, these people are not clustered along the Atlantic shore; they live inland many hundreds or a thousand miles. Their wealth is not in money ... not much money.... By and large they are bringing their households and herds. When they get here, they are going to be hungry for land.

"Our Mexican friends have no idea what they are sitting on." He leaned forward. "Now is the time to get in on the ground floor. You as a trader understand how important it is to be ahead of the times."

Stephen nodded emphatically.

Hastings snapped his fingers at the waiter for more coffee. "Annexation is coming, mark me. No one wants to talk about it openly." He spread his palm as if hefting a melon. "You have this many Mexicans owning the whole shebang. Thousands upon thousands of acres of land, each of them! Covered with herds. Ever *see* better land? Not to mention the *mission* lands, my word! Now, when annexation comes, all that land is going to be up for grabs."

Stephen shook his head. "It's in land grants. . . ."

"My eyes!" Hastings snorted. "Those won't be worth the paper they are written on. You look like a smart man, Davis. You already have an in—"

"Not an in," Stephen protested. "The Bandini-Warners are friends."

Hastings shrugged. "Now, what about the folks back in Boston? And the trading company family—what did you call them, Roebuck? What about the Roebucks? It is our duty as Americans to see that good people, our *kind* of people, get the word and get it fast. I could form up a new emigrant party out of Saint Louis. If a prominent family like the Roebucks backs a train, I could sign up a hundred families in a day."

Hastings produced a folded sheet of paper from an inner breast pocket and called for pen and ink. "Give me those names again." Stephen hesitated, and Hastings looked up. He smiled. "If you like I would personally ride by your wife's—that is your betrothed's—family home and deliver a message about their daughter."

"Oh, not that she was injured! I do not wish to alarm them without cause. Alissa and I will want to inform them about that ourselves."

Hastings nodded. "Of course. And you want them to get a copy of my immigrant guide."

"That is very kind of you."

"Not at all! We Americans have to stick together." Hastings returned the paper to his pocket and patted his coat. "You—ah—don't happen to be on your way back to Boston yet, do you?"

"No. I plan to return to San Diego to visit my betrothed and then sail north again."

"You carrying any furs?"

"Not yet. I hear Indian trappers from Fort Vancouver will be coming down to Fort Ross soon, with prime beaver pelts."

Hastings's lynx eyes leveled at him over the rim of the coffee mug. "I happen to know of a cache of quite good furs that was abandoned at a Sierra camp," he said slowly. "It's there for the taking. But it has to be somebody who can get in and get out quick."

An alarm bell rang in Stephen's head. "They aren't smuggled goods, are they?" he said quickly.

Lansford laughed. "No. But I'd like to get them out of California without the *cholos* taking a cut."

Stephen nodded sympathetically. "Had a run-in with them myself once."

"Then you know." He waited. "How about it?"

Rapidly Stephen sorted his options. "Perhaps when I reach Monterey I could take a look at them."

Hastings shook his head. "Not soon enough."

"Where are they?"

"Still in the Sierras. You and I would go together. We could take a flatboat up the Sacramento to within a league or two of the cache. Load them and no one would be the wiser."

"Why such a mystery, Hastings?"

"Because nobody knows about it!" Hastings chuckled, as if it were a huge joke. "Look, I swear to you as an American citizen that they are not smuggled, and they belong to no trader. Good enough? But if another trader happens on them. . . ." He shrugged. "I'd bring them out myself, but I lack resources in that part of the country. A deal?"

"I'll think about it while I am visiting my—"

"That won't do, dear chap. It is my good fortune to have happened upon you at this opportune moment—you with a ship at your disposal and me with a tidy cache of furs for sale. But entrepreneurs must seize the moment, right? And what are Americans if not entrepreneurs? We could be there and back within two weeks, man! You would handle all details of the sale. . . . Half to you and half to me. Easily two thousand apiece!"

Two thousand! Enough to give him and Alissa a wonderful start on their life together. "But what about your appointment with the American consul?"

"That can wait. It wasn't a definite appointment."

"I couldn't pay you for your share now. . . ."

"Of course not! I understand. You'd pay me when you sold the furs. You could deposit it to my account. I have an account in a bank in San Francisco. Friends must trust one another."

"I'll write up an agreement—"

"I trust you, Davis."

Stephen smiled. "But I am a lawyer. What kind of a lawyer would I be without my paperwork?"

Hastings chewed the inside of his lip, cast him a sidelong look, then said, "Done. You write it and I'll sign it. And we can talk about land grants on the trip!"

"Land grants? I don't think you understand—"

"My dear friend, there are ways. There are always ways!"

Wealth and land! Such prospects appearing in his future so suddenly! Dame Fortune was certainly smiling upon him! Stephen got up from the table and threw down his napkin with a flourish.

"Well, then, let us go!"

8

A month later, Lansford Hastings was cooling his heels in the outer office of the American consulate, a two-story wood structure sandwiched near the docks of Monterey. It had been a hour since he'd sent in his card. The American consul, Thomas Larkin, was taking his own sweet time about seeing him.

At last a door opened, and he was ushered into a small office. The furniture was sparse, but good. The man behind the Sheraton desk rose graciously, a well-built, slightly portly gentleman wth immaculately barbered blond hair and whiskers and English gray wool frock coat. Hastings felt foppish by comparison. He disliked feeling at a disadvantage and wished he had worn his brass-buttoned regimental coat rather than clothes of a gentleman that were so obviously less expensive than the consul's. "If unable to compete, be different" was a motto that had served him well. It bore the advantage of removing him from comparisons as well as keeping people off balance.

"Won't you sit down, Mr. Hastings?" said Larkin. He picked up a card from his desk. "Lansford W. Hastings. You are American."

"Exactly." Hastings watched the manicured fingers toying with his card. Larkin had something on his mind. "It must be gratifying to you to see so many Americans coming into California these days." When Larkin didn't answer, he added, "I brought some of them myself."

"Yes, I know." The expression on Larkin's face remained guarded.

Hastings leaned back in the chair and steepled his fingers. "Yes, sir, I've sold a lot of folk on California. So much so that I'm prepared to make application for a grant of land for myself."

Larkin's eyebrows lifted. "Why come to me? I have no authority here, other than to help Americans avoid problems that arise from living under a foreign government."

"Which you do well, consul. Governor Micheltorena speaks well of you, and we both know that the governor isn't given to praise." Hastings allowed himself an insider's smirk. "You've probably smoothed the path for scores of grants for friends."

Larkin put down the card with a snap. "For me to do so in your case would not be honorable."

Hastings dropped his hands and leaned forward. "May I ask why not? I am not without reputation."

"Indeed, your reputation has preceded you."

"I brought a train of folk through to the Oregon Territory last month," Hastings protested with an uncertain smile. "And led a party of those men on down to Captain Sutter's ranch on the Sacramento. Never lost a man."

"Never lost a man on your side."

Hastings moved uncomfortably in the chair. "What do you mean?"

"I received a complaint against you, Lansford Hastings, signed by six of the party you brought in from Oregon. It is to do with an episode of wanton shooting into a camp of Digger Indians in the Sierras. The men of your party are remorseful and admit their culpability. But it is you, Hastings, as leader of the group, who had the authority, nay, the duty as a Christian man, to prevent any such incident." Larkin's voice shook with emotion. "Rather, you instigated it. You saw it as nothing more than a gentlemen's sporting event like potting ducks in a pond. If word of this were to reach the governor in Los Angeles, you would be banished from California, or worse."

"We were but defending ourselves!" protested Hastings. "The Diggers were just waiting for a chance to make a surprise raid on our camp. We were only a dozen men, they were probably hundreds. We were forced to teach them a lesson. Not too many of the rascals had rifles, and we took a couple potshots at them. So what?"

"According to your companions, none were seen to have rifles, and you convinced them—although it is hard to see how sober men could make this judgment—you convinced them that taking potshots at local Indians was common entertainment. Among you, you killed several men and women."

Hastings flushed with anger. "It is my word against theirs."

"Yes. One against six. Six who admit guilt. You may file a protest, but I would advise against it." Larkin rose and stepped back from the desk as if to put more distance between himself and Hastings. "Frankly, Mr. Hastings, your actions are so abhorrent that instinct tells me to turn you over to Governor Micheltorena."

Hastings held his breath, waiting for Larkin to go on, his mind furiously churning out plans to alter the situation.

"To my own sorrow, I am forced to allow your scurrilous conduct to go unremarked. Relations between our two countries are very tenuous with so many Americans coming in. Governor Micheltorena has the authority to close his ports to American vessels at any time."

"He would not dare!"

Larkin threw him a look of undisguised contempt. "That attitude, Hastings, is typical of men of your ilk. Don't you realize, man, that Micheltorena would leap at a chance to close off the borders to Americans? Overland as well as by sea? Your actions would provide that justification, and all the protests I might lodge would not alter it. Good day, sir. And may I wish you speedy passage back to the United States. Permanently."

9

"We'll run them down the east arroyo, to that mesa directly south," Ramon was saying. His elbows rested on his outspread knees as he leaned toward his father. Juan Julian was seated on the opposite side of the fireplace.

His nose is beautiful in profile, Alissa decided, watching the play of flames on Ramon's fine features. *It is exactly like his mother's.* She glanced at Arcadia. Arcadia's full mouth drooped in relaxed contentment. Her fingers flew in concert as she crocheted an exquisite piece of lace. Alissa studied the small, partly finished square of petit point in her own hands. She was working it to cover a cushion for Mariana and Felipe, since she had not yet given them a wedding gift.

As the two women bent over their needlework Ramon and Juan Julian worked out the details of the *matanza,* the annual fall cattle roundup, which was to commence at dawn.

"Last year we got in trouble because the vaqueros could not bring the hide carts close enough to the mesa."

"Because the floods washed out the way to the mesa," said Don Juan Julian. "Do not blame yourself for that."

The quiet crackle of the logs in the fireplace, the men's voices, and the warm glow bathing the room from the candle sconces filled Alissa with an ineffable sense of family.

Ramon reached down abstractedly to scratch the huge head of the yellow hound resting on the top of his booted foot. His eyes strayed in Alissa's direction.

Alissa returned his smile. Arcadia caught the look passing between them. A brooding frown knitted the black eyebrows. She lifted a finger wound with crochet thread and touched Alissa's arm lightly. "Talk of bringing the cattle out of the hills for slaughter must be distressing to you, Alissa."

"I do not think of it like that, Dona Arcadia. Only how quickly summer has gone." She brushed away a thread clinging to her white skirts. She sat straighter, her breasts a firm, rounded curve against the starched front of her white linen waist.

Arcadia nodded. "Your Stephen will be back any day now. Is that not what he told you in the letter last week?"

"Last month." The blue gray eyes gazed with raw honesty at Arcadia. "But the letter before that also said he would be back any day."

Ramon broke off the conversation with Juan Julian to interject, "If you want my opinion, a man who—"

"Ramon," came Arcadia's soothing voice.

The yellow hound arose and padded to the door. He sniffed and dusted the tiles with his tail. They heard the patio gate swing open, a servant's voice raised in welcome, and then a strong, deep voice with an American accent.

"It's Stephen!" cried Alissa. She shoved aside her needlework and rushed to the door and threw it open just as Stephen came through the patio gate and across the courtyard. He was as properly dressed as any Bostonian setting out for his bank.

In a moment she was in his embrace, feeling giddy and breathless. He seemed at once strange and familiar to her. Odors of pine and eucalyptus, salty ocean spray and tobacco infused her with the reality of his presence. His moustache was new. The dark bristles scratched her face as they kissed. She gazed up at him. The determined mouth was transformed by a broad smile.

"I had forgotten how beautiful you are!"

"Oh, Stephen! I missed you so!"

"How's my girl?"

"All well again. Why did you—?"

But Stephen was already glancing past her to the Bandini-Warners, going around her to clasp hands with Juan Julian and kiss Arcadia's hand. "Hello! Hello!" He pounded Ramon on the back and clasped him in a hearty embrace.

Ramon quickly stepped back. His moustache twitched. He threw a glance at Alissa. "You see, Alissa? The coyotes did not get him after all. What fine adventures have kept you away, Don Esteban?" The welcoming words were spat out like the crack of a whip.

"I've had plenty. I'll tell you all about them. But first—" Stephen turned back toward Alissa, but again his eyes were not for her but the man behind her, waiting on the threshold. "Please, come in! This is Pastor Finnegan, Abraham Matthew Finnegan."

He is making such an effort to sound hearty, thought Alissa.

His arm swooped around her waist to draw her in. "Pastor, this is my Alissa."

Parson Finnegan extended a ham-fisted hand. "A pleasure to make your acquaintance."

The dry, quick clasp of his fingers on hers set off a swarm of misgivings. Finnegan's sandy hair looked as if it had been trimmed by a sheepshearer. His scuffed, sweat-darkened, buckskin jacket pulled under the arms and barely met across his suspenders. The dark trousers fairly reeked of dirt. This man was to marry them? Stephen could not have insulted her more deliberately if he had tried.

Without a word she turned away and headed back into the house. The warm glow cast over the room by the tallow candles seemed suddenly illusory.

Stephen caught up with her and appropriated her elbow. "I met him at a camp meeting in Yerba Buena."

"Just happened to run into him, I suppose, and pressed him into service! Stephen, how could you?" Alissa snatched her cherry colored shawl off the back of a chair and pulled it about her shoulders.

Stephen followed her to the hearth, stretching his hands behind him to the warmth of the blaze. He bowed in the direction of Juan Julian, who was settling in a chair next to his wife. To him he said, "Parson Finnegan agreed to join me on shipboard for a couple weeks so that—with your blessing—we might have a proper Protestant wedding."

Alissa stared at him, openmouthed. Announcing to the world, never mind her feelings, that he was ready to pick up their life together after disappearing for four months! And behaving as if he had just personally given the Bandini-Warners a gold mine, for heaven's sake! Arcadia was responding with gracious pleasure, as was her nature. Ramon's face wore an angry scowl.

"We must make a toast," said Juan Julian.

"Yes," said Arcadia. "And then I'll have the servants prepare some supper. Have you eaten?"

Finnegan's stubby fingers immediately clapped his stomach. "Not so's I couldn't eat more, senyora."

"Good idea!" Stephen rubbed his hands together. "I am well enough sick of galley cooking."

In minutes they were all crowded around the long oak table in the dining room. Stephen and Parson Finnegan dove to with a will, devouring the remains of a roasted pheasant Ramon had bagged early in the day, eating cold tortillas, sweetened mashed pumpkin, and washing it down with a mellow port.

Stephen hoisted the glass like a salute toward the candelabra. His deep-set eyes shone in the candlelight as he looked around at the Warners and Alissa. "A toast. How glad I am to be back with you. I have a gift for you in my saddlebags, Juan Julian. Your friend, Don Luis Vignes, sends you six bottles of his good port."

"Just how did you meet him?" Ramon exclaimed bitterly.

Stephen's eyes rested on Ramon. Then he said briskly, "Business, dear friend. Vignes is going to make wines for Boston now, and I—Roebuck Trading Company, that is—will sell them for him. In my opinion they are as good as European wines." With a sudden movement, he quaffed the entire glass.

Arcadia was talking softly with Finnegan. Stephen shot a swift look in their direction as Finnegan said, "He was comin' out of the Sierras, ma'am. If ever a man received divine help, it was him and his friend. They were right proper exhausted, him being more a merchantman than a hunter."

"What were you doing in the Sierras?" Alissa said.

"Yes, what were you?" chimed Ramon. "No one has goods to trade in the mountains. The tribes are still wild."

"Not true," said Finnegan. "There's furs—"

"Ah, well, that's a story for another time," Stephen cut in. "Say, Ramon, you ever eat pilot bread?"

"I do not think so. You, Father?" Ramon glanced at Juan Julian.

Juan Julian nodded. "Of course. Good bread. A specialty of galley cooks. They love it in Yerba Buena."

"That's right! That's it! And it's a fine way to get around those sharks in the customs office."

"How do you mean?" asked Juan Julian.

"Simple. Ships anchor off Monterey and have the cooks bake up extra bread. They pack their import goods in water casks and deal a layer of pilot bread on top. Toss 'em over the side. Pick 'em up on shore, and before you can say 'skinned beaver,' you have half your cargo ashore, duty free. The bread's light, and if customs does snare a barrel, they all know how everyone likes the bread, and chances are you get away with it."

"But that's dishonest!" sputtered Alissa.

"That's *business*, dear Alissa. You want those wharf sharks getting half your uncle's cargo? What did Micheltorena and his gang of *cholos* do to earn half the profit of your cargo?"

Alissa stared at him, sick at heart, angry, and suddenly aware how very vulnerable she was. She had never realized this tough, aggressive side of Stephen. "What aren't you telling us?" she blurted.

An awkward silence engulfed the table.

"What sort of goods did you find in the Sierras?" Ramon prompted.

Stephen's eyes glittered. His lips parted in a calculated smile. "Suffice it to say I am now well able to support a wife and to pay you for her board."

"Now you are insulting my hospitality," said Juan Julian lightly, but there was an edge to his voice.

"I only meant, when I left Alissa here, that I did not intend to be gone so many months. I did not realize that you would have her care and responsibility this long. It was only with the knowledge that she was in such capable hands that I was able to accomplish all that I have." He leaned over to squeeze her fingers.

His proprietary tone made Alissa seethe. She attempted to withdraw her fingers, but Stephen's grip became unpleasantly tight as he said, "I have brought gifts for all of you from Monterey, right off the China trader. Before the customs house got their fingers in them."

Suddenly Alissa burst out, "I didn't want gifts, Stephen, I just wanted you. Why didn't you come when you promised?"

An irritated frown marred the congenial exterior. "Can't it wait?"

"Don't you realize how many months I've waited?"

This time the silence grew uncomfortable.

"Pastor Finnegan," said Arcadia, "have you a church in Yerba Buena?"

"My church is God's out-of-doors, senyora. Marryin', buryin', and baptizin' are what I do most, with a right hearty sermon now and again."

Alissa could have curled up and died of shame. This man was a man of God, like her father. Like Padre Zalvidea. She watched him lick the cold grease off his fingers. She said little the remainder of the long evening, aware of a growing detachment from Stephen, as if she were observing a stranger. She felt more akin to her adopted California family than to him.

At last she rose. "I am going to retire, Dona Arcadia. Good night, Don Juan Julian . . . Ramon . . . Parson Finnegan." She studied Stephen's face, the hard face of jollity. "Good night, Stephen."

Stephen was on his feet with alacrity. "I'll walk you to your room."

"No need. Good night."

10

She dressed quickly in a dusk blue wool skirt and bodice, wrapped a matching shawl around her bright hair and went outside. After a restless night, she had risen before dawn. The air felt moist and cool in her nostrils. Softly she made her way across the patio, through the gate, and back toward the vegetable garden beside the cookhouse. A heavy dew laced the tomato vines, drooping nearly to the ground with their heavy red fruit. Varieties of chilies and sweet peppers, red and purple and yellow, fist-sized ones shaped like bells, and shiny, dainty cones no longer than an inch gleamed softly in the fading shadows.

A rustle of tomato leaves distracted her. In another moment she discovered the shape of the cook bent down between the rows of foliage. "Good morning, Ben Gee. You are gardening very early."

The Indian rose respectfully. Without looking at her he said good morning. She waited.

Ben Gee glanced in both directions then down at his plants. "I am all through, thank you, *donita.*"

Alissa watched in surprise as Ben Gee trod silently past her and back to the cookhouse. She tightened the shawl around her and pulled her thick hair around to the front of one shoulder. Her fingers began to braid the taffy colored tress as she thought about Stephen. In four months' time she had received only three letters, letters in which he never faced the fact that by deserting her he had humiliated both her and her family. Now he had come, with no real explanation. Did she still love him? A rueful smile lifted the corners of her soft, pink lips. She was losing sleep over him. Had he ever lost a night's sleep over her?

"S-s-s-t!"

Alissa glanced around. The sound came from the garden.

"Please do not cry out," begged a youthful male voice in Spanish.

"Why should I?" she demanded. "Why are you hiding?"

A barefoot figure clad in white cotton shirt and blue drill trousers rose from among the tomatoes. "I am Gregorio, *Doncella* Alissa." His voice sounded both pleading and desperate.

She recognized the stocky figure immediately. "You are the young man who ran away from the mission."

"Yes. Guadelupe told me she believed you were a good person who would help us."

"Is she the young woman whom Padre Zalvidea will not let go?"

"Yes, *Doncella* Alissa, that is right." His voice was soft and deferential. He stared at her with the wise-eyed watchfulness of a deer primed to take flight at the first sign of danger.

"You speak Spanish very well."

"Padre Zalvidea taught me. I can also write and read, a little."

In spite of the turmoil of her own problems, Alissa felt compassion for the young man. The idea of being made to stay forever at a mission did not appeal to her, either. Perhaps it was naive of her, but she thought it was very courageous of him to seek out help. "Why did you come here?"

"To speak to Ben Gee."

"Ben Gee?" she said in surprise. "Why?"

"He is our leader. He was there, at the mission." Gregorio's voice grew bolder, though he remained several lengths away. "I told him this morning I wanted to ask you to help us. He said I should not. Our lives mean nothing to you. You are not even of the Faith."

"I am faithful to our Lord, Gregorio. Many belong to him who believe they do not need a priest in order to talk with God."

"I heard this same thing many years ago from Che-Muc-Tah."

"Che-Muc-Tah again! Who is he?"

Gregorio shook his head. "For a time he was there, in the hills. Men from the mission would leave the fields, and they would talk. They would take him food."

"Did the padre know him?"

"Oh no, *Doncella* Alissa," Gregorio said earnestly. "The padre would not have treated him as much man, and he is. Many from the mission left to go with him. I was too young. He would not take me."

"What did Che-Muc-Tah tell you and the others when you met?"

"That Indians must not be owned by a priest and made to live on his rancho and do his bidding. He told us of other people who live as we do. They are called slaves. Their masters also tell them it is the will of God."

"Where did he go when he left the hills by the mission?"

Gregorio shrugged. "Far away. His head was like a nest full of things he thought about, and he had many things to do. He will come back someday." He glanced toward the cookhouse, where a trail of smoke drifted up in the still air. "I must not be seen here. The *ranchero* would have to tell the priest."

"Surely not!"

"He is very strict."

Alissa reached a sudden decision. "What can I do to help?"

A light burst over Gregorio's broad face. "You can ask the priest to let you have Guadelupe as a serving woman and then give her to me."

"No one can give one person to another, Gregorio." Alissa clasped her shawl against her breast and paced a few thoughtful steps. "But I shall talk to Dona Arcadia. If she is willing, then I will ask Padre Zalvidea to permit Guadelupe to be my servant."

"Oh, senorita!" Gregorio started toward her as if to throw himself at her feet.

Quickly she stepped back. "Don't do that! But promise me that if she is allowed to come, you will not take her away without her permission or without telling me."

"Yes, senorita. Yes! God bless you!" Gregorio turned and scanned the fields, then sped off down the mesa toward the distant rim of scrub and safety.

Alissa stared after him, awed by her own boldness. What would Arcadia think? Surely she was stepping into affairs where she had no business. Swiftly she returned to the house.

"You've changed."

"*I've* changed!"

Alissa's gloved hand gripped the fence rail separating her from Stephen. Hours had passed since she'd seen Gregorio scurry like a jackrabbit away from this mesa.

Stephen was studying her neat figure in the riding costume, his mouth pursed in judgment.

The riding habit could have been designed for her, the froth of lace down the front, under the short black jacket, the split riding skirt accenting her lean waist and thighs. Her thick hair was drawn back into a black net snood snugged at the base of her neck under the black felt hat. In her ears were the pearl stud earrings that Stephen had given her at their betrothal party in Saint Louis.

"I don't wonder Ramon was hoping I would never show up," he said suddenly.

"That remark is beneath you!" she said angrily. She glanced at the vaquero, ten paces away, holding the horses for the morning ride that she had proposed at breakfast.

"You are just angry because I wasn't here wringing my hands while you were recuperating," Stephen accused. "What could I have done if I had stayed? It was all for Roebuck Trading Company! Blast it, Alissa, what did you think I was doing? You have a proprietary interest in the cargo."

"I wasn't worried about my share, Stephen," she said quietly. But she could not keep the hurt out of her voice as she added, "You left me in the care of strangers when I was helpless. One could have sailed to Yerba Buena and back a dozen times in the time you were gone!"

For the first time Stephen did not meet her gaze. His dark eyes were fixed on the horizon, his mouth set in an unbending line. He said, "Sometimes I wonder what your father and your uncle were doing allowing you to come out here. It's no place for an American girl."

"And what does *that* mean? That I was responsible for getting smashed with a broken spar? That I am a millstone to your ambitions?"

"You were afraid I wasn't coming back to marry you. You're angry I brought a parson."

Alissa was so dumbfounded by the accusations she was speechless. Suddenly she realized that even this morning he was wearing a brown business suit. "You look ridiculous wearing that to go riding," she snapped. "Why didn't you ask Ramon for some decent clothes?"

"Like that get-up you are wearing? You are a fine-looking woman, Alissa MacGowan, but you don't need to flaunt it to the world."

"It is the same costume Arcadia and Mariana wear. Further, it is practical!" They glared at each other, her blue eyes betraying her pain, his gaze as stubborn and dark as a log caught in a frozen pond. The vaquero, a small, wiry figure, slid nonchalantly down to his haunches and began to roll a cigarette. For the first time since she had regained consciousness on this rancho, Alissa was thankful for somebody who could not understand English.

"Oh, Stephen, *why* did you leave me?"

He expelled a sharp breath of exasperation. "How many times do I have to tell you? For the Roe—"

"No! What if I had taken an infection? What if I had died? You would not even have known. My family—"

"Don't overdramatize. I hate a woman who overdramatizes."

Fear clutched her chest. *Stop! Stop! before you drive him away.* But she couldn't stop. She had to know the truth. "Is this what our life together will be like? My needs coming second to the trading company? And when we have babies, and when they need you—"

He hissed with impatience. "You'll be there! All I want to do is be a success for you. When I told your father and your uncle Harmon that Roebuck could become the biggest trading company in California, I wasn't just spouting air. You have no idea the potential—"

"Just don't tell me it's for me," she said, so quietly it was almost as if she were musing to herself. "Just don't tell me it's for me, when you never asked me."

The handsome face settled into the firm lines she had thought so dashing back in Boston. Now they seemed merely uncompromising. "I don't understand you," he said.

"I don't want to ride after all, Stephen. I need time to think." She came around the end of the hitching rail and headed back toward the hacienda.

Stephen planted himself in her way. "It's Ramon, isn't it? The only mistake I made was leaving you in the hands of a man who couldn't be trusted. That's what it is, isn't it?"

"Please move out of my way, Stephen."

"Where is he?"

"Up and gone hours ago."

"Oh, so you know that, do you?"

"Everyone knows it! The matanza has started. He and the vaqueros went out to start the roundup. It's time for the slaughtering, so great business successes like you will have lots of hides and tallow on your next trip!"

Alissa was fuming as she strode into the hacienda. And what nerve, criticizing her dress after the generosity of her hosts in providing for her so well. She could not have felt more at home if the Warners were her own family. And in this riding habit, dress that was a hallmark of the vigorously active life of the Bandini-Warner women and their friends, she felt freer than she had since her early adolescent days, growing up on the homestead in Saint Louis, when she had been allowed to wear jeans like the farmhands.

She was beginning to realize that women of the ranchos, the aristocracy of California, had more personal freedom than any she had met in Saint Louis or Boston. And she was beginning to see that the more freedom or position or money people held, the easier it was for them to ignore tradition.

She stopped. That was it. That was what had been bothering her about Stephen's behavior since last night. It was his attitude that anything was permissible as long as one justified it as "business." One might cheat the customs at a country's port—excusing it on the grounds that the customs were unfairly high—or one might acquire cargo that one had no right to (what *had* Stephen gone into the Sierras after?). In a flash her thoughts leapt to Padre Zalvidea. One might even tell Indians God willed them to be slaves if the end—turning them into Christians—justified it.

Dangerous thoughts! Her mind in turmoil, Alissa strode through the family rooms. Arcadia had gone to visit Mariana and Felipe this morning and taken many of the servants with her. It was doubtless a discreet effort to allow her and Stephen time alone, so like Arcadia. But now the empty, sunny rooms suffocated her. She turned slowly, allowing her anger to diffuse.

From the window she could see through the open patio gate. Stephen was talking in impatient gestures to the vaquero. The man shrugged his shoulders. Finally he clambered to his feet and pointed twiglike fingers, pinching a cigarette in the direction of the suede brown hills east of the rancho. The two of them mounted the saddled horses and left at a run.

Going after Ramon, she thought. *Good. I hope he makes a stupid fool of himself!* But deep inside her loomed a sadness that would not be denied. She had walked away from him. And he let her go.

11

An hour's ride from the rancho, Stephen and the vaquero spotted Ramon surrounded by a herd of grunting cattle kicking up dust.

"Hola!" the vaquero called.

Ramon hailed them with a wave. He pointed with a handful of coiled whip toward a knoll out of the stream of cattle. Reaching the shade of the oaks ahead of the other two men, he hooked a leg over the pommel and waited, as comfortable in the saddle as if it were an easy chair.

Look at him. A hundred tons on the hoof milling in all directions, and he acts as if he's got nothing on his mind but smelling the flowers. Stephen gritted his teeth, suppressing his anger under a blanket of icy control. Alissa had deliberately picked a fight with him. She was in love with Ramon. Of course that was it. Something had to have happened to have changed her so drastically. Stephen's business instincts took over. It would not do to confront Ramon. Play him along. Let him believe he suspected nothing. He forced a hearty grin. "Need some help?"

"Stephen, my friend, that is so like you," said Ramon. His eyes swept the constricting suit worn by the American. "I apologize that I did not think to find you something suitable to ride in. Your fine suit could be ruined."

"Hang the suit!" The words came out a bit more angry than he intended.

Ramon nodded. "Well, come then, wait with me." He signaled the vaquero to leave.

"What are we waiting for?" Stephen asked.

Ramon grinned, the master now. He turned his attention to the cattle. They streamed through the groves around the men, dozens of them, stringy and shaggy, brown and white, herded by half a dozen vaqueros uniformly coated with suede colored dust.

Stephen said, "Are these what they call longhorns?"

"I do not think so, no."

The cows and the vaqueros disappeared. They were alone. Ramon eyed him without speaking. Reaching overhead, he snapped a twig from an oak branch and placed it between his teeth. "Have you seen Alissa this morning?"

"We had the place to ourselves." Stephen glanced around. Distantly he heard squeals that sounded like animals being slaughtered. Why wasn't

Ramon there, helping? Why was he waiting here, on a small mesa overlooking a mass of arroyos filled with chaparral? "Now what, Ramon? What happens next?"

Soon the men will call the next *rodeo.*"

Conversation was forced for the next few minutes. Then Ramon's vaqueros appeared, singly and in pairs, exchanging banter with Ramon, then scattering up the arroyos. Stephen could hear them shouting at the top of their lungs, calling and screaming fit to waken the dead. He looked at Ramon in disbelief.

"They're calling the cows."

"*What?*"

Ramon shrugged, continuing to chew on his twig.

The racket went on, sometimes faint, sometimes louder, then joined by a faint series of cow calls. Soon Stephen heard the rumble of hooves. The combined shouts and mooing and hoofbeats grew louder, until again the gullies around them were filled with cattle streaming toward the rodeo ground.

"They actually *call* the cattle, and they come?" Stephen shouted over the din.

"Of course. Why waste energy rounding them up when all you have to do is call them?" Seeing the incredulity on Stephen's face, Ramon laughed.

"Each spring, after calving, we drive the herds to the rodeo ground. We keep them there for a few hours, feed them, then drive them away. We do that a couple times a week, then once a week, and then perhaps in another month. They learn the vaquero's voice. They learn to come when they are called. In the spring we brand, in the fall we slaughter. Whichever, all we need to do is ride up into the arroyos and the canyons and call them when we are ready."

In spite of himself, Stephen had to laugh, impressed by the simple ease of the Californians' solution.

For the next two hours the two men rode together, saying little. As nearly as Stephen could figure, there were about twenty-five vaqueros in the drive. Several times he spotted Juan Julian, always in the thick of it. They drove the cattle to a broad, level clearing, where a chute fed into a corral. Twenty-five steers were let in at a time and killed. Then the heavy work began, flaying the animals and trimming out the white tallow and *manteca,* the prized fat that lay closest to the skin. This was tossed aboard mule carts and hauled to rendering vats nearby. The skins, eight feet across and over a hundredweight apiece, were heaped together for preliminary dressing.

The meat was largely ignored, harnessed and dragged off the field through the dirt by ropes wound around saddle horns. When Stephen questioned Ramon about it, Ramon replied offhandedly, "The bears will eat it—and the coyotes and the buzzards."

Stephen's mount jerked its head as a steer let out a particularly curdling death scream. Ramon reached over and seized Stephen's reins to gentle it. Stephen's hands shook as he took over the reins again. The sight of cattle being slaughtered on such scale sickened him. The slaughtering grounds were drenched in blood, as were the perspiring vaqueros and the horses and wheels of the carts moving constantly back and forth.

Ramon watched his face turn a sickly white. "Had enough?"

Stephen nodded. "I can find my way back."

Ramon said, "I will go with you until I am sure you will not get lost." As they moved away from the shouts and screams Ramon looked at him curiously. "Why did you come back, amigo?"

"For my wife."

"She is not your wife yet."

"She is betrothed to me."

"A man does not leave an injured woman alone with complete strangers if he loves her."

"You are my friend. I left her with you. Was there anyone else in California in whom I placed more trust?"

Stephen had struck unerringly where Ramon was most vulnerable, his sense of honor. "But she was well enough to travel after three weeks." Stephen continued to ride in silence, and Ramon ventured, "If you don't love her, it would be kinder to let her go."

"Who says I do not love her?"

Ramon shrugged. "We do not treat our women as you have treated Alissa."

"The *New Horizons* was the first brig from Boston this spring," Stephen said stubbornly. "She'll be carrying back prize cargo. Do you know I've got the padres of twelve missions contracted to take all the hides their Indians cure this year—"

"What does Alissa think of your conquests?"

"I don't have to answer to her," he snapped. "Women don't know what it's all about, you know that. . . . I was doing work for our future together. I don't suppose she told you that."

"She is a lady. A lady does not discuss her private life with a stranger." All humor was gone from the Castilian face as he added, "When we first met last year and rode together on a bear hunt, I called you *amigo*. I called you *Californio*. I was wrong, Yankee trader. My father married my mother to get her rancho. They both knew it. It is fortunate that they also seem to love each other. What did you win in the trade for Alissa? Are you a *hijo*, a son, in Roebuck Trading Company now? Roebuck and Sons? Business will always come first, no?"

Stephen had not used his fists to settle an argument since he was a boy. But now, spouting a volley of oaths he didn't know he had acquired, he reached over and seized a lapel of Ramon's jacket and tried to yank him from his horse. Ramon was too quick. The horse shied away, and his whip was in his upraised hand before Stephen could fairly right himself.

The men eyed each other. Quivering with tension transmitted from the riders, the horses danced on nervous feet.

"*Con su permiso,*" Stephen said in a voice heavy with sarcasm, "I will marry Alissa and carry her out of your life."

"It is not my permission you need, Davis, it is Alissa's. And that I doubt you'll get!"

Ramon's shouts followed him as Stephen wheeled away and galloped for the hacienda.

12

In June the garden in the patio had been lush with a giddy cascade of purple jacaranda blossoms and streaming fronds of pepper trees that gave ear to every breeze, bent but did not break, and entertained Alissa with a whispered stream of promises.

Alissa thought about promises and remembrances of happy times. *What a difference the end of summer makes.* She buried her chin in the stiff white lace at her throat, her arms clasped across the wool broadcloth riding jacket. Slowly she paced the brick walk, her riding boots making a hollow sound on the bricks, kicking aside the jacaranda blossoms, which were now just a scattered litter of unsightly brown clinging to her soles.

The patio gate opened and thudded shut. She turned. Stephen came to halt in an angry stance just inside the gate. His suit was stained with sweat, the trousers spattered with a darker substance. He whipped off the brown beaver and rubbed the felt with his elbow, leaving a wet band of dirt around his forehead, where dust had mixed with sweat.

"We're leaving. Get your things."

"What on earth are you talking about?"

"Look, Alissa, these people used to be my friends. I don't know what you've told them, but suddenly I'm the villain of the piece. You'll have to hurry. I want to make the ship before dark."

"But Stephen, I can't—"

"Stop it, Alissa! First you moan I'm not here to marry you, now you moan about coming with me! Which is it to be? Where's Finnegan? He can marry us on the ship."

"Stephen, you're behaving in a dreadfully childish way! No one is against you! What is it? What is wrong?"

Stephen's jaw clamped shut. "I don't have to answer to you or anybody. I'm doing my job."

Alissa gave a little laugh of bewilderment. She came to him, placing her palms on his rumpled coat. "Darling . . . , come on." She could feel the rigidity of his frame beneath the fabric. "Stephen. . . ."

Stephen turned away from her. "Are you coming, or aren't you?"

Alissa could hardly breathe. *O dear God, I am so frightened. He could leave me alone, in this strange country! My family will be sick with worry. I came with Stephen of my own choice. They will believe I have been compromised. What is to become of me?* A wave of nausea overtook her, and she felt herself swaying. Through a roaring in her ears she heard herself saying, "No."

"What?" Stephen stared at her.

"I love you, Stephen. I—I think I do. I thought you loved me. But—but you have shown me what is most important to you, and it isn't me." Her voice tailed up and she fought down her tears.

His jaws tightened again, refusing voice to the words Alissa longed to hear.

"Oh, Stephen—"

A wall as icy as a blast from the Arctic dropped between them.

"If that's the way you feel." Stephen sidestepped her and strode into the house.

Alissa sank to a bench and clutched her face tightly with both hands, wanting to feel the pain, wanting to know that this moment was real and not some nightmare she could escape. *It was said. It was true then, the feeling she had had when he came last night. O God, why doesn't Stephen love me the way I want him to?* Alissa doubled over on the bench, hardly able to bear the pain. Minutes passed. Then she felt a hand touch her shoulder.

"Miss MacGowan."

She swallowed. "Yes." It was the Protestant parson's voice. She could see his shoes, scuffed and old.

"Stephen says we're leavin' and that you aren't coming."

Alissa took a deep breath and looked up at him. He had changed his clothes and wore an awkwardly mended version of parson black. She brushed the tears from her lashes and willed herself to her feet. In an unconscious gesture of piety from her Sunday-school days, she clasped her hands before her. "That's so, Parson Finnegan."

The straggly eyebrows lifted as he peered closely at her. "You look poorly, miss. Care to chat a bit?"

Alissa was touched by his gentleness. Tears belled in her eyes. "It would be a relief. But Stephen does not like to be kept waiting."

"He'll wait," Finnegan predicted.

They walked through the afternoon, Alissa doing most of the talking, with an occasional emphatic nod of understanding from her companion. As she spoke, she grew calmer and more certain of the rightness of her decision. "My parents reared us to believe that one must not turn away from the hard choices. But—but I never thought . . . ," her voice trailed away.

Finnegan grunted in sympathy. "I have joined many couples, and I have seen more workin' marriages than geese in a flyover—all kinds, Miss Mac-Gowan. Now let's face it. Something kept you young folks from marryin' back there in Saint Louis, where you got betrothed. You say you could have gotten married again in Boston, but you didn't. 'Twas unfortunate your accident kept you apart when you reached California—or then again maybe it wasn't. Maybe the Lord used that space to give you the chance you needed to be apart. Now Davis here takes off and goes with this here Hastings into the Sierras, gone longer'n a man pinin' of love ought. And whilst you're angry about that, you got a load of second thoughts about the kind o' life you'd be sharin' together."

Alissa gave a small laugh, part sadness, part relief. It had been said, and he was right; she did have second thoughts.

"Did I tell you I'm a preacher's daughter myself? Preachers' daughters are taught to think first about doing what's right." She glanced at her companion, making sure he understood. "Growing up, I thought a lot about doing what was pleasing to the Lord and to my parents. Stephen came to work for my uncle Harmon. He was from Boston and came to work at the Saint Louis office. He was handsome, of good moral character; he had a good position with good expectations; he respected my parents and had such elegant manners. I liked the way he took charge. I felt so—so *safe!*"

"You wanted to be taken care of, what gel doesn't?" nodded Finnegan.

"I thought I did. . . ."

Finnegan had stopped. His hands went behind his back. He questioned her with raised eyebrows. "I notice you ain't yet said 'love.' "

"I thought that all those things *were* love!"

Finnegan was silent. Their gazes met and locked for a long moment.

"I guess love means different things to everyone, doesn't it? Those things are nice, but they are all surface things. Without a desire to share the feelings inside, they don't necessarily mean love at all! I feel so empty inside! Stephen only wants to tell me what to do, as if I were a little girl."

"Love does not insist on its own way; it is not irritable or resentful—" said Finnegan.

Alissa smiled, a quick, bright smile that brought a warm light to her eyes. "First Corinthians thirteen. I shall make love my aim, Parson Finnegan," Alissa said softly, "as Saint Paul said we should do." Impulsively she gave the grizzled parson a quick hug.

They resumed walking.

"But now I must decide what to do."

"If you was back home in Saint Louis, you'd likely remain in the bosom of your family a mite longer. Here you ain't got family. You're stuck between a rock and a hard place. What do you see as likely? Goin' back home?"

She shook her head. "I have a brother. He might be in California. . . ."

Finnegan nodded. "Stephen told me you had a Shawnee half brother by some brave your ma married first."

She shuddered at his crude words. "Daniel is a fine Christian person, Parson Finnegan!"

Finnegan screwed up an expression meant as apology. "So you want to stay. Well, pretty young gels are scarce out here. You'll have your pick o' the crop."

His words embarrassed her, but she realized how practical they were. With no family and a not unlimited supply of money, she could not live on the hospitality of the Bandini-Warners forever. "It's not that I have no money. Part of the ship's cargo belongs to me. Although it was meant as a betrothal gift."

"I'm sure your uncle Harmon would understand, Miss MacGowan."

They had reached the end of the mesa. In the distant south, huge thunderheads were building up in the faultless sky. "Yer a brave lass. Most gels alone in a strange country would fear to do ought but marry. If you change your mind, you could always find me up around Yerba Buena—San Francisco they're callin' it now, had ye heard? Plenty of Americans up there, more comin' in every day, unchurched, missin' their Lord, Protestant like you an' me." Finnegan pushed his nose back and forth with his hammy paw. He nodded. " 'Tis a good callin' fer a man like me."

Alissa laughed, testing the waters for the possibility of happiness.

Finnegan pointed a stubby finger at the distance. "There's an Injun over in those bushes, if I'm not mistaken, tryin' to get your attention."

Alissa shaded her eyes. "Gregorio!" She glanced around. They seemed to be alone.

Gregorio stood where she could see him. "Guadelupe. . . ."

She couldn't hear all his words, but the meaning was clear. "Tomorrow," she called softly. "Come back tomorrow. At dawn. In the vegetable garden." She glanced at Finnegan. "He wants to get the girl he loves away from the mission where she lives. I said I would try to help."

Unexpectedly Finnegan laughed. "Well, God's blessing on you. I have an idea you'll do all right, Alissa MacGowan."

"She'll change her mind," Stephen was predicting confidently at that moment to Arcadia. "When I hoist sail, she'll be on that ship."

The proud Castilian heritage that was Arcadia Bandini-Warner's was never more evident. Her magnificent eyes flashed angrily as she stalked around the living room. "Do not be certain of that! This is a dishonorable moment for you, Stephen. My son has made a poor choice of friend in you."

If the words stung, they served only to fuel his anger. "Dona Arcadia, if I let Alissa dictate to me now, she will never submit to me! Wives must submit to their husbands. Her own father would tell her that! My mother did."

"And was she happy?"

Stephen looked surprised. "I never—that doesn't have anything to do with Alissa and me."

"If women submit, it is from love and respect. And husbands also submit to the desires of their wives, because they also love and respect them." She scowled at him, as if forcing comprehension of her words into his closed mind. "I learned this from my husband, not the priest. My husband, having been reared a Methodist, has read much more of the Bible than most Catholics."

Stephen pulled his watch from a pocket and glared at it. "Where is that rascal, Finnegan?"

The words were no sooner out of his mouth than Finnegan and Alissa came in the door. Arcadia gazed anxiously at the girl, relieved to see that the strained face was nevertheless filled with determination.

"Well?" demanded Stephen.

Alissa drew in a deep breath. "I shall need my portion of the cargo money. I am not going with you, Stephen." She glanced down at her hand and pulled off her betrothal ring. "Here."

Stephen stared at the ring. "There is little cash," he said slowly. "Most of the cargo will have to be sold in Boston before the full profit is realized."

"Then give me what you can."

Anger crossed his face and disappeared. The face presented to Alissa across the chasm was without emotion. "I will. I will render you a full accounting." He turned to Dona Arcadia. "If you will permit a man you trust to accompany me to San Diego, he can bring it back tomorrow."

Stephen glanced at Finnegan.

"Ready anytime you are. I travel light."

"Then let's go. I've wasted too much time already."

Alissa was stung by the cruelty of his words, by the rapidity of change since her decision. It was as if Stephen had goaded her into a position he knew she could not tolerate. As the men left, she and Arcadia looked at each other.

Without a word Dona Arcadia crossed the tiles and gathered Alissa to her. Alissa felt tears coming again as she allowed her weaker side to merge in the warmth and strength of the older woman. They held each other close for several moments, then Arcadia stepped away and took her by the shoulders.

"You will stay with me."

"If you will allow me to. I can pay—"

Arcadia smoothed the blond hair back from Alissa's face. "We have little need for money here. Our currency is on the hoof, as *Juanito* likes to put it. And the land is given us by God, no? Come. Have Concepcion bring you a bit of food while I change, then we will go for a glorious ride!"

Only minutes later the two women were jogging across open hills, feeling the wind of the approaching storm. "Let's run!" Alissa shouted.

"Hi-hi-hi!" cried Dona Arcadia, plunging ahead.

A surge of joy filled Alissa as they streaked down and up the endless brown hills. The reckless running, the dangerous, driving hooves, the half-wild animal carrying her made her so giddy with exhilaration she could not speak. The feeling of joy lasted as long as the run. As they gradually slowed the heaving horses to a walk, she discovered in its place a sense of calm. She would be all right. Stephen was gone. She was alone. But she would be all right.

On the way home, as the horses cooled out, Alissa told Arcadia about Gregorio. To her surprise, Arcadia's mouth tightened in a line of disapproval.

"How did you get involved in this? The Indians in the hills are dangerous, Alissa. This is not a place for misguided sympathies. When Gregorio ran away from the mission, he became an outlaw. Padre Zalvidea is right to discipline him. It would be wrong to help him by helping the girl go to him."

"But they are in love!"

Arcadia's black brows lifted like wings, as if to say, *Haven't you had enough of love for the moment?*

Alissa glanced down. She reached forward and tugged ruefully at the horse's mane. "Padre Zalvidea does not treat her well. I do not think he likes her."

"That is nonsense! Who worries about whether an Indian is liked or not liked?"

"Might she come here to the rancho and be a servant?"

"Your servant, you mean?"

"Well, yes. I would pay her—"

"No! You do not pay them."

"All right," said Alissa meekly.

"Very well, then, I'll see what may be done. But you must not forget one thing: If you bring Guadelupe to live with us, then you are responsible for her. And if she and Gregorio marry, they must marry in the Christian faith. Her immortal soul must not be lost. You must be sure you can trust her and that her word is good."

"But—"

"We have service in our chapel, Alissa. She will be permitted to join us. There are too few priests in California, so we worship as best we can. On special occasions, Padre Zalvidea comes." Arcadia smiled. "As for your own soul, you will have to do the best you can."

"I will," she said seriously.

A whole new world of thinking was rushing into her mind. Wherever it led, she must not allow herself to be lured astray. If Zalvidea and the masters he served really believed that converting the Indians justified forcing them to live and work for the mission, she must not come to feel comfortable about it, as the Californians apparently did. She was the daughter of Micah MacGowan, pastor!

And if Stephen really believed that business justified any means to success, she must not accept that, either. Her mother, Hannah Roebuck MacGowan, had always lived according to her own standard of rightness, even when it was hard, even when it ran counter to what was proper and expected.

And she, Alissa, was Hannah's daughter.

13

After spending two day making idle conversation and surveying the extensive holdings of Roebuck Trading Company in Saint Louis, Lansford W. Hastings rode slowly through a double row of red and gold poplars, up the road leading to a house. It stood on a broad bluff just north of Saint Louis, overlooking the Mississippi River, a gracious, wide-spreading home of deep red brick and weathered shingle. Still, after spending two days making idle conversation and surveying the extensive holdings of Roebuck Trading Company in Saint Louis, he had expected something more opulent. Of course, this was the preacher's house. The houses of Harmon Roebuck and the other partners might be another matter altogether.

With several hundred yards to go, he guided his horse to the side of the road, crushing a scattering of dry leaves underfoot as he dismounted. Pulling a coarse bit of cloth out of a saddlebag, he scrubbed the dust from his new buffalo-hide boots. Next he extracted a cambric handkerchief from a pocket inside his satin brocade waistcoat and wiped along either side of the sharp nose, blotting at the pencil moustache and finely drawn lips. It was a handsome face, made less so by his habit of glancing at something, then quickly away, then fixing a stare—as if preappraising territory he planned to conquer.

It was late fall of this year of 1845, but an unreasonably hot afternoon. Hastings pulled the waistcoat away from his shirt momentarily to allow a cool breeze to reach his sweating skin. Then, patting the ruffled, false shirtfront in place, he slid a thumb along the gold chain crossing his vest from pocket to pocket and flicked at the sleeves of his fawn topcoat. Finally he withdrew a tiny silver vial of scent, sprinkled some on his handkerchief, and applied it to his face.

Once again he mounted his horse and headed for the shingle and brick house.

"Yore ol' sin nature's gonna get you in trouble, Miz Molly!"

Red-haired, blue-eyed Molly MacGowan tore down the stairs to the landing, lost her footing, and slid into a potted fern, which then bounced down the several steps to the foyer and spilled dirt on the polished oak floor as it rolled.

Her father came out of the study just as Molly leaped the last three steps and plunged into him.

"Oh, Papa, did you know that—"

"*Don't you dare!*" came a stentorian command from the second floor, followed by the thumping footsteps of a large black woman.

"No disr'spect to you, sir, but if Molly ain't a typical preacher's daughter! She fairly *teeters* with sin."

"What have you done, young woman?" Micah MacGowan demanded with tired affection.

Molly's face changed. The sparkling, teasing gaiety disappeared in an instant, like the sun behind a cloud. She clasped her hands. "Nothing, sir. I am sorry if I disturbed you. I forgot that you would be working on tomorrow's sermon. I'll clean up the pot; it didn't break. Lavinia won't have to do it." She glanced up the stairs at Lavinia, poised magisterially on the landing.

MacGowan's faded blue eyes stared out at his daughter another moment; then he turned and disappeared behind the heavy walnut door of his study.

"I'll help," offered Lavinia.

"Papa acts like he hates me sometimes," said Molly as she bent to pick up the urn and scoop soil back around the rootbound plant.

Lavinia knelt beside her. "He ain't never forgive you for running off with that no-good Larsen boy last year."

"Running off!" snorted Molly. "We went rafting. We were back by midnight. Pa's always preaching forgiveness. Wouldn't hurt him to practice a little of it himself."

"Nineteen ain't too old for a chaperone, an' you knows it," Lavinia reprimanded her. " 'Specially for preacher's young'uns."

"I feel like a prisoner," sulked Molly. "Alissa was lucky. She went to Boston to meet her feller. Nobody told her she couldn't go."

"She allus had better sense 'n you, Miz Molly."

Molly burst out laughing. "But I always get what I want, Lavinia."

Lavinia eyed her thoughtfully. A slow smile spread over the pleasant chestnut brown face. "You sure did this time, didn't you?"

Molly put a comforting arm around Lavinia. "Honest, Lavinia, I just wanted to know for sure if you wore purple satin unmentionables. I'd never tell a soul, certainly never Papa."

"Yore Pa'd mos' likely show me the door."

"He'd never!"

"He might, if the mood was on him."

The young woman fell silent as they finished cleaning up. Her Pa sometimes did get a mood on him, as Lavinia put it. She knew, from listening to servants who had been with the family for a long time and from words that slipped out when the MacGowans took part in family get-togethers with the rest of the Roebuck clan, that her pa and ma had had some awful fights when they were married, and even before, when her mother had been a widow and Daniel a little baby.

She heard the sharp clunk of the door knocker and edged out Lavinia to answer it. "Yes?"

The gentleman on the broad, shaded verandah removed his hat. She could not see his features well at first, against the strong sunlight behind him. "How do you do, miss? I am Lansford W. Hastings. Here is my card. Is the Reverend Micah MacGowan in?"

"Git away from that door!" hissed Lavinia behind her.

Molly smothered a laugh, inviting the handsomely attired stranger to join her mood, then stepped back.

"Yes, sah?"

Hastings repeated himself. Lavinia accepted the card. "Won't you come in, sah? You kin wait right in there."

Lavinia took his hat, gloves, and riding crop, then glared a warning at Molly, who had preceded her into the parlor as she ushered Hastings in.

He's a beautiful man, Molly decided, even if his voice was pitched a little

high. At once she determined to be so ladylike not a soul could fault her, even
Pa.

Hastings betook himself to the center of the room, bowed slightly at Molly,
then sat gracefully on a Queen Anne settee, where he assumed a courteous in-
difference to her presènce. His eyes beaded on the doorway through which his
host would enter.

Molly ran a practiced eye over his dress. He was clothed as expensively as
anybody in Pa's congregation and wore it well. He must be extremely wealthy,
she concluded. She arranged herself decorously in the window seat, where the
light would wash out the freckles, which she had hoped in vain would disappear as she grew up. They remained, a pale brown scattering across her pink
cheeks and small, straight nose. She set her full lips in a prim, demure line.
What could he want with Pa? Her hand? The thought quickened her pulse. He
was older than the beaux who pestered her now. Why, he looked thirty-five if a
day.

A little old, but ripe for love, Hastings was thinking, aware of the scrutiny he
was under. *Perhaps even nearing twenty, as she did have an affair once,* or so he
had heard. Her eyes were lively and knowing. He noted appreciatively how the
blue bodice strained over her firm bosom. She was dressed immaturely for her
age, he judged, as if someone were trying to deny her womanhood. A door
opened across the foyer, and Hastings sprang to his feet.

MacGowan was a tall man, thin, but without the hard trimness of some men
of his age, which Hastings guessed to be in the mid-sixties. His hair was a faded
metallic rust, with sideburns channeling in like pincers toward the no-nonsense
mouth. In his youth his hair had undoubtedly been as red as his daughter's.
MacGowan glanced first over Hastings's shoulder, to his daughter, then he extended his hand. "How do you do, sir?" he said in a slightly testy tone. "This is
an odd hour to call. Most of my parishioners know that Saturday afternoons I
work on my sermon."

"I am deeply sorry, Reverend MacGowan. Shall I call at a more convenient
time?"

"Oh, not at all, sir." MacGowan relaxed slightly, as if pulling himself out of
the web of his creation aborning in the next room. "Molly, perhaps you could
find something to do elsewhere. . . ."

"Of course, Papa." She turned to Hastings and dropped a curtsy. "Good day,
sir."

Hastings bowed gravely, switching a quick glance to her father to gauge his
reaction.

MacGowan was immediately businesslike. "Now, sir, sit down, please. How
may I help you?"

Chameleonlike, Hastings adopted a parallel attitude of sober rectitude and said, "I have just returned from California, Reverend MacGowan. Mr. Stephen A. Davis told me he would take it kindly if I were to call upon you."

The effect of his words on the reverend's stern countenance was remarkable. The face lighted, age and care dropping away. "Stephen! Well, young man, why didn't you say so at once? Excuse me, please." MacGowan crossed the room and threw open the door. "Hannah, my dear! We have a visitor from California. He has seen the children!"

Hastings heard a squeal from Molly. "Alissa and Stephen! Pa, really?"

MacGowan returned, followed by Molly, who looked ready to burst with questions. In a few moments a tall, gracious lady entered, with a sweep of iron gray hair across her forehead, arranged in a soft bun at the crown. Her face was beautiful, age distilling the skin and crow's-feet to highlight a truly extraordinary bone structure.

As soon as proper introductions had been dispensed, Hastings was bombarded with questions.

"How is he?"

"Where are they?"

"He's a fine young man, works for your trading company, he told me. He's a sharp trader. I predict within a few years that he—"

"Excuse me, Mr. Hastings, but my daughter—have you seen Alissa?" asked Hannah.

Striking a dramatic pose, Hastings stroked the pale bristle of his moustache. "Madam," he said gently, "I did not have the privilege of meeting your other daughter. If she looks like her mother, it is a pleasure I would not willingly miss."

Micah brushed the flowery words away from his wife like a busysome bee. "Then tell us what you do know, sir!"

His audience hooked, Hastings leaned forward. "He was trading in Santa Barbara, I believe it was, out of a ship called *New Horizons,* and being fellow Americans we struck up a friendship, and I continued with him on his ship to the city of Yerba Buena—er—I believe they are now calling it San Francisco. This is where Hudson's Bay is putting in a store, Reverend MacGowan, although most of their trade is up in Ore—"

"And Alissa was not with him?" demanded Micah.

"No, sir."

"But then—," began Hannah.

"A moment, dear lady, let me remember. . . . Of course. Mr. Davis mentioned a family of Californians—wealthy Californians, landed gentry—who were their friends. Your daughter was staying with them while Mr. Davis saw to business. Fine young man, a first-rate mind. As a matter of fact, I have encouraged him to apply immediately for a land grant."

"We haven't had any letters at all from them, Mr. Hastings," said Molly, in a plaintive tone. "They told us not to worry, it could take months, or a year even."

"Did he not send any letters with you?" asked Hannah.

"Unfortunately—"

"What did Stephen look like, Mr. Hastings?" MacGowan demanded suddenly in a cold voice.

Hannah threw a startled, embarrassed gaze at her husband.

Hastings gave a self-conscious laugh, then said lightly, "It sounds as if you are impugning my honor, sir. However I will believe that it is only concern for your daughter and her fiancé that prompts such a question. As I recall, young Davis was of regular height, his hair was dark and waved becomingly at collar level. He dresses most properly and speaks with a Boston accent."

A collective sigh broke the tension.

"I am sorry I doubted you, Mr. Hastings," said MacGowan, coloring above the stiff collar. "Please make our house your home while you are in Saint Louis."

"Thank you, sir," said Hastings with sincerity, "but I fear my hours would be disruptive to your household. I am quite comfortable in an excellent hotel. Although my greatest joy was naturally to bring you the good news that your children are safe, it was not the primary reason of my visit."

MacGowan stiffened warily. "Oh? What might that be?"

With a becoming affectation of modesty, he confessed, "I am on a mission for the government."

14

Hastings returned the next day after church. He could hear merry laughter from a range of voices almost as soon as he spotted the rooftop of the MacGowan house. Arranging a congenial smile on his features, he prodded the horse into a smart trot.

Several people were on the porch. He recognized Molly first, by her red hair, fetchingly youthful in a bright yellow dress, the skirts billowing out over the porch swing as she pushed back and forth. Beside her was another girl near her age, in a rose colored frock. On the step below them in full sun were three young men and a young lady, garbed in what Hastings took to be their Sunday best. His smile did not alter as his eyes searched out the elders. Yes, in rather prim poses, it seemed to him, as if still churched. Five of them sat in a semicircle of straight-backed chairs, behind the line of shade crossing the verandah floorboards. There was MacGowan, leaning forward, cosseting a pipe, Hannah beside him, and three others. He wondered what they had said about him.

"Good day!" Hastings called out heartily.

"Here he is," he heard MacGowan say.

"Good afternoon, Mr. Hastings!"

"A splendid sermon, Parson MacGowan," said Hastings, dismounting. A groom appeared to lead away his horse. He removed his hat and inclined his head courteously to the assemblage. He was aware that the swing had stopped and the two girls' heads tipped to each other.

MacGowan introduced everyone. Nearly everyone was a member of the Roebuck clan, as Hastings had surmised. "I thought it only proper that you present your proposition yourself, sir."

"I only thought that with your natural eloquence—," Hastings began.

"Nonsense," MacGowan said. "If you had need of another calling, you'd be a fair man in the pulpit yourself."

"Very well, sir." Hastings cast a second glance at Hannah MacGowan and the man seated on her other side. They looked remarkably alike. "May I be so bold as to enquire if you might be twins?"

"Right you are," said Harmon Roebuck. Roebuck was as handsome and youthful looking as his sister, with the same healthy sweep of iron gray hair.

"Isn't that amazing?" declared Hastings. He turned a jocular gaze on the children and grandchildren of the Roebuck clan, seated on the porch steps or playing in the yard. "And the young people, any twins here?"

"Not so far," piped up a boyish-faced young man from the porch steps. "But we got a bet on that Uncle Micah don't know about, first set of twins wins a heifer from all t'other families." Proudly the young man hugged a young woman sitting beside him, who was dressed in so many layers of clothing that it was entirely possible she was already expecting a child.

"You think Uncle Micah doesn't know about," MacGowan observed brusquely.

A servant fetched another chair. Hastings waved it away, preferring the advantage of looking down on his listeners. He accepted a glass of lemonade, which he set carefully on the porch rail and immediately forgot. "Well then," he began, "yesterday when I called, I left a copy of my book, *An Emigrant's Guide to California,* and the pastor was gracious enough to invite me back today to speak to all of you. I'm in the business of organizing folks who want to make a move to California. In my book I give step-by-step all the information needed to bring everyone safely and happily to this incredible land."

"You've been overland to California, I take it?" said Harmon Roebuck.

"Why, indeed I have, sir. And by ship. I have been called upon to assist our government in Washington to adopt policies favorable to new immigrants." As if by merest chance, Hastings's gaze dropped tranquilly on the girl, Molly. Her ripe lips were parted, her eyes shining windows that betrayed the course of her imagination.

He lowered his voice a theatrical notch and went on: "Lands so vast and so fertile you've only to plant in order to harvest more grain and more produce than you deemed possible this side of heaven's gates." Almost in an aside, he added, "One has only to tour the missions to realize that."

"What about the people living there already?" asked Hannah MacGowan.

"California is still a Mexican territory, madam, to be sure, but in one hundred years the Mexicans have never settled more than a few miles in from the coast. They have little interest in farming. There's thousands upon thousands of acres of prime farm land, untouched by a plow since time began. Thanks to my book, and, ah, to earlier explorers and guides, word is spreading like the pla—like wildfire. Folks from all the states are forming up to cross by land to California."

"Is it a safe place to live?" asked the girl in the swing beside Molly.

"Why there's bears and other game—"

"No, sir, I mean Indians. When our folks came west to Missouri, they tell of fearful times—"

"Now that's the remarkable thing, miss. Indians in California are not warriors, they are more like children. The Mexicans have got almost all of them put in places where they work hard and learn how to lead good, Christian lives."

Harmon threw a skeptical glance at Micah.

"There are a few savages abiding outside the missions, to be sure," Hastings conceded, catching the look. "But more and more Americans are reaching California from the States, and they are *crying out* for a man of God to bring the word into the wilderness."

"Are they now?" said Hannah.

"Mexico's state religion is Catholicism, isn't it?" asked Harmon. "Some Papists don't take kindly to folks of another persuasion movin' in on 'em."

"Surely that would not keep out true Christians like yourselves."

"Oh, Pa, let's go!" said Molly. "Let's go to California."

"You'd go to Madagascar on a mattress," drawled a handsome black-haired youth sitting on the steps.

"I would not, Jared McCloud!"

All the young people laughed. Molly's taste for adventure was well-known. Her father scowled. Hastings wisely kept silent.

"Mr. Hastings," said MacGowan, "yesterday I wasn't quite clear what you wanted of us. Mrs. MacGowan and I, and Mr. Harmon Roebuck and his wife, we are beyond the age of wanting to test ourselves against new frontiers."

Hannah MacGowan nudged her twin. Her eyes still gleamed with the high-spirited call to adventure. Harmon erupted with a chuckle.

"My sister and I did a fair amount of traveling in our day, Mr. Hastings. But Micah's right. Now we leave it to the younger ones."

"Why have you come to us, Mr. Hastings?" Hannah glanced at her husband as if to fathom whether he was entertaining a scheme she knew nothing of.

Hastings rocked back on his heels, his fingers sliding in along the waist of his trousers. "You folks are the best people in Saint Louis. Other folks listen to you. Not that I'm saying you all will want to take up roots," he added hastily. "But when you need things done, go to the best, I always say. If you people, sitting right here on this porch, were to say to your friends and neighbors, 'That Mr. Hastings is a man you can trust to get you to California in safety,' why, a lot of people would go. Just on your say-so."

The young people on the porch stole glances at each other, filled with self-conscious awareness. Were they really the best people in Saint Louis?

MacGowan compressed his lips as if to say this bit of foolery didn't sit too well.

When no one spoke forth, Hastings shifted to a new tack. He frowned in his most businesslike manner. "Now, first of all, a train of God-fearing folk setting out for a new Canaan needs a shepherd. A simple man like me, I can lead them, but we all need a leader above us. The way is sometimes hard, and having a man of the cloth along is comforting. My first thought, of course, was that you, Reverend MacGowan, would entertain thoughts of evangelizing in that godless land. Failing that, it is my earnest hope that you might help me locate some young minister who'd take up a call to California."

Micah glanced at Hannah. "Might be some young man willing to go. When are you hoping to leave the States?"

"Next spring, sir. As soon as the ice melts and the rivers are fordable. That's when the pasturage for the herds is best, and there's plenty of meat for the hunters."

Molly felt a delicious shiver ripple up her spine. "Ooh, Pa, doesn't that sound *wonderful?* I *do* wish we could go!"

Jared McCloud leaned back on the step and looked up at Molly, his eyes filled with longing. "I'll take you, Molly."

There were a few chuckles. No one else spoke. Hastings picked up again.

"There is a very practical way in which you folks might participate in this endeavor. In order to further the Lord's work, you might sponsor a pastoral family."

"How's that?" said Micah sharply.

"Get your congregation to pledge a stipend for a pastoral family, say a hundred dollars for a year."

Micah tugged at one sideburn.

"That is a marvelous idea," said Hannah. "When my husband came to our country as a young man from the London Missionary Society, he was given a stipend for two years. This way we could pass along some of our blessings."

"Claim it for the Lord!" declared Hastings.

"And you, sir," said Hastings, addressing Harmon Roebuck. "Everybody has heard of the Roebuck Trading Company. When Hudson's Bay Company opens up new territory, the first thing they do is send out a man to set up a store. California is just sitting out there like a ripe peach, waiting for someone to come along and pluck it." Hastings spread a hand and swept it in a broad arc. His audience was hanging raptly on his words.

"And if we don't intend to allow her Britannic Majesty Queen Victoria to plunk the crown of England on our land, why, ordinary folks like us have got to do something about it. I'm offering you a chance to put Roebuck Trading squarely in California."

"That's what Stephen is supposed to be doing," Harmon Roebuck said dryly.

"To be sure." Hastings turned his attention to the young folks. "Just before I met Mr. Davis, I had brought a party of one hundred and sixty emigrants across the continent to Oregon, and some of those worthy pioneers expressed a desire to cross down into California, so I brought them. Now, you young folks, you will appreciate this: In the northwest, the Oregon Territory, there was a tree so big it took five grown men with their arms outstretched to reach around it. Man never made a monument almightier than that tree. And there's forests of them that size!" His eyes strayed to Harmon and some of the other listening men. "You could build a dozen houses from a single tree.

"Just the other day I was saying to President Polk—"

"You were *talking* with the president of the United States?" Jared interrupted, incredulity in his voice.

"That's right." Hastings glanced down and fingered his watch fob with becoming modesty. "Knowing I'd been to California and the Oregon Territory, he wanted to know what I thought about the mood of our people living out there. About being subjects of a foreign government. Oh, I tell you, folks, there are fortunes to be made, just waiting for those to follow in the steps of the men who made this country what it is today. Another thing: Do you know that there are thousands of wild horses in the southern part of the territory? So many that they have to go out and thin the herds so there's enough forage for the cattle."

"Mr. Hastings," said Hannah. "Please do not take offense, but what do you get out of this? Are you acting as someone's emissary?"

"No, ma'am, it's my good fortune to be able to conduct my own business in an honorable way and to serve the interests of the United States at the same time. I'm collecting families to sign up on my wagon train at a dollar a head. Never has a soul come to harm when he was under the experienced guidance of Lansford W. Hastings. And Divine Guidance, too, of course. If some of the Roebuck or MacGowan families decided to travel on my train, citizens near and wide would want to come along."

Lavinia came out to the porch and whispered in Hannah's ear. Hannah rose. "Mr. Hastings, will you join us for Sunday dinner? We want to hear everything you can tell us about Stephen and about California."

Hastings swept off his hat. "It will be my fond pleasure, ma'am."

Micah MacGowan and Harmon Roebuck hung back as the others trooped inside, Hastings surrounded by youngsters eager for more tales. "A dollar a head don't seem like much for guiding folks across two thousand miles of wilderness," mused Harmon.

"He wants something for nothing and expects other people to pay for it," decided Micah.

"A pastor to go with his train, you mean? The Lord could still be working through him."

"Hm."

"It's not a bad idea, Micah. It would make a lot of folks rest easier, knowing that a man of God was traveling with them."

"Do you trust him?"

Their eyes met. "Well . . . , no reason not to, until we know him a little better," decided Harmon.

Micah nodded. "I may help him find a pastor, but I won't be counseling my congregation to pull up stakes."

The brothers-in-law went inside.

Hastings prepared to ride back to town near dusk. Molly lingered at the edge of the fence, her fingers idly playing with the brittle stalk of an exhausted sunflower drooping over the fence bordering the drive. After her parents and her uncle Harmon said their good-byes, Hastings mounted and, seeing her waiting, walked his horse slowly along the fence until he was opposite her.

"Are you going back to California right away, Mr. Hastings?"

"Not until spring."

"And you have wagon masters and scouts, like you told us at dinner?"

"Yes. By April the train will be fully provisioned and ready to go, hopefully with eighty-five to a hundred families."

Molly tossed her red hair. "I suppose if a body wasn't happy living where she lived, a body might want to start life over like that."

Hastings smiled. "A body might. I'll be in Saint Louis for three months, Miss Molly. May I call on you again?"

"Mm. I suppose so. If Pa says so."

"Pa did."

An enchanting smile broke over Molly's face. Unexpectedly her voice grew shy. "Then I would like that, Mr. Hastings."

"Thank you. Good evening, Miss Molly."

"Good evening, Mr. Hastings." Molly could not see the smile on Hastings's features as he turned and headed back down the poplar-lined avenue.

"P-s-s-st! Molly!"

Molly turned around. Jared was standing in the middle of the yard, his fingers jammed in the waistband of his trousers.

"What'd you two talk about?"

"None of your business! How dare you spy on me?"

"Love talk, warn't it! He's too old for you."

"He is not."

"He's twice your age." Jared took a step toward Molly, then another. "Molly?"

She turned back, pretending she could still see Hastings. Jared's fingers crept tentatively around her shoulder. When he pressured her shoulder she turned to him.

"Molly. I love you. Don't you know it?" His voice was poignant with the pain of an emotion he did not want to reveal.

Molly looked wistfully up at the handsome, unhappy face. "Yes, I know it. . . ."

"Well?"

She lifted her shoulders. "I don't know if I love you."

"You don't *not* love me, do you?"

"No, I don't *not* love you."

"Would you let me put my arms around you?"

"I guess it would be all right."

Tenderly, as if she might break, Jared held her. "Would you let me ask your pa if I could start courting you?"

"Jared!"

"Please?"

"You're so young."

"I'm older than you!"

Molly pushed his arms away. "Let's go inside. Mama will wonder where I am. Coming?"

"No! I'm going home. See you tomorrow."

"If that's the way you want to be. Good night." Molly turned back to the house, Jared disappearing from her thoughts before he was even out of the yard. *Wouldn't it be something!* she was thinking. *Wouldn't it be something to go to California. And wouldn't Alissa be surprised to see me!*

15

R amon entered the room so quietly that Alissa did not hear him until he spoke to her.

"Good morning. You are up early."

"Oh!" She turned to smile at him. Ramon was dressed for work in a well-worn leather jacket with gloves stuffed in one pocket. His black hair glistened as if he had doused it with water before combing. "Good morning. Juan Julian offered to take my letters to San Diego today."

Ramon prowled behind the small writing desk. The scratch of her quill filled the quiet air. "Writing to Stephen?"

She shook her head. "My family."

He leaned over the high, wooden back of her chair. "All those letters?"

Alissa smiled, her fingers rearranging the stiff, creamy sheets of paper. "No. One is to Thomas Larkin, the American consul in Monterey. He may be able to help me find Daniel. If he is here."

As he leaned close to her head, Alissa could smell the fragrance of sandalwood soap. She turned and glanced up at him. Ramon's eyes were eloquent with emotion. Hastily she picked up the quill.

"I'm also writing to the governor. Don Juan—"

Then Ramon's hand was under her elbow. Without a word he lifted her to her feet and turned her to him. He took the pen from her hand and placed it deliberately on the table. A little smile danced on his face as his fingers curled under her chin.

She caught his fingers. "You are a dear friend," she said quietly.

"A *friend* is not what I hoped you would say."

"To me, you are like a wonderful brother. You will make some girl—"

"Don't say it! Please, don't say it. You can learn to love me."
Her eyes grew moist, but she gave a little smile and shook her head.
"Is it because I am Catholic and you are Protestant? That's it, isn't it?"
"No, that isn't it."
"But you love me, I know you do!"
Alissa turned back to the desk and began to pull her letters into a pile, as if seeking from these links to her family the strength to shore up her shattered life. "I am still trying to get over Stephen."
Ramon was immediately penitent. He stepped away. "Of course you are, dear Alissa. I am sorry I rushed you. In time we will see, eh?" With a gallant bow he strode from the room.
Alissa watched him go with a tiny shake of her head. Someday he *would* make a girl a wonderful husband.

"I am delighted that you decided to come with me today, Ramon."
The stallions' heads bobbed in peaceful unison as father and son rode southwest through the rolling countryside in the direction of San Diego. Behind them several vaqueros attended the horse-driven carts stacked with hides or barrels of tallow and manteca. The hides would be finish cured at San Diego, while the barrels of fats would be loaded directly on ships destined for American ports.
"Was there any particular reason?"
"What?"
"That you came."
"Oh. No. Yes. Father, when you married my mother, was it hard leaving your faith? Learning to be Catholic?"
Father and son exchanged glances. The erect, sandy-gray-haired Bostonian, even after twenty-five years in California, sat more in the saddle after the English mode. His blue eyes, under the flat-brimmed hat, were a pale wash of their original color from years in the unrelenting sun. "I became a Catholic because I fell in love with your mother. I could not marry her unless I became one. I could not have become a Mexican citizen, or owned property under Mexican law."
"Yes," said Ramon impatiently, "but was it *hard?* What did you have to give up?"
This time Juan Julian took longer to answer. "I was not a faithful churchgoer in my youth. Not going to church was sinful, but not like—" Juan Julian shrugged.
"Not a *sin* sin," acknowledged Ramon.
"Exactly."
"So you have not missed it—not being a Protestant."
"Not much. But, Son, even now—to you I say this, but I would not say it to

your mother or to the padre—a lot of what you Catholics do does not carry the same meaning for me. All the Latin and the incense. You know?"

"Yes. But then, Father, why should Alissa find it so hard to change?" Ramon struggled to keep the misery out of his voice.

"Alissa!"

"She loves me, I know she does!"

"Did she tell you that?"

"I love her!" Ramon said defiantly. "But she doesn't want to give up her faith."

"Ah, Son . . . ," the father reached over and clasped his shoulder. "All I can say is that Alissa's faith is stronger than mine ever was. Her father is a parson, a minister trained in London, England, I believe she told me. I can understand it. If your mother had been asked to give up her faith to marry me—well, I do not believe she would have married me."

Ramon spurred ahead, not wanting his father to see the tears scalding his eyes.

By midafternoon they had exchanged their hides and tallow for credits and handed over Alissa's letters to the captain of the trading ship in San Diego's coved bay. Then the Bandini-Warners headed north to the mission at San Juan Capistrano, sixty miles up the coast.

"Why are we going to visit the padre?" Ramon wanted to know.

"Your mother wants one of his Indian girls for a new servant."

"Any special one?"

Juan Julian nodded. "One who is in love with a renegade."

"That one!" said Ramon.

"Your mother insisted."

"Asking for trouble."

Padre Zalvidea, a few hours later, concurred. "The one whom you ask for, my dear friend, is not a pure-bred Indian. Her father was white, probably Mexican."

"Have we your blessing to take her, if she is willing?"

Zalvidea nodded. "I would not deny any of my children a good, moral family life."

They enjoyed Padre Zalvidea's hospitality overnight. The next morning Guadelupe, with her eyes shining, clambered aboard a mule for the journey to her new home and a new life as a serving girl at the Bandini-Warner hacienda. No sooner had they left the mission behind than she dug her bare heels into the mule's flanks and prodded it up beside the horses and bombarded the men with questions.

"How is Gregorio? Are you taking me to him? Are we free now? Truly *free?*"

"I am not taking you anywhere but to my rancho," said Juan Julian sternly.

"It will all be clear." How, he did not know. But he could not deny Arcadia anything.

They found the women in the parlor.

Arcadia crossed to the door and kissed her husband's cheek. "Welcome home, dearest. Did the sale go well?"

"Yes, *mi paloma*. And I brought your new serving girl with the padre's blessing."

Ramon sought Alissa's eyes. "We gave your letters to the captain," he said by way of reestablishing a friendly footing between them.

"Thank you. Did you have a pleasant trip?"

"Very. Thank you."

"This is Guadelupe." Juan Julian pushed the girl gently into the room.

Guadelupe gazed from Arcadia to Alissa. She recognized the latter immediately and ran over to her. "May the Blessed Virgin be with you forever and ever! Now I can be with Gregorio!"

Dona Arcadia's eyebrows lifted. She exchanged a glance of alarm with her husband.

"She's all yours," said Juan Julian.

"You want to marry him, you mean," Alissa corrected her.

"In our way, the way of the Luisenos, we are already married."

What have I gotten myself into? Alissa stared at the girl standing before her, dressed in a clean cotton waist and full skirt that ended about six inches above her bare brown feet. Guadelupe appeared to be no more than fifteen. Yet she was already a wife, in her own sight.

"You and Gregorio must be married by the padre."

"No, Dona Alissa."

"*No!*"

"The padre would make Gregorio come back to the mission. He would put him in the *carcel*."

Alissa glanced at Arcadia.

"Jail," supplied Arcadia.

With Guadelupe gazing anxiously at her, Alissa said in English to Arcadia, "How can I promise her that Padre Zalvidea won't put Gregorio in jail?"

Arcadia turned to the girl. "You are right, Guadelupe," she said in Spanish. "We cannot ask Gregorio to go back to the mission to be married."

Guadelupe's tense body relaxed.

"We must find another padre who will marry you. Will you give me your word that you will remain here and not try to run away, until we can do that?"

"Yes," she said.

Arcadia smiled, and Alissa recognized again the warm love shining forth, which so endeared her to all the servants and vaqueros. "If this Gregorio wishes to visit you, he must come to me first. And he is never to see you unless Concepcion is present. Will you give me your solemn promise, before God?"

"Yes, dona." Swiftly Guadelupe crossed herself. She would have knelt at her feet, but Arcadia anticipated her action and pulled her up. "Concepcion!" she called. While awaiting the appearance of the servant, Arcadia pushed the girl's coarse hair off her neck with an affectionate smile. "Concepcion will give you something to eat and a place to sleep. Tomorrow she will begin to teach you how to serve Dona Alissa. We will try to get in touch with Gregorio and let him know you are here."

"Gregorio knows, dona." Guadelupe followed Concepcion out of the parlor, leaving Arcadia and Alissa staring at each other in astonishment.

"I hope you will not regret taking responsibility for the child, Alissa."

"I do, too. I had no idea. . . . How do you think Gregorio knows she is here?"

Arcadia's smile disappeared. "One of the Indians at the mission must know where he is and how to send messages."

A door opened. A chink-chink of spurs announced Juan Julian's presence. A moment later he entered. "Well, is Guadelupe all settled?"

"I hope so," said Arcadia. "She has given us her promise to remain here until she and Gregorio can be married—What is that in your hand, my dear?"

"This?" Juan Julian held up a letter. The red seal on the flap had been broken. "An invitation to a ball in Los Angeles next month, given by Governor Micheltorena in honor of the American consul, Thomas Larkin."

"Oh, good!" said Alissa, then blushed immediately. "I'm sorry, I didn't mean—"

"Not at all," laughed Juan Julian. "Of course you are invited. Senor Larkin will be pleased to see every American. Upon my soul, look, Arcadia! Our girl looks happy enough to dance here and now."

16

"Are you an official of the United States government?"

Thomas Larkin looked up at the young man entering the consul offices near the Monterey wharf and sized him up quickly. Prosperous, American, exuding that peculiar confidence he had begun more and more to identify with other Americans who made it to California. He smiled. "Semiofficial."

The stranger's clothes were new, cut in the Spanish mode, dark gray trousers that hugged muscular legs, a maroon frock coat and vest, with an oversized white stock at the throat, a hat that he was now removing and placing carefully on a Sheraton side table. The costume suited his lean body very well.

"Stephen A. Davis, of Roebuck Trading Company, Saint Louis and Boston." The deep-set brown eyes that met Larkin's were unwavering and serious. His handshake was firm, his hair and fingernails neatly cut.

"Davis! Yes, I have heard of you. Come in." Larkin led the way into his private office.

"Really?" Stephen was pleased. "Word of our enterprise is getting around then. I should have paid my respects before this, but frankly, I have been too busy. I am here to formally request your help in purchasing enough land to house our firm's California branch."

"Whoa, young man! Tea? Or coffee, perhaps?"

Stephen shook his head, showing a trifle of impatience.

"You haven't been in California much, have you, Davis?"

"This is my second voyage. You seem surprised."

Larkin nodded. "The Mexican way of doing business is much more leisurely than you seem accustomed to."

Stephen laughed apologetically. "It is a hard habit to break, all right. I will have some tea, thank you." He settled into a springy horsehair chair with carved walnut arms, placed his portfolio on the floor beside him, and appeared to relax.

With private delight, Larkin gentled his impatient visitor with ritual talk about the weather, the *cholos,* the whaling industry, pilot bread, public eating houses, fur seals, and finally the import-export trade. "I trust you made it through customs satisfactorily," he finished.

Stephen ran his tongue up into his cheek, as if deciding how much to take Larkin into his confidence. "I paid customs on goods, yes."

Larkin's eyebrows edged upward. "But not necessarily on all your goods?"

"Their duties are exorbitant."

"Yes. It would be understandable if one decided to take matters into one's own hands. But dangerous, Mr. Davis, if one is caught. Bear that in mind."

Stephen stirred in the chair. "It's not as if their own ships were offering the same goods. Besides, government officials and military officers are my best customers."

To tell this Stephen Davis that what he was doing was wrong, unethical, and morally unworthy of the fiber of an American seemed pointless. He knew it, else he would not have defended it so rashly. But Larkin could not resist saying, "You youngsters are so sure that you can outfox everyone. You will undoubtedly get rich. What is the hurry, young man?"

"What is the hurry?" Stephen looked blank. "Why not?"

"Interesting," Larkin said. "Tell me. What is the mood in the East regarding California?"

Stephen leaned around to glance into the outer office.

"We are quite alone."

He sank against the back of the chair and clasped its arms with both hands. "That is easy to answer, sir. In the coffeehouses of Boston, the talk is not 'if' but 'when' our country will annex California. Russia we no longer have to worry about, since they pulled out of Fort Ross a couple years ago. Now, it seems to me, the United States is hovering around California, ready to pounce should either Britain or France make a move."

Larkin was grudgingly impressed by Stephen's acute assessment. "Had you a profession before you became a factor for your company?"

"A lawyer, sir. But I've always loved the sea, and I love driving a good bargain!" Stephen confessed with relish. "Besting an opponent in court cannot hold a candle to beating him to port with a full hold of goods and the wind driving your sails!"

"Hm. So you see Britain and France circling, too, do you?"

"Yes. But I believe it is our manifest destiny to occupy this whole continent."

"Manifest destiny! That has a mighty ring to it."

"Doesn't it? I took it from a magazine I received from Washington." Stephen pulled his portfolio onto his lap and extracted a folded clipping. " 'Our manifest destiny is to overspread the continent allotted by Providence for the free development of our multiplying millions.' " He glanced up expectantly at Larkin.

"That is what they are saying in Boston, sir. Everyone says that our territorial expansion must be divinely sanctioned, for the march of the United States has met naught but success."

"What an extraordinary idea."

"Indeed. If proof were needed, just look at Texas."

"Oh, yes. I heard that a push for annexation is underway."

"I predict California will not be far behind." Stephen leaned forward, his body coiling around the intensity of his words. "I have heard, Mr. Larkin, that coal has recently been discovered on this coast. Is it true?"

"Why, I don't know . . . ," Larkin was hard put to keep up with this whirling young mine of information.

"Well, if it is true, it will greatly facilitate the introduction of steam navigation in the Pacific. It could be the means of making California one of the most important commercial positions on the West Coast of America, particularly, if ever a communication should be opened by means of a canal across the Isthmus of Panama."

Larkin nodded. "There has been a lot of talk about a canal. When it happens, one might visit and return to the United States in half the time."

"Yes. The outward navigation is terribly long and tedious, a journey I must make again in two weeks."

Especially for young men in a hurry, thought Larkin. He poured them more tea. "What else have you observed, Davis?"

Stephen cradled the teacup and at last appeared truly relaxed. "If we but wait, and the Europeans do nothing, California is ours." The intelligent brown eyes gazed candidly at Larkin. "I have no quarrel with the Mexicans. I remember something a friend told me once. He's Ramon Antonio Bandini-Warner, the son of an important landholder in the south—he said that anyone who migrates to California soon becomes one of them. As you have said. The pace is one of leisure. Even in business. One loses one's nationalism and simply *becomes* Californian, no matter the origin of birth. This may be true. But this is what will cause Mexico to let California slip out of its grasp in the end."

"This would not happen to you, this—addiction—to leisure."

"No. Not to me. Never," he added with emphasis.

"It is dangerous to say 'never,' my friend. For that is just when 'never' becomes 'ever' and bedevils the life out of us!" Although disapproving of some of his guest's attitudes, Larkin found himself liking the young man. "By the way, Davis, in two weeks the governor of California is hosting a ball in my honor."

"Congratulations, sir."

Larkin laughed. "Thank you. I did not tell you to garner congratulations, but to extend an invitation. The ball would present an ideal opportunity for you to extend your acquaintance with men who are important to California's future."

Stephen looked as if he could not believe his good luck. "Why, sir, that is— that is very *noble* of you. Where is the ball to be held?"

"In Los Angeles."

Stephen nodded. "Yes, we shall be in port then, I could be there—"

"Splendid! Several important families from the south will be there, the Picos, the Alvarados, the Bandini-Warners. And I understand that a very beautiful young lady, an American girl, is visiting with the Bandini-Warners. Her hair is said to be the most remarkable shade, like light shining through a goblet of liquid honey."

The change that came over Davis startled him. A slow stillness settled over his features. His mouth took on a hard line, a mixture of defiance and something resembling guilt.

"Miss Alissa MacGowan."

"You know her!"

"Yes," Stephen said brusquely. He thrust himself up out of the chair. "I am sorry, sir, but I think it will be impossible for me to attend the ball after all.

Perhaps there will be another occasion when I return to California. For now, I have taken enough of your time."

"A moment." Larkin reached for a card. Dipping his pen in the inkwell, he scribbled rapidly on the reverse side. "This man is a land broker. He is well versed in Mexican land law. He is also honest."

The barb was not lost on Stephen. He took the card and shook Larkin's hand. "Thank you, sir." He hesitated for a moment, and Larkin thought that for the first time he perceived a glimmer of uncertainty.

"I thought Miss MacGowan had gone back to Saint Louis. It is her family's interests I represent."

"Her family is associated with Roebuck Trading Company?"

"*Roebuck* is her mother's maiden name. The company represents a consortium of several brothers and a sister." The sharply tailored shoulders of Stephen's frock coat appeared to sag momentarily. "If she . . . , no, never mind. Thank you again."

Larkin did not offer to see him out. His brow clouded in thought. *Pity. A fine young man, of pleasing appearance and good mind. But Caesar was ambitious. . . .*

17

Alissa MacGowan, descended of Scotch-Irish and French forbears, born an American citizen when Missouri was its newest state, was fast becoming a Mexican. She adored the climate, the horses, the dashing good looks of Latin men, *asadera,* anything with chili in it, the scent and hand of well-tanned leather, the fun-loving, spirited dispositions of its aristocratic, athletic women, and the wonderful, velvety rhythms of its language.

On the other hand, indolence, *machismo,* and a lack of ambition by many men for the future of their northernmost province had produced for the Mexicans a peculiarly backward region. Nowhere else had a conquering country so failed to recognize and capitalize on the potential of a conquest.

In the months since breaking her engagement to Stephen, Alissa had busied herself learning not only to speak Spanish fluently but to write it. She had used a little of the money Stephen had rendered to her account for her share of the cargo of the *New Horizons* to purchase fabric for clothes suitable for riding.

The Mexicans had not bothered to build roads to connect the coastal towns of San Diego, Los Angeles, Santa Barbara, Monterey, and San Francisco; therefore carriages were little used. Travel by horseback suited the Californians well and required nothing more than periodically capturing and breaking new mounts. Alissa had graduated from a very gentle mount to a satiny, compact, black stallion nearly as spirited as those ridden by the others.

The Californians were a sociable society. At the time the Bandini-Warners were setting out from the rancho to attend the governor's ball in Los Angeles, landed aristocrats from all over California were without doubt similarly enroute. A branch of Arcadia's family owned a rancho that sprawled across the eastern foothills, only a few miles outside the dusty town. Thus the ball created occasion for an extended visit of the clan.

Alissa could hardly wait for a real glimpse of Los Angeles. The Bandini-Warners had mentioned it casually for months, yet she remembered nothing that revealed its presence when she and Stephen had sailed south from Santa Barbara nearly a year ago.

Ramon and Mariana were riding with her. Mariana was talking about the governor's cholos.

"Don't worry, Governor Micheltorena would not dare give them free rein with so many of us there," said Ramon.

"I was terribly afraid, that day at the mission," Alissa put in.

"They are sneaks and cowards. They would not attempt to rob one of us if the odds were anywhere near even."

"Even Micheltorena could not permit such behavior," agreed Mariana.

The horses moved smartly through the dappled shade of groves of oaks. The stamina of the range-tough horses never ceased to evoke Alissa's admiration.

"You look so happy. What are you thinking?" Ramon asked her now.

"That I am glad to be alive! It is spring, and I have never been to a ball." She glanced at Dona Arcadia, riding behind her. "And I have never, *ever,* gone visiting on such a grand scale."

Dona Arcadia flashed a beautiful smile. "If it were not a ball, we would have gone visiting soon anyway. There are several young men in my family who have been clamoring to see you again."

"Really?" Alissa blushed with pleasure. Breaking up with Stephen still bruised her spirit, despite the arguments she had with herself that it was all for the best.

"Of course. The last time you met them, at Mariana's wedding, you were betrothed. And much shier."

"You're teasing me! Well, yes, I suppose I was. But only because I couldn't understand what anybody was saying."

"You speak beautifully now, Alissa. Your American accent is charming."

Alissa twisted around to check on Guadelupe. The girl jounced along with the stiff posture of a novice rider, among the other servants. Her face shone with delight, as if in all her young days at the mission she had never imagined so grand an adventure. Alissa knew exactly how she felt.

It seemed to Alissa that the longer she was with them, the stronger grew the girl's enthusiasm for life at the rancho.

"Are you happy here, Guadelupe?" she had asked her last week.

"Yes, Dona MacGowan."

"Have you seen Gregorio?"

"Yes. Don Warner told Gregorio that he could come and work at the rancho, too."

"What did Gregorio say?"

Guadelupe's hand shook as she inserted the needle carefully in the fabric of the ball gown she was helping Alissa make. "He will not come. Also Gregorio says that he does not see a reason to be married by any priest. We are already married."

Alissa had put down her handwork. "Oh, Guadelupe! What did you tell him?"

"I tell him that I promise you, and I promise God. I keep my promise."

The knobbed hills sloped gently downward as the party neared Los Angeles. After the warm spring rains, the hills were blanketed with vibrant greens and masses of yellow mustard. Soon a small hacienda covered with fuschia bougainvillea vine came into view. As they rode to the higher ground of the house Alissa's gaze swept westward. They were at the center edge of a plain crisscrossed with small rivers and streams that rolled on to the Pacific. The plain was contained like a bowl in a rim of sheltering hills. A smattering of buildings lay at the heart of the plain, under a hazy sky, with smaller outcroppings built here and there, all the way to the shore.

"Where is the smoke coming from?" she asked.

Ramon answered, "They call Los Angeles the bay of smokes. It is just the way the air is." He lifted his gaze to the sky. Alissa followed. In awed silence they watched a flight of Canada geese pass overhead. The graceful black and white birds flapped steadily northward, never breaking formation.

The procession drew up before the flower-decked house. The others were dismounting, walking around Alissa and Ramon, cries of greetings and welcome filling the air. Alissa hung back.

"Not afraid, are you?" Ramon teased.

She shook her head, smiling into the lively brown eyes. "Thank you for being a good friend."

His eyes were eloquent testimony to his own thoughts.

She gave his hand a squeeze. "May I ask a favor?" she said impulsively.
"Anything."

"Will you accompany me to call upon Mr. Thomas Larkin tomorrow morning? I'd rather not wait until the ball. If he knows anything at all about Daniel—"

"Yes, of course. I'll ask my cousin to ride in today and present your card."

The family of Pio Pico were second-generation Californians, grown wealthy from a score of land grants, far more at home with the other powerful rancho families than the rapacious governor, General Manuel Micheltorena.

Thomas Larkin and Pio Pico had enjoyed an amiable friendship of several years, so it was no surprise that Larkin chose to guest at the Pico's rather than at the more pretentious mansion of the governor on his visits from Monterey.

The spacious inner courtyard of the Pico mansion was entirely surfaced with fine red tiles, an attribute of the Picos' love of dancing and entertaining. A pink adobe fountain circumscribed by a seating wall of decorated, glazed tiles invited relaxation, giving an illusion of coolness on even the hottest days.

Here Ramon and Alissa were shown to await the American consul. Alissa immediately recognized something about the man striding across the red tiles that marked him an American. It was a sense of self-confidence, of rightness about the world. The recognition shocked her. Until then, she had not thought about such things.

Thomas Larkin welcomed them with a gracious smile accompanied by an outstretched hand. "Welcome to Don Pio Pico's home. He is not here at the moment, or I should have asked him to join us."

After introductions, Larkin asked how Alissa had come to be in California.

"Aboard the *New Horizons,* sir, out of Boston. My family owns a trading company, Roebuck Trading."

"Yes, I have heard of it," he nodded.

Alissa found herself being easily noncommittal as she said, "Our representative is Mr. Stephen Davis. You may have met him."

"Indeed, Miss MacGowan. As a matter of fact he—," Larkin stopped himself just in time and covered the pause with a cough. The brig *New Horizons* was at this moment docked offshore, not twenty miles away. If Davis and Miss MacGowan were at odds, then he, as a gentleman, should certainly not create any awkwardness that might be avoided. "Excuse me. He presented his credentials at Monterey just two weeks ago."

"Oh? I expected he would have sailed for Boston. However he did have some business to conclude with an associate, Mr. Hastings—"

"Oh, surely not!" said Larkin, with a quick glance at Ramon. "Don Ramon, are you acquainted with this Mr. Hastings?"

"No sir."

Larkin pursed his lips. At last he said, "Well, how may I be of assistance to you, Miss MacGowan? I have no real authority here, but I am able now and then to help Americans avoid some of the problems that arise naturally from living under a foreign flag."

"I am looking for my brother. . . . "

"That should not be too difficult," Larkin said when she finished, "providing he did not go on to become a solitary trapper who only surfaces in the spring and fall."

"Not difficult! Really?" Alissa said in astonishment.

"Why do you say it should be easy?" Ramon wanted to know.

"In the census six years ago, in eighteen forty, there were only six thousand people living in all of Alta California," explained Larkin, "not including the native Indian population, of course. They do not count. Of the six thousand, only six or seven hundred are foreigners, most of whom are American and most of whom are registered with my office."

"But that is wonderful! Then it is possible that in your office right now is an address for Daniel!"

"Indeed it is possible, Miss MacGowan," Larkin smiled. "And I will be delighted if it is so. If you will write all the particulars for me before I return to Monterey, I will check that very day and send a rider to you with any news I can discover."

Ramon pumped Larkin's hand. "Thank you, sir. You have given Dona Alissa new hope."

Larkin said with pleasure. "It is nothing. Shall I see you both again?"

"At the ball tomorrow night."

"Good! Then may I ask now that you reserve a dance for an old man of forty, Miss MacGowan?"

Alissa broke into a dazzling smile. "I shall be honored. Thank you so much, Mr. Larkin, thank you!"

"Now, shall we have some refreshments?"

"A moment, Mr Larkin. . . . "

"Yes, Don Ramon?"

"You have heard of a Mr. Hastings, eh?"

Larkin considered his words. "If it is the same man, I would urge you and your friends to have no more to do with him. Now, shall we have that cool drink?"

18

The air was pungent with the heady scent of blooming roses as twenty women and men on black horses set out from the Bandini rancho in the foothills east of Los Angeles. Their voices were gay, infected by a splendid winter moon, glowing like an enchanted pearl cast against lavender velvet.

Alissa heard the clear call of a meadowlark. Tiny bats hurtled by, low to the horizon. She was surrounded by ladies gorgeously garbed, wearing jewels that would be at home around milk white throats at the courts of Europe. The dresses rustled. New leather creaked. Moonlight gleamed off silver conchos. She drew in a sigh and felt blissfully happy.

Hundreds of torches planted in the ground lighted the pathway to General Manuel Micheltorena's mansion, a large, square structure of white and rose stucco with neither veranda nor balconies. An imposing Moorish arch framed a pair of heavily carved double doors. Two stone carvings flanked the arch, each depicting an eagle wrestling with a serpent, symbols of Mexico's freedom over oppression.

The doors opened. As the Bandini-Warner clan assembled in the foyer, Alissa felt an indefinable sense of foreboding. Of evil. An involuntary shiver rippled up her back, and she glanced up at Ramon for reassurance.

Ramon clasped his hands behind his back and smiled down at her. "Ready to brave the serpent in his nest?" he murmured.

She laughed, relaxing. A footman took her white wool cape, revealing a gown of amethyst taffeta that shimmered in the candle glow. At her throat she wore an antique lavalier of white gold and pearls suspended from a necklace of irregular pearls as large as peas, lent her by Arcadia.

Juan Julian and Arcadia had started through the reception line. Alissa and Ramon followed. An aide in a short red jacket with gold epaulettes took their names. "Dona Alissa MacGowan and Don Ramon Antonio Bandini-Warner," he announced. "His honor, Governor Manuel Micheltorena, general of the army of Mexico and governor of the Department of California."

Micheltorena was a small, pock-marked man almost overwhelmed by his trappings. A general's gold epaulettes and braid decorated the shoulders of his white uniform. A palm-size medallion of office emblazoned with a red enamel eagle and serpent hung by a silk ribbon around his neck.

Alissa offered her hand. Micheltorena's gaze traveled slowly the length of her gown, dwelling pointedly at the soft hollow between her breasts. Then, imprisoning her fingers in a hard, deliberate grasp, with his other hand he fondled the lavalier at her throat, resting thick, hairy fingers brazenly against her skin.

Alissa gasped and stepped back. Micheltorena released the lavalier and her fingers so smoothly she was uncertain if his ill-mannered behavior had been by intent or ignorance.

"What a lovely piece," he said. "The gift of a lover, perhaps?" A glance flicked Ramon's way, accompanied by a lascivious smile.

The unease Alissa felt when she had entered returned, intensifying her anger. For the first time she realized the presence of cholos. No money for uniforms there, the men looked exactly as they had that dusty afternoon at the mission. They lounged in twos and threes about the quickly filling ballroom, with the arrogance of men secure in the power of their leader. Ramon, tight lipped, guided her to join his family.

"Those men are wearing pistols," she whispered.

Ramon nodded.

"What did that man say to you?" Arcadia asked her, as if she could not bring herself to refer to him by name.

"He admired your lavalier." The women's eyes met in perfect understanding.

"Santa Anna should have known better than to send such a man to us," Juan Julian said in an undertone. "He has been here three years and earned Mexico a host of new enemies. Do not judge California by anything that happens tonight, Alissa," he told her. "Times were better a few years ago."

"Presidente Santa Anna has made it a point to ship the most worthless men in his government up north," said Arcadia. "Micheltorena is the worst of the lot. Even his cholos despise him."

"He cannot control them, therefore he is afraid of them," added Ramon in a scathing tone.

They were all relieved when the musicians struck up and the dancing began. Juan Julian took Arcadia in his arms and whirled away. Ramon turned to Alissa.

"Let us forget our host and his problems and enjoy his party." He bowed crisply to her. "Now?"

"Now?"

"You would not dance with me at Mariana's wedding. But *now.* ..."

She laughed. "Now I will!"

The next two hours passed in a whirl of rampant, giddy fun. Alissa felt herself the toast of the ball. Occasionally she caught the governor watching her, quite casually, as if his glance just happened to travel over the dancers in concert. Each time this happened, Ramon's cousins or friends would descend to beg a dance.

At one point Thomas Larkin took her hand to lead her out for a courtly *jarabe*, inserted as a breather among the livelier rounds. "Have you thought about visiting Monterey yourself?" the American consul asked in English as he led her in an execution of the intricate steps. "It would be a shame to return to Saint Louis without coming and without visiting San Francisco. That is the most American of the Mexican cities. Mrs. Larkin and I would be honored to have you stay with us."

"I shall consider it, Mr. Larkin."

At ten o'clock the dancing stopped. Guests were herded rather unceremoniously through the foyer into another room, where stewards had set up long tables of food. Alissa glanced around. The room was practically bare. A fortune in silver, crystal, and plate gleamed from the linen table coverings, but guests helping themselves at the food tables were apparently expected to eat at benches or standing up.

"Did you see the bottles of mission wines?" remarked Ramon as they carried their plates to one of a cluster of short benches set about the dining hall. "You can bet he didn't pay for them." Soon they were joined by Ramon's parents and Mariana and Felipe.

Mariana glanced over her shoulder as she sat between her brother and husband. "The governor keeps looking over here. It gives me goose bumps!"

"It is outrageous, the way he flaunts his mistress in proper company," said Arcadia.

"His mistress!" said Alissa.

"I hear he has a wife and several children at home in Mexico," Mariana said.

A man strolled casually across the hardwood floor to station himself against a wall near them.

Alissa glanced up at him with a shock of recognition. She was positive he was one of the cholos who had threatened them at the mission. She glanced at Ramon. He had recognized him, too, but shrugged it off with a devil-may-care grin. She was relieved, as they finished eating, when Ramon suggested a stroll outside.

He led her through the French windows to a large patio. A crisp breeze was rising. She inhaled deeply. The night air in California was simply intoxicating. It was like nowhere else. Alissa smiled at Ramon, admiring the way the wind whipped through his hair, transforming the thick natural wave into breakers of curl.

"Alissa, Alissa. . . ." He ran a hand tenderly down her bare arm. He clasped her fingers and brought them to his lips. She could feel his warm breath against her skin, the sensuous brush of his moustache. "Come here...."

Ramon's arms went tenderly about her. The music from the ballroom traveled out to the fragrant patio. Suddenly, perversely, she wanted his kisses. Their lips met, and she could feel the pressure of his fingers against her back. She caressed the nape of his neck, feeling stirrings in her own body. Suddenly she broke away.

Ramon was breathing heavily. "Stephen was a fool to ever let you go! Please, please marry me, Alissa."

She shook her head, ashamed, knowing that she did not love him.

"How do you think it is for me? Living with you, day after day, learning what makes you laugh, listening to your strange ideas, the rides, the picnics—oh, darling—"

"I am so sorry. I should not have let you kiss me. It isn't fair. You should be courting. You are a wonderful young man. You are giving and generous and beautiful."

"Beautiful!" he said scornfully. "I am not playing games, Alissa!"

She hung her head. "It is time for me to leave your family. I have taken your hospitality for far too long."

"Alissa, please," begged Ramon.

She glanced away. "Did you know that there is a boardinghouse for American ladies in San Francisco? Mr. Larkin told me about a very respectable place—"

"Don't! I can't let you go someplace like that!"

"Dear Ramon. Come with me, and then you will see that I shall be all right."

"And then what?"

"Then I shall make a life for myself." She could not stand the pain in his eyes. She moved to the edge of the patio and stared at the cactus garden. Sharp spines of cactus leaf glittered in the moonlight. How could she tell him that the thought of leaving the protective warmth of his family was nearly unbearable?

She turned back to Ramon, a tall, silent, and slender shadow waiting against the moonlight. "If I can learn nothing of Daniel, perhaps then I shall sail back to the United States."

The shadow did not move.

Alissa hesitated. Then she returned to the ballroom alone.

19

Sir George Simpson, governor-in-chief of Hudson's Bay Company, peered into his shaving mirror. His jaw was broad, as firm as it had been in his youth, his sable moustache as vigorous. The dim reflection did not do justice to the full head of dark hair, the broad shoulders, and stout frame of the Englishman. He had been invited by the governor of California to attend the ball given in honor of the American consul, Thomas Larkin. By jove, Simpson decided, he would look his best, even if Micheltorena was a dishonorable rascal.

Micheltorena had even sent his personal sloop to San Francisco to collect him. Simpson suspected that the governor's hospitality had little to do with furthering international relations. Americans were circling around California like dogs at a rabbit hole. He himself was undoubtedly a cleverly considered diversion intended to set Briton and American butting heads while leaving the governor free to pursue his rapacious ways. The tactic suited Simpson's purpose even better than Micheltorena could have guessed.

While he completed his toilet in the cramped, upstairs guest room in the governor's house, Sir George thought back to his audience with Queen Victoria several months ago.

He had reminded the young queen that Mexico's debt to England now exceeded $50 million. If Mexico could be persuaded to cede California to England to cover the debt, he and the Hudson's Bay Company could govern California for the British Empire. Hudson's was already in place, with links through Canada. Under good management and with an English population, California would most certainly realize all that had been predicted of her. Land grants parceled out to native citizens would of course be nullified. . . .

Simpson's audience with the queen receded into a brown haze as guitar rhythms gradually insinuated themselves into his consciousness. He stood in the center of the guest room, an ear cocked to the music rising from the party below. By all that was holy! He, George Simpson, knight of the realm, stood to go down in history as the man who brought England the richest prize since India! He ran his thumbs behind the lapels of his new frock coat and opened the door.

Simpson descended the stairway to the rising sounds of merriment. He crossed the foyer to the ballroom. Larkin's tall, sandy-gray-haired figure stood out in the sea of darker heads. Next to him stood John Warner, an American who had given up his citizenship and his religion and Mexicanized his name in order to marry into the wealthy Bandini clan.

Ah, but look at the lady he won! Simpson thought, appreciating the beauteous Arcadia Bandini-Warner, standing tall and dignified beside her husband. Arcadia was reputed to be the best dancer in all California. And surely the dashing young man next to Arcadia was their son. And next to him, a beautiful English flower, a vision in amethyst. Simpson quickened his step.

"No wonder it is so difficult for traders," Larkin was telling Alissa. "Last year's laws are this year's jokes." He paused, recognizing the newcomer headed their way. "Simpson! I didn't know you were in Los Angeles." He reached across the circle to shake the hand of the Britisher and introduce him.

Simpson lingered over Alissa's hand. "By your accent you are American. Allow me to voice my sorrow that a lady as radiantly lovely as you is not English."

Alissa laughed. "I am not sure if I have received a compliment or not, Sir George."

Simpson allowed a wide smile, deliberately at his engaging best. "A compliment, my dear."

"How are things with Hudson's Bay Company?" said Larkin.

Simpson hesitated slightly before answering. "We are establishing an office in San Francisco."

"So I had heard. Do you expect to get enough furs to warrant another station?"

"Captain Sutter does well enough in California. I do not see why Hudson's should not also."

"Who is Captain Sutter?" Alissa asked Ramon, fascinated with the cosmopolitan turn of conversation.

"He was a French citizen born in Switzerland," supplied Larkin. "He applied for Mexican citizenship, which he received, and then petitioned for a land grant in the wilderness. All this was some years ago. No one understood why he wanted land so far away from the Pacific."

"It is prime wheat land, for one thing," interjected Simpson. "In my opinion, Mexico should have looked twice before deeding him so much acreage."

Larkin studied Simpson speculatively, wondering why Simpson had made it his business to learn about Sutter. "Have you ever seen his place? What does he call it?"

"New Helvetia? No, but he has built quite a fortified town, I understand. Completely self-sustaining, even to military enforcements."

"Sutter is a strange bird," Larkin mused. "One would suspect that he does not want other people to become too interested in what he is up to."

Simpson laughed. "There is that tad of an emperor complex about him all right," he said smoothly.

"Have you had a good look at this land, Simpson?" said Larkin. "Here on the very threshhold of the country, barely awake. All kinds of people. . . ."

"Nature doing everything, and man doing nothing."

"California in a nutshell," Larkin agreed with a smile. "But not for long." The determined glint in Larkin's eye was not lost on Simpson.

A shrill laugh drew the attention of the group. It issued from the throat of a gaudily dressed woman strutting in the wake of the governor. Governor Micheltorena was making the rounds, throwing extravagant compliments at the ladies, greeting most men with small nods of the head. As they proceeded from party to party, the length of the ballroom, attended by half a dozen hard-eyed men, Warner and his friends watched the approach in deepening silence.

With ill-disguised contempt, Micheltorena accepted the congratulations of Juan Julian and Arcadia, Ramon and Alissa, Larkin and Simpson upon the success of his ball.

"You *should* feel honored," he said, brushing aside Juan Julian's attempt to draw him into civil conversation.

"I beg your pardon, Your Excellency?"

"You should feel greatly honored, especially you, Dona Arcadia." Micheltorena smiled, revealing long, tobacco-stained teeth. "Senor Larkin here believes I make all this expense just for him. No. I have done it for only one purpose."

Alissa was shocked by the malice in his eyes as he glanced at Thomas Larkin.

"What purpose is that, Governor Micheltorena?" Arcadia asked with an even smile.

"Call me Manuel, please, dear lady. I make all this expense just to dance with you! You do not invite me to your daughter's wedding. I am a big man, I shrug it off. And now we dance." Micheltorena extended his arm. Arcadia laid her fingers delicately along the white sleeve of his coat. He turned back toward Alissa and paused, his gaze once again moving over her with insolent freedom. "Do not be disappointed, *pajarita.* Your governor will not neglect you—Senora?"

Juan Julian stared after them with an expression of disgust.

"I say, he's a rude brute," Simpson said in a low voice.

"The only thing—nearly the only thing—that I bitterly detest in California is that we are sometimes at the mercy of amoral, greedy pigs. Think twice before giving up your American citizenship, Alissa."

"I do not plan to do that," she assured Juan Julian.

"Californians have more in common with Americans than with the Mexicans down south," suggested Larkin.

"Oh, I would not agree with that," Simpson put in. "True Californians behave more like the British. They are independent, resourceful, brave— What do you say, Warner? You have a foot in both camps."

"Right now, foreigners nearly outnumber native Californians," he said slowly, still watching his wife.

"And most foreigners are Americans, right?" Sir George Simpson said. "You see, Larkin? You fellows already have a disproportionate share of influence."

"Come, Simpson, how can you say that? Britain's habitual pattern of conquest is to establish industries in foreign lands and fill the upper ranks with Englishmen. Frankly, it is no secret that Hudson's is less interested in furs than in future conquest."

"You are imputing American motives to simple English enterprise, sir," said Simpson with an air of injured dignity.

"The United States claims nothing below the forty-second parallel," Larkin retorted.

The two men were glaring at each other when the musicians stopped playing and Micheltorena led Arcadia back to her husband's arm.

"What is this, senors?" Micheltorena said, his eyes flicking from Larkin to Simpson with relish. "Not getting along?"

"Only a slight discussion about the Oregon Territory, Your Excellency," Simpson said.

"No! That is a relief. As long as you do not try to carve up *my* borders. Mexico has no interest in extending its northern boundaries," he added virtuously.

"I should hope not!" Ramon said. "Our *presidente* ignores us as it is!"

"You feel ignored, young Ramon?" Micheltorena's head swiveled like that of a toad considering an insect. "That is not what my *cholos* tell me. They tell me that you are very fond of strutting for your lady. They tell me that you interfered with them while they were on *my* official business at San Juan Capistrano Mission."

"Official business? Extortion!"

A hush fell over the group and spread to others close by. Several cholos crowded nearer.

"Perhaps a tour of service in my personal army would cure you of feeling ignored, young Ramon. Perhaps I shall conscript you here and now, eh?"

"Fortunately we are not at war, governor," said Juan Julian in an effort to smooth over his son's rash words.

Alissa's heart began to pound as she cast about for a way to divert Micheltorena. "Governor Micheltorena?"

His gaze swiveled to her.

She swept him a curtsy. "I am still waiting for our dance. Do your musicians know how to play, 'In a Garden in Castile'? It is a song my Aunt Isabella taught me when I lived in Saint Louis. Have you ever been to Saint Louis, Your Excellency?"

Alissa took his arm and smiled down into his face. "I could sing it for the musicians."

As Alissa led the governor away, Arcadia gazed after her. "There is a true *hidalga,* a noblewoman," she said with conviction. Then she turned to Ramon with anxious eyes. "You must leave now."

"Without Alissa?" he protested.

"We will bring Alissa," said Juan Julian. "Your mother is right. You must get out of sight. Felipe and the vaqueros will go with you." The Bandini-Warners began a seemingly casual progression toward the entrance.

Larkin watched them go. "I hope young Warner is smart enough to keep out from under Micheltorena's nose," he said to Simpson. "There is a man who enjoys carrying out threats."

The tempo of the music changed again. Soon Larkin noticed Arcadia and Juan Julian dancing perfectly together as if they hadn't a care in the world. Alissa came toward them, laughing, her cheeks alive with color.

"It appears she survived her dance with the governor," Simpson observed.

"You look charming, Miss MacGowan," smiled Larkin. "Are you having a good time?"

"Yes, thank you! Dancing is such fun. I have come to invite you to be my partner, sir."

"Me?" said Larkin with pleasure. "With so many young gallants around, you want to dance again with an old codger like me?"

"Mr. Larkin," Alissa said urgently as they began dancing. "Ramon's father begs a favor of you."

The crinkled gaze of carefree enjoyment never left the politician's face as he gazed out over the floor before coming back to her eyes.

"Soldiers were waiting for Ramon when he and Felipe went for their horses. It is lucky we had so many vaqueros. Juan Julian says Ramon must leave California. Ramon will not do it, but he would come with me if I take up your invitation to visit—"

"By all means, Miss MacGowan." After a moment's thought, he added, "I can get Ramon aboard an American trader tonight."

"You *can?* That's wonderful!"

"You will travel with me. I'll remain a couple more days. Then we will collect him up in Monterey. He is not known there. He will be safe."

Tears of gratitude brimmed in her eyes.

Larkin smiled down at her. "You have had quite an initiation tonight, Miss MacGowan. May I say that I am proud that you are American?"

"Thank you, sir."

20

The night had turned cold. In contrast with the trapped, moist air inside the ballroom, the air that met Ramon and Felipe was frigid, leaving an impression of bits of frost hanging from their breaths. The moon had gone down, but a haze hovering over the night seemed to reflect a glow that pushed back the blackness, giving hills and trees mass and moving shapes substance.

They rode several miles without speaking, in the core of a dozen vaqueros whom Juan Julian had instructed to accompany the two men back to the Bandini rancho in the San Gabriel foothills before returning for himself and the women. Micheltorena's men followed close behind.

Over the hoofbeats of their galloping horses they could hear the soldiers ragging them with catcalls and crude epithets. Ramon's contempt for them increased. His humiliation at being ordered home like a boy was fusing into anger. What would Alissa think of him? At last the anger exploded. He pulled his horse up sharply.

"Let's teach them a lesson!"

"No! Not here, it is not worth it," Felipe urged. "Think of your parents, Ramon!"

Resentfully he spurred onward. After an hour the cholos began to drop farther and farther behind, until at last there was no sign of them.

"It is no use to sulk. What did you say to the governor?" demanded Felipe.

"That his breath stank. Pah! In truth, the governor is still angry that I caught his men robbing the San Juan mission. Hold it!"

Felipe threw up a hand to halt the men behind. Immediately they scrambled the horses into a tight circle, facing outward, whips, pistols, and rifles in hand.

The flying hooves of a single horse pounded down the road they had come. "Don Ramon!" came an urgently whispered call in an American accent.

"Here!"

The horseman pulled up so sharply that his steed's legs bunched in a four-

footed stall. The rider's face was blacked out under the silhouette of an American cowhand's hat. "I'm from Thomas Larkin. He's got a ship waiting offshore.
It'll take you to Monterey."

"Don't believe him," said Felipe. "How could the American consul get a
ship ready so soon?"

"What ship?" Ramon asked.

"I don't know. He sent another aide to the coast to make arrangements. My
job was to follow you with orders not to approach until the cholos got off your
tail—following you, you understand? Larkin says if you want to come, come
alone. It's safer."

"I'll come."

"Ramon—"

Ramon leaned out of the saddle to clasp his brother-in-law in a quick, hard
embrace. "Take care of Mariana and my parents. Tell the vigilantes. Micheltorena may try to take it out on my family."

"I will," promised Felipe. *"Vaya con dios."*

"Con dios," said Ramon, and to the American, "Let's go."

"Which way is quickest?" the American asked.

Ramon forged ahead, giving the main road to Los Angeles a wide berth. The
hardened range horses raced through the night with the endurance of fresh
mounts. The sky was paling to gray when they reached the patches of marshy
lagoon that spread inland from the coast into the Los Angeles valley.

At San Pedro, the air reeking of tar, they were met by two more of Larkin's
aides, who led the way south. The ship was anchored a mile below the usual
shipping anchorage in the lee of a jutting promontory of rock. Ramon sprang
from the saddle.

"I shall see that your horse gets back to your people," said the American.

"No, he is yours, with my thanks," said Ramon. A rowboat was waiting.
Ramon waded out and jumped aboard. How on earth had Larkin managed it?
He seized an oar, only to have it taken good-humoredly from his grasp. "Here,
I can do it faster," said a voice.

Ramon laughed. "So be it, eh?" A quarter of an hour later he was clambering up a rope ladder.

"Welcome aboard," said a cool, familiar voice as he climbed over the rail
and dropped to the deck.

"Stephen!"

Stephen hoisted a lamp. *"Mi casa es su casa,"* he said mockingly. My house
is your house.

"How did you get here? Alissa said you were on your way to Boston."

"I was. Come." Stephen led him down a narrow passage to his cabin. "Don't
get seasick, do you?"

Ramon followed, feeling his way through the near darkness. "I don't know. I've never been out to sea before."

Stephen placed the hurricane lamp on a tiny varnished table. He pointed Ramon to a storage bench built along a curved wall of the cabin and sat opposite in the only chair. The two men looked each other over without speaking, their features distorted by the lamplight, black shadows thrown up on the narrow berth. A few shelves and sacks hung from hooks behind them. Stephen appeared as trim as always, his dark hair combed and neatly cut, the dark business suit in no way marking him a man of the sea anymore than Ramon's formal coat and stock.

Ramon pulled off his hat and tossed it on the table. The dangerous proceedings, had diluted his anger into a sense of adventure, erupting in the tiniest flicker of a smile. "Thank you, Stephen. I owe you my life."

Stephen shook his head. "We are even. You saved mine two years ago."

Ramon reached across the table. "Friends again?"

Stephen looked at the hand, then turned away, more, it seemed to Ramon, in coldness than in anger.

Ramon studied him, decided to overlook the insult to his honor, and withdrew his hand. "Tell me how you happen to be here; then I will tell you what happened tonight."

"Was Alissa with you tonight?" demanded Stephen.

"Of course, as a guest of my family. Where you left her."

"Where *she* decided to stay."

"She could hardly do otherwise. You insulted her!—ah, I am sorry, Stephen. Alissa is well. More than that you will have to ask her."

Stephen's deep-set eyes impaled him with an unreadable gaze. Abruptly he said, "I am here as a favor to the American consul. He knew the *New Horizons* would be docked here."

"Lucky for me."

Stephen rose and prowled the cramped quarters. "What is it about you? You live life as if there were no tomorrow. Why can't you plan better? Why can't you think things through? You'll never make a businessman!"

"Why should I?" His attack left Ramon mystified. Had Stephen changed, or had he always been so deadly serious? No wonder Alissa backed away rather than submit to his will.

"Can't you see what is happening, Ramon?"

"You mean Micheltorena? The only way to get around him is not to let the coyote know what you are up to." Ramon leaned back and hooked one heel over the edge of the table. "So I got in his bad graces tonight. That was bad planning, you are right. What could I do but leave? He had the idea to conscript me into his army. It is a favorite way to keep the rancheros in line."

"He would take you like a hostage?" Stephen said incredulously.

Ramon flashed a smile. "One is not allowed to refuse the honor."

"Tell me about tonight."

"I have to go back and tell you what has been happening since you left. Micheltorena's cholos have gone more and more out of control. One day they raided the mission at San Juan. I happened to be there."

"Their idea to raid?"

"His, that time. After that, the rancheros met. We formed a vigilante band with vanqueros from each rancho. Today the cholos raid the missions with impunity. Tomorrow it may be the ranchos, eh? The vigilantes will stop them."

Again Stephen was staring at him, as if seeing him for the first time. "You don't see, do you?"

"See what?"

"Micheltorena has nothing to do with it. He no longer even counts! Those thugs he calls soldiers do not count! Mexico and the United States will be fighting over California before the end of the year, Ramon! The United States will win. There is no question. All you think about is being happy, getting into mischief. What about your mother's rancho? Don't you know there are at least a dozen Americans jockeying to take it away from her? From all of you down here in the south?"

Ramon's heel dropped to the floor with a thud. "That is impossible! Our grant is from the king of Spain. Not even Mexico can touch it."

Stephen shook his head. His voice dropped in tone and pace as though he were explaining to a child, "Some of your own countrymen are against you. Do you have any idea what the Mexicans who are in business around Monterey and San Francisco call you? Horse-happy *caballeros!*"

Ramon laughed. "That is hardly an insult, Stephen."

"They have been sweet-talked by the United States until they think that everything will be the same as it is now, only better. Even they are waiting and planning how your ranchos can be stolen away from you. Even now you should be hiring lawyers. Not that the United States necessarily wants war. From what I read and hear from Washington, we are pushing Americans into California as fast as they can be convinced to migrate, so that when it comes to a vote, the people of California will say, 'We choose to be governed by the United States.'"

"That is crazy!" Ramon cried. "If a vote comes, we will vote to stay with our mother country. It is true that our country does not protect us. They leave us alone. We protect ourselves. We are free Mexicans, and that is what we will always be."

Stephen shook his head. "Then you will lose everything."

"Tch-tch! Cool down, my friend. Business is not everything. There is honor.

There is friendship—you coming here for me! Now that is friendship, in spite of what you say!"

Stephen looked down at him with undisguised contempt. "There is nothing so stupid as a man who will not see."

Slowly Ramon got to his feet. "I wish we had let the cholos kill you in Santa Barbara!"

The men glared at each other. The ship creaked suddenly as if it were no longer riding at anchor.

"Where are we heading?" Ramon asked.

"Monterey. Larkin feels you will be safe there. You are to go to his house."

"How do you know that?"

"He sent a message with his aide. Also this." Stephen tossed a pouch of coins at him.

Ramon caught it deftly. "I am sorry to be taking you out of your way. I know how you hate to waste time. But you have discharged two obligations tonight, eh? You no longer owe Larkin a favor, and you no longer owe me a life. That is very good business!"

"That's right," said Stephen. "Just good business. You can sleep here. I have moved my things."

"Thank you."

Stephen turned to go. As he opened the door, Ramon said, "Stephen! I may not be a businessman, but I know one thing. One can save time and lose other things that are precious. You are not stupid like me. Maybe you will learn that sometime, eh?"

Gently Stephen closed the door behind him. He trudged up the companionway to the deck, feeling like an old man. Dawn was breaking. Enough light to pull from his pocket and read again a portion of Larkin's message.

> . . . Hastings mentioned by your friends. In the event it is the same man, it is my opinion that Mr. Hastings should not be considered a trustworthy business partner. It would be unfortunate for the American cause if this were to go further, Mr. Davis, but after meeting you I feel assured that you and I have the same interests at heart. So I will tell you frankly that I believe this Mr. Hastings to be the same man who led a massacre against a tribe of hunters and trappers in the Sierras. If they were to come upon him, he would surely not escape with his life.

Stephen stared off to port with gritty eyes. Santa Catalina Island was emerging from the flat horizon of the Pacific like a melting bar of gold. A new day. A new day.

21

It was nightfall on a bitterly windy January day in 1846. Inside the fortress of New Helvetia in the Sacramento Valley, Johannes A. Sutter was informed by a messenger that Governor Micheltorena wanted to see him.

"He sent for me like a common flunky!" he stormed after ordering out of his presence the hapless aide who had brought the letter. "Who the blazes does he think he is? I'm a busy man!"

"Sh-shall I send him away—," stuttered his secretary.

"No! Who knows what that conniving weasel has up his sleeve." Sutter seized a pipe and tamped it furiously as he paced up and down the carpet in his parlor. His Indians had woven this carpet. The wool had come from his own sheep, the dyes from native plants. Knowing this as he paced over the carpet usually gave him immense satisfaction. Little existed inside the walls of New Helvetia that had not originated somewhere on his domain.

"Give the beggar some food and a berth."

"Yes, sir."

"First bring me my dinner."

"Yes, sir."

A night's sleep relieved his physical exhaustion but not his temper. Nor did a nagging worry about the purpose of Micheltorena's letter. Micheltorena was the sort of man who rarely placed himself in the upper position unless he was sure he already occupied it.

With a single attendant and a spare pair of horses, Sutter set out for the governor's mansion at his provincial capital of Monterey. Micheltorena had followed the lead of former governors in shifting the capital seat of government from city to city as suited his fancy.

Sutter affected an easy joviality as he was shown into the governor's presence. Micheltorena's unhealthy smile, exposing long, stained teeth, was not a particularly pleasing sight.

"Sit down, please. I understand you were in Monterey just four days ago," said the governor. "I've only returned, myself. Pity you had to make an extra trip."

"Something important, was it?" Sutter teetered impatiently on the balls of his feet.

"You have more important things to do elsewhere, Captain Sutter?"

"No, Your Excellency." Sutter glanced around and decided to sit after all. Micheltorena's beady gaze crawled over his face. "And how will the fur harvest be this spring?"

Sutter shifted in the chair, suddenly uncertain where the conversation was going. "It is too early to tell, Your Excellency."

"Do you know Sir George Simpson?" the governor demanded suddenly.

"Hudson's Bay Company, yes."

"Furs."

"Yes."

"Rivals?"

"Could be—"

"Rivals?"

"Yes, Governor."

"I want him out."

"But—"

"He has applied to the federal government in Mexico to open an office in San Francisco in the name of the company. Spies!" Micheltorena said bitterly, "Spies!" He whirled and pounded a fist on a heavy table. "They want my California, Captain Sutter, he and that American rascal Thomas Larkin. I know this, I heard this in my own house, at a very expensive ball I gave for Larkin in Los Angeles. *I gave!* In my own house! You and I are going to stop them, in the name of the Holy Mother Church."

"You must be mistaken, Governor Micheltorena. A powerful man like you, your soldiers . . . the people behind you. . . ."

"It is all for the Holy Mother Church," Micheltorena insisted stubbornly. "That is all I care about. With Simpson comes the Church of England. The Americans are worse yet, godless pagans who do not care what a man's beliefs are!"

"It's a little late to close the borders. . . ."

A crafty gleam entered Micheltorena's eyes. "Not necessarily."

Sutter heaved an impatient sigh. "I do what I can—"

"We appreciate your close ties with our church, senor. And your donations. But then, with the income from the lands we have granted to you, that must be a pittance."

Sutter was growing angry as well as impatient. "I have always been a friend of your Catholic government. I am a naturalized citizen of Mexico. I remind you that I helped Governor Alvarado get rid of the last of the Russians at Fort Ross."

"You were well paid, Sutter. I have never seen New Helvetia, but it is very large, I understand. With navigable rivers that reach from Sacramento to San Francisco."

Sutter decided to change tactics. "Obviously, Governor, as you are a man of action as well as man of reason," he said in a conciliatory voice, "you have already formed a plan of action."

Micheltorena smiled and clasped his hands behind him. He stalked in a small circle before answering. "I have decided that Hudson's Bay Company has no business in California. I am formulating a decree against foreigners taking furs out of California."

"Oh, excellent," Sutter cried, praying that a show of enthusiasm was all the governor required. "That will certainly solve your problem."

"And for your part, you are to use your soldiers to see that no more immigrant parties cross over the mountains from the United States."

"What? But that is impossible, Governor! My soldiers, as you call them, are to protect New Helvetia from—," he stopped short of saying *cholos*. "From the hostiles. They come down out of the hills—"

"As a loyal citizen, Captain Sutter, from this time on you will make it your business to turn back foreigners from our borders."

Sutter stared at the petulant face and thought, *Mexico has squandered a prize to feed the arrogance of a fool.*

"Yes, Your Excellency."

The Indian scooped a bucket of water out of the swiftly running stream. He paid no attention to the icy Sierra-born water splashing over his bare calves and arms. Trotting back to his vegetables, he poured the water carefully down the row, as Padre Gonzales Rubio had taught. As he turned back to the stream, he noticed some dully gleaming nuggets at the bottom of the bucket. He examined them curiously. Heavier than other stones and shinier. On an impulse he tucked them in the deerskin bag hanging from a cord at his waist. He would ask his padre to tell him what they were.

22

Two weeks later, Thomas Larkin's ship reached the harbor at Monterey. Alissa had welcomed the breathing space aboard ship, time to think, time to face her future. If she did locate Daniel, what then? From the day he had left Saint Louis, the family had not heard from him. What if he did not want to be found? She refused to consider any more dire possibilities.

The hurly-burly of the approaching docks captured her attention. The lure of California was inescapable, but so were its drawbacks: no public schools, few churches outside the Catholic missions, no hospitals or doctors, and law and order simply didn't exist as they knew it in the States. Larkin had told her about some women from Oregon who had set up a missionary school. She meant to find them and offer her services. If they had no place for her, she would ask her uncle Harmon to find her a situation with Roebuck Trading. Some women worked, after all. On a frontier like California, one did what one had to.

She heard Guadelupe's voice tail into a high-pitched laugh and saw the captain's cat leap out of the companionway onto the deck. The girl came bounding after. The cat was too quick. Panting with laughter, Guadelupe threw herself against the rail beside Alissa.

Alissa smiled at her. Guadelupe had become like a different person on the voyage, like a sparrow uncaged. She had not planned to bring her to Monterey, but the girl had begged, and Alissa had realized that propriety would be better served if she had a companion.

"We are almost there. You will have plenty to tell Gregorio when you get back."

Guadelupe faced the rail, gripped it with both hands, and swung herself gently from side to side. "I do not want to go back, Dona Alissa."

"Guadelupe!"

An eloquent shrug.

"Did you and Gregorio quarrel when he visited the rancho?"

"I tell Gregorio I no longer want to marry him. I like living at the hacienda, in a house. I do not want to live under a tree. That is worse than the mission!"

"But—"

Fire flashed in Guadelupe's dark eyes. "I have good talk with Senor Thomas

Larkin. Plenty of good Catholic men in Monterey. One hundred for every girl! He promise that if I stay long enough, many men will want to marry me. He will find me a good man who will—will. . . ."

"*Court* you?"

Guadelupe beamed. "Yes! Court me. When I am ready." She glanced at Alissa. Her mood changed like quicksilver again, and she said, "Do not look so worried, Dona Alissa. I know you promise Padre Zalvidea that I will keep my faith. I will."

At last Larkin came to escort them ashore. Monterey was teeming with life. Fresh-faced Americans were everywhere, on the docks, on horseback, hurrying along on foot, heavily armed, carrying themselves like soldiers although not wearing uniforms. Wealthy-looking Mexicans with black lacquered walking sticks marched along like Spanish grandees. From the docks stevedores of all races and nationalities shouted and cursed in a babble of tongues. Eagerly Alissa scanned the faces. Wouldn't it be thrilling to discover Daniel among them.

"I had better get directly to my office and see what is going on," Larkin said. "I've arranged for a carriage to take you and Guadelupe up to the house with the luggage. You'll probably find Ramon there."

Ramon had been in Monterey a week. Stephen had hustled him ashore in a dinghy by night, with not even a change of linen, and immediately turned back for the long run to Boston.

Ramon had not wasted his time. He had never been as far north as Monterey. His countrymen here seemed like a different breed. Saloons, with rooms above to let to travelers, were used as meetinghouses. Every day they were crowded with men who wrote public newspapers, with men who were shippers, importers, storekeepers, lawyers, and politicians. Even the *rancheros,* who in the south would be found at home or visiting on a neighboring *hacienda,* were caught up. On every tongue was takeover. Not if but how soon California would pass into American hands. Jockeying to consolidate, to extend; schemes for quick enrichment, prophecies of glory.

Ramon had listened, stunned, fascinated, struggling to orient himself to this foreign order that existed parallel to his own. This was Stephen's element. This was what he was about, what he had tried to tell the Bandini-Warners, what he had tried to warn Ramon was happening.

The mission lands, the mission herds, the ranchos. *Easy pickin's,* said the Americans. . . .

He was waiting at Larkin's when the servant announced Alissa had arrived.

"Ramon! Thank goodness you are safe!"

He bent over her hand. "Thanks to Stephen and Thomas Larkin," he said coolly.

He ushered her from the foyer into the quiet, tasteful parlor. Alissa shepherded Guadelupe ahead of her. She had a swift impression of deep green velvet settees and velvet drapery that screened out the noise of the bustling streets.

Guadelupe darted to the window and thrust aside the drape to stare out at the street.

Ramon threw an irritated look at her back.

"Your mother said she might come with me," explained Alissa in English.

"Of course. You could hardly travel alone."

"Guadelupe doesn't want to marry Gregorio after all."

"You should not have interfered in the first place. I should not have allowed it."

"She is very bright, Ramon."

"Of what use is that to an Indian?" he said scathingly.

Alissa felt a surge of anger. "She is eager to learn, and she speaks better Spanish every day."

Ramon uttered an oath. "I do not wish to talk about the servants."

"Excuse me, miss, shall I just leave your trunk in the foyer?"

"Senor Larkin said to put her things in the corner guest room," Ramon snapped. He pointed up the staircase. "What is so hard about that? And take Dona Alissa's maid with you."

Alissa spoke to Guadelupe, then as she left, turned to Ramon with a speculative gaze of her gray blue eyes. She unpinned the gay little blue felt hat and removed it. "I thought Mrs. Larkin was here."

"She is, but not right now."

There was a new, unsettling maturity about the young Mexican. Alissa was not quite as comfortable with him. "Tell me about Monterey," she said.

Somehow they made it through the afternoon.

When Larkin returned later that evening, Alissa's relief was heartfelt. "We expected you *hours* ago. Mrs. Larkin is still away."

"She is a nurse. She would be gone twenty-four hours a day if the people of this town had their way."

Larkin's gray suit was rumpled. The skin below his eyes sagged with tiredness, but his eyes were bright. With Ramon and Alissa hanging on his words, he downed a cup of coffee and caught them up on events.

"Micheltorena is out. President Santa Anna has ordered him back to Mexico. And his cholos. You are a free man, Ramon."

"Praise God," said Alissa.

"Pio Pico is the new governor," added Larkin.

"An old friend," said Ramon. "Good!"

"The rumor is that he has been ordered to begin selling off mission lands. Supposedly to finance a war effort," said Larkin. "But personally I believe that the Mexican government knows there is no way they can stop the United States, and they are trying to rake every *real* out of California that they can!"

Ramon jumped to his feet. "I must object, Don Thomas. That is an insult! The Picos are an honorable family."

"I am sorry, Ramon," Larkin replied wearily."I didn't mean to impugn Don Pio's honor. Honorable men are often given distasteful tasks precisely because governments know people will follow them."

Ramon glanced aside with embarrassment. Slowly he said, "Stephen said that once the mission lands started to go, you Americans would go after our ranchos."

You Americans! Alissa felt like crying. The new void between them stopped her from going to him, to offer comfort.

Larkin turned up his hands in a gesture of not knowing.

"But your ranch is clear," said Alissa.

"Stephen says that is not enough."

Ramon turned to Larkin. "How can I protect my mother's land grant?" he said somberly. "And my father's? He added thousands of acres to the rancho."

Larkin massaged his temples with a viselike grip. "I've heard rumors, too, Ramon. Sometimes I hate this business! I can't answer you. I don't know how to advise you— Did your father also retain his American citizenship? If he has not renounced it, Juan Julian's holdings may be safer than Arcadia's."

"I do not know. I never bothered to learn," he added in a tone of self-recrimination. Slowly Ramon got to his feet. It seemed to Alissa that he had aged five years since meeting her at the door a few hours ago. He did not look at her. "I must go back, Don Thomas. Thank you for helping me get away from Micheltorena. No matter what comes, you—you have been a good friend."

Larkin rose and shook his hand. "I will do what I can, when I can."

Ramon gazed at Alissa as if filling his memory with her.

She started to her feet. "Ramon, I will always be your friend." Tears blurred her vision. Larkin gave a small, discreet cough and looked away. Alissa would never forget the pain in Ramon's eyes, dulled like those of an animal who does not comprehend the whirlwind but understands it may be dying. "*Vaya condios.*"

"*Con dios,* Alissa."

A small tap came at her door an hour later. Guadelupe opened it. Larkin stepped inside.

"This may not be the time, my dear, but I thought you would like to know that I have found the name of a Daniel MacGowan—"

Part II

Molly

23

Molly MacGowan gazed out eastward across the Mississippi River. The early sun crisped the red hair with golden highlights. The blue eyes were placid and dreamy. In place of the broad river she saw a broad mesa of hot, parched land. She heard foreign shouts and saw riders in dashing black costumes nigh kill themselves showing off for the ladies. She pictured proper, businesslike Alissa wearing a scandalous riding suit with skirt split like a man's trousers. Oh! She wished she was there and Alissa had a blueberry pie in her eye!

Here she was, cooped up on a farm, while her older sister was having all the fun! Maybe Uncle Harmon could put her on a trader. Of course she always did get seasick, even in a rowboat.

But she could go overland. More and more folks were coming into Saint Louis every day to join Mr. Hastings's wagon train. How could Pa not want to go to California?

"Miss Molly!"

Molly turned and shaded her eyes. At first she thought the man standing a few feet away on the grassy bank was a stranger. Then she saw that it was Lansford Hastings. He was dressed in a light blue topcoat piped in dark blue velvet, with dove gray trousers and a gray satin brocade vest. His walking stick was knobbed in silver.

"You look as pretty as a picture in that peach colored gown," Hastings smiled. He walked over and sank to his haunches. "What are you doing out here all alone?"

"I come when I want to be by myself," she answered. "You can't see this part of the riverbank from the house, because of all the trees."

"Oh, I am sorry. Shall I—"

"Oh, no, don't leave! We got a letter from my sister, Alissa, Mr. Hastings."

"Splendid! Is she all right?"

Molly sighed. "She is having such wonderful adventures."

"There, see? What did I tell you?"

Molly gazed wistfully at the smooth, handsome face, the pencil-thin moustache. "I wish I was going with you—Lansford."

Hastings took her hand and helped her to her feet. "I wish you were, too," he said sincerely. "We have barely gotten to know each other. Molly."

Molly held her breath, feeling a new sense of excitement. "Can't you stay just a few more days?"

He shook his head. "We have to start. I have eighty families signed on."

"I talked to Pa again last night. I tried every persuasion I knew. He just plain didn't want to budge!" She glanced at Lansford's face. It was remarkable how well he controlled his disappointment. "It's tomorrow, isn't it?"

"Yes, tomorrow."

Molly's upturned face was wistful with unsaid longing.

Slowly his arms went around her, and his mouth bent to hers. Molly returned the gentle kiss.

"I want to go, I *will* go!" she said against his neck.

"Not without your family."

"If you—," she started to say, *If you marry me,* but she held back, wanting him to say it.

"It's different in California, for a man and a woman," Lansford said.

"It is? How? How is it different?"

He smiled and cupped her face in his hands. "It's different, Molly." Slowly he brought his lips down on hers again, pressing her body into his, moving his hands with sureness.

Molly broke away, her eyes large with alarm. "I—I shouldn't stay away any longer. I have to go back. Are you coming?"

He dropped his hands, making no attempt to stop her. "No. I already thanked your father for finding us a missionary couple," he said indifferently. "It was you I came to see, to say good-bye."

"Don't be angry with me! Maybe if you asked him again. . . ."

A mirthless smile flitted over Hastings's lips. "If he would come to California, so I could court his daughter?"

"*Court?* But Lansford, you never—"

"There wasn't time. You know that."

"I couldn't go without his permission," she said.

"Of course you couldn't. Good-bye, Molly."

Molly watched Hastings spring gracefully back up the bank and saunter toward the horse tethered a few yards away. Her mind was a welter of confusion. Did Lansford really want to court her? She had never met a more exciting man. Why had he not said something sooner? Or had he said something to Pa, and Pa discouraged it?

Suddenly she picked up her skirts and dashed up the bank after him. "Lansford, I *do* want to go with you!"

He paused, one hand on the bridle. She placed her hand on his chest. "Take me with you," she whispered.

"Darling girl! They would be after you in a trice. Can't you see it would be impossible?"

"If I—if I come to California. . . ." She stared up into his eyes, entranced by the mysterious pleasures he seemed to promise.

A smile played over his face. "If you come . . . I'll be waiting. Good-bye." Without a backward glance Hastings swung up on his horse and cantered leisurely down the drive toward the road back to town.

A feeling of excitement trembled inside her. If she did not run or jump, she would explode! Someday, some way, she *would* get to California!

The wagon train had been forming up for days on a broad prairie east of town, a constant stream of men and women and children carrying supplies, pulling reluctant milch cows, making last-minute arrangements to dispose of property they were leaving behind. The morning they left, there were so many white-topped wagons and cattle as far as the eye could see, that it seemed impossible they would ever sort themselves out.

Lansford Hastings seemed to be everywhere at once, calling orders in a sure voice, assigning point riders, and offering expert advice on everything from placement of tar buckets and butter churns to trail discipline for the youngsters. Not once did he glance toward the gathering of traps and the horse riders assembled to wish them farewell.

Molly felt depressed all over. She had had several glimpses of Lansford, usually surrounded by teamsters. As far as she could tell, he had not even realized that she was one of the onlookers, and she was too proud to embarrass her mother by calling attention to herself. She and Hannah had driven out alone, after Micah had expressed no interest in seeing the adventurers off.

Suddenly a rider shot through the ranks of townspeople, on a horse flecked with foam. "Mr. Hastings! Mr. Hastings!"

Hastings trotted forward. Workers and observers alike dropped their work and crowded in to hear what the newcomer had to say. The young man was bony, angular, with a shock of black hair, wearing an ill-fitting jacket.

"They's five more wagonloads o' folk wanting to join your train."

"Good! Where are they?"

"Springfield. They got detained. They figger to be here in about three, four days. They sent me on ahead to make sure you'd wait for them."

"I can't wait three days! These folks are ready to go now. You can't have them eating up their provisions, just marking time."

The young man looked ready to cry. From his appearance, he'd ridden night and day to reach Hastings.

Hastings shook his head. "I'm really sorry, Son." He settled back on one foot and stroked his moustache, staring at the ground. After a moment he looked up. "Tell you what. You have any guides at all with you?"

"No, sir."

"No mind. Tell them they should come ahead to Saint Louis. Like as not, within the week other folks will be making up their minds to go. It's only May, they have plenty of time to make the crossing. Now, it shouldn't be too hard to find a guide here. He's to bring you to the Green River rendezvous, near Jim Bridger's trading post. It is not hard to find, every trapper knows it. I'll be waiting there with my people, and I'll guide you all together over the Wasatch Mountains."

Hastings reached over the back of his horse and fished a small book out of his saddlebag, which he gave the youth. "Here. You read, Son?"

" 'Course I read!"

Hastings tapped the book with a manicured finger. "This is my guidebook. It's got maps and trail markers for a special shortcut that'll save you four hundred miles off the regular route. It's a bit tricky, but you don't have to worry, I'll be there taking you through it. You got all that, Son?"

"Yessir!" The lad began to look less crestfallen.

"What name is your party traveling under, Son?"

"Donner, sir. George P. Donner. That's my uncle."

Hastings gave him a dismissing nod and glanced around. His quick gaze fell on Molly. He removed his hat and trotted over to the trap. "Good morning, Mrs. MacGowan, Molly."

"Good morning, Mr. Hastings," said Hannah. "We said a special blessing this morning for you and all our friends traveling with you."

Molly nodded, suddenly tongue-tied.

"Thank you, dear lady." Hastings looked at Molly, looked through her, she felt. "Will you write to me, Molly?"

"Oh, yes!" She glanced at her mother, then said in a more proper voice, "Where shall we direct our letters, Mr. Hastings?"

"Care of the American consulate in Monterey."

"Then, good-bye." *The American consulate in Monterey. That is where I will see you next, my darling.* "Good-bye," she whispered again.

Hastings put his hat back on and trotted smartly toward the waiting wagons. He waved to the trail boss. A cry rang out, changed and echoed and rang again. "Let's go! Let 'er roll! Roll 'em!"

As Molly and Hannah watched, the bulky wagons lurched forward and tailed into line. Several youngsters on ponies were riding out with the train for the first part of the day and coming back that night. Watching them, Molly wished passionately that she were one of them right now. Only she would not come back! She would hide, she would—As the dust started to settle from the herds, most of the townspeople began to put the spectacle behind them and head for the day's work. Still Molly sat, the reins resting in her idle hands, gazing westward.

"Someday, Molly," Hannah broke into her thoughts, smiling. "Your turn will come. You won't always be the one staying behind, not unless you want to."

"Good morning, ladies!" Jared McCloud rode up on a sleek bay he had been training for the Fourth of July races. He was wearing a white collarless shirt, open at the throat, black broadcloth vest and trousers, and a new hat, which he tipped to them.

"Good morning, Jared," smiled Hannah. "I was talking to my brother about you last week."

"You were?" Jared snatched a peek at Molly. She was gazing off as if the conversation didn't interest her in the least.

"He says you are an excellent worker. He expects you will someday become an important force in the company."

Jared straightened. "Thank you, ma'am, but like I told Mr. Roebuck, I don't intend to stay with the shipping company."

"I'm sorry to hear that, Jared. Have you had a better offer?"

"No, ma'am, but I'm going to be a cattleman. Go out west. Almost signed on with Mr. Hastings," Jared's glance fell casually on Molly, "but I wasn't quite ready to leave Saint Louis."

Molly's glance flew to Jared's face.

"Harmon will be sorry to hear you are going," said Hannah. "Molly, dear, take me home now."

"Yes, Mama."

"Molly?" Jared trotted around to her side of the trap and glanced down at her.

She looked up at him.

"You think anymore about last night?"

"What about?"

"You know."

"Oh, I guess," she said indifferently.

A smile spread over his face. "Good! See you tonight."

Hannah studied her with amusement as they drove off.

"I hate it when you get that superior look, Mama."

"What superior look?"

"You know. Besides, Jared's just a friend." She glanced at her mother. "He thinks he's in love with me. Last night he tried to make me say I love him."

"Oh, Molly. . . ."

"Oh, Ma!"

24

"Good morning, Mrs. MacGowan!"

"Good morning, Mr. Samuels."

"Fine day!"

"Indeed." Hannah Roebuck MacGowan swept past Samuels, her spine as straight at sixty-eight as it had been thirty years ago. Her iron gray hair was nearly as abundant under the wide, smart hat as it had been when Micah brought her to Saint Louis as a new bride.

The recently planted trees lining Saint Louis's main street were beginning to leaf out. In a reminiscent mood this morning, Hannah recalled the dusty, reckless French port city as she had first seen it. She hadn't been exactly a *new* bride, she reflected. A second-time-around bride.

It was a letter from her daughter Alissa that now brought Hannah into town.

She found her brother Harmon in his dark-paneled offices on the second floor over the largest of the warehouses of Roebuck Trading. He was standing before a block of square-paned windows overlooking the wharves and loading docks of the city. They exchanged an affectionate kiss. Nearly seventy years of different life experiences had incomprehensibly etched identical crow's-feet, the same sweep of gray hair up and across the forehead, the same wide mouths bracketed with firmness and humor.

"I was about to knock off early and ride out to see you."

"Isn't that a coincidence!" Hannah said. She waited.

"You first."

"You first."

They chuckled, each enjoying the other's company. "We received a letter from Alissa that has me a little worried," Hannah said, drawing a stiff, ivory envelope from her bag. "Micah thought perhaps you could shed some light on it."

"Dear mother and father," Harmon read.

> You will see by this that I am still "yr obed. dtr. Alissa MacGowan" and not Mrs. Stephen A. Davis. Stephen has discovered that business is truly that—"busy-ness"—and that he has no time to be a proper husband, too.

["The scoundrel!" Micah had raged.] Harmon, Hannah noticed, merely lifted his eyebrows thoughtfully at this passage.

> I am well and safe. The family that befriended Stephen on his earlier voyage is very gracious, and I am treated as a daughter of the house. The Bandini-Warners have offered to send a servant to accompany me, should I wish to return to Saint Louis.

Harmon lowered the letter and looked questioningly at his sister, the brown eyes carefully withholding judgment.

"She goes on to say she has become a horsewoman in the California style, whatever that is. . . . Harmon, I am so frightened for my daughter. She is all alone. She is too young to realize how vulnerable she is, how totally without resources if Stephen has abandoned her, which it certainly sounds like!" Her voice had risen steadily in pitch. Suddenly she stopped and glared accusingly at Harmon. "I must say, you don't seem very surprised."

Harmon retreated to his desk and waved a heavily creased paper at her. "A letter from Stephen."

"What!" Hannah bristled.

"Now, don't get angry, Hannah. The boy is—"

"He's not a boy! He's older than you where when you were a father."

Harmon nodded. "When he worked for me here, he was a regular workhorse. It isn't hard from his letter to see that he has continued to be that in California.

" 'Dear Mr. Roebuck,' " Harmon read.

> I don't know how all this happened, but my business venture has—[*has* is crossed out here—] for the trading company has met with truly astonishing success. So much so that I have had little time for the more proper obligations to my dear Alissa, believing, as I am sure you will agree, that it is at once more necessary and more desirable to get the jump on one's competitors than to play the lovesick swain.

"Lovesick swain! That he never was. I knew that young man was too ambitious for his own good!"

"Is there such a thing?" Harmon asked mildly. "I seem to remember our years in Paris, when I wanted to come home and marry Isabella, and you refused to sail with me, giving business as your reason. . . ." Hannah flashed a guilty smile at her brother, and in it he recognized the headstrong woman of twenty. "What does Micah think of all this?"

"Oh, Harmon, he is ready to horsewhip that young man. We should have *known,* when they were 'too busy' to marry in Saint Louis, and 'too busy' to marry in Boston. . . . Have you any sherry?" she asked, suddenly sitting down on a plush-covered straight chair and removing the pins from her hat. She lifted the hat off and placed it carefully in her lap while Harmon poured a dram of sherry in a dainty glass.

He dragged a chair across the thick carpet and faced her thoughtfully while she tasted the sweet sherry. "Marriage should be for all time, Sis."

"But he's compromised her."

"I doubt it. Alissa is a strong young woman. She'd not put up with any non-sense. Nor would Stephen. I have faith in both of them."

"But what is she to do? Her letter has caused such an uproar you wouldn't believe. Molly is all ready to pack up and go after her sister. And Lavinia says if Molly goes, she's going, too! Can you beat that? And all of Micah's talk of a horsewhip—why, I swear, Harmon, sometimes that man behaves downright unchristianly!"

"He's human. Something even Micah has trouble accepting sometimes." Brother and sister exchanged a rueful glance of perfect understanding.

Hannah felt herself relaxing. Years of trying to be the leader in moral recti-tude had had the strange effect of rendering Micah frequently dour and un-communicative, as though mixing too much with his parishioners might tempt him to reveal how human he really was.

"So now Molly is talking of going to California. . . ."

"Yes."

"Why?"

"It's in there."

Harmon scanned his niece's letter. " 'I considered coming home, but I have not yet abandoned hope that Daniel may be in California. I have written to a Mr. Thomas Larkin in Monterey, begging for his help. Mr. Larkin occupies a consular position to American foreigners and is by all accounts an honorable gentleman.' " Harmon let his breath out in a soundless whistle.

"Molly wants to go look for her brother, too." Hannah smiled. "You know, Harmon, I've half a mind to go myself. I did speak to Micah about it, but you know him."

"Hastings stirred up a hornet's nest," said Harmon. "One of my best young men is talking of leaving—"

"Jared, you mean."

"Did he say something to you?"

Hannah nodded.

"Jared wants to cross by land. He's a farmer. The year he's worked for me, I know he's saved every cent he could."

"By land! I cannot help thinking of the hardships!" Hannah shook her head. She caught Harmon's glance, and they both smiled, remembering their own great adventure of youth.

Then Harmon drummed his fingers on the desk as if mulling something in his mind. "Sis, did you notice the way Hastings and Molly looked at each other?"

"Y-yes . . . , but he's *years* older than Molly! And there was something about him I didn't trust."

Harmon waited.

She shook her head. "Nothing I can put my finger on. He was just too—too slick."

"I felt that way when I first met him."

"Did you?"

"But I never heard anything against the man, Hannah. True, he was not 'down home,' but that should not reflect on his character."

"Micah gave him permission to call on Molly while he was here." Hannah slumped against the bristly fabric and gazed out the window. "Frankly, I am glad he is gone."

"Be thankful you and Micah have reared good children." She nodded. "And as for Alissa, I have every confidence that if she says she is all right, that's just what she is."

"Thank you."

Harmon began gathering papers on his desk. "And as far as young Jared goes, if he wants to travel by wagon train to California, he's got a good brain under all that hair. I've talked to plenty of folks in the last week who have decided to sign on with the Donner party, and it wouldn't surprise me a bit if he ups and leaves, too."

"Harmon Roebuck! I've seen that look before. You'd like to be on that train yourself."

His smile grew boyish. "By golly, I *wish* I was going!"

"I can imagine what Isabella would say to that," Hannah laughed. She rose and replaced her hat on the neat gray hair. Then her expression changed. A sense of loss invaded the timeless beauty of her face. "I've only three children. Our friends the Pelliers have seven grown children, and every one of them lives in Saint Louis. First Daniel left and then Alissa. I could not bear it if Molly left, too."

25

One morning a week later Hannah came into Molly's room with an arm-load of linens. It was nearly noon. Molly lay in bed, with the covers pulled up under her chin.

"Molly! I thought you were up and gone hours ago! Are you ill, dear?"

"I'm not ill, Ma, I'm . . . I'm lonesome."

"You miss your sister, don't you, honey?" Hannah sat on the edge of the bed and stroked her daughter's cheek with the back of her fingers, tucking aside a wisp of red hair.

Molly nodded morosely. "Now even Jared's going. He told me."

Hannah's fingers stilled. She started to get up, and Molly seized her hand. "Stay and talk, Ma."

"I was just going to draw your curtains back and let in some fresh air." All her life Molly had taken occasional spells of feeling lonely. Hannah returned to the bed and sat down beside her daughter again. "I wish you and I were closer, Molly. I feel that you kept your thoughts too much to yourself, when you were hurting and even when you were happy. I always had to guess how you were feeling from your face."

Molly mustered up a rueful smile. "How do I look now?"

"Lonesome." Impulsively Hannah hugged her. "Don't be lonesome! You have so many friends. Being a pastor's daughter isn't always easy and perhaps you feel that your father has been too strict with you." Molly made such a com-ical face that Hannah had to laugh.

"I have a feeling that life will get a lot more interesting very soon. Jared's not the only young man in Saint Louis. The mother of a certain person—"

"Oh, Mama, I know who you mean, and he's such a *child.*"

"He's older than you are."

Molly shrugged. "Boys are different."

Hannah said, acutely feeling the gap between herself and her daughter, "Maybe if I had been younger when you were born. . . . Did you know that I was considered an old lady by the time you came along?" Hannah chuckled. "Some of the elderly ladies in your father's congregation were quite outraged that I was having another child when most of them were becoming grandmoth-ers."

Molly grinned. "I guess they didn't think you and Pa still slept together."

"Molly, honestly!"

Molly giggled. "Tell me about when you were a young woman."

"The years in Paris?"

"After, when you married Daniel's father, before you married Pa."

In a gesture from her girlhood, Hannah clasped her hands over her knee and rocked gently back and forth. "We were married just about the time the war started between the United States and Great Britain. The United States Army had sent in a force and massacred all of Tecumseh's people, and he vowed that he would fight them as long as he lived. . . ."

She had been living in Detroit, with other wives of British officers, during the bitter winter of 1812–1813. Inside the fort, Hannah and the other women and children had waited in enforced idleness for news of the men. The waiting was hard, but for Hannah it became an agony of loneliness and ostracism. Not only was she American, and therefore an enemy, but she was the wife of an Indian and with his child. It mattered not to the outraged sensibilities of the other wives that Hannah's husband, the famous Shawnee warchief, Tecumseh, was now a British general. He was Indian, and as far as the British wives closeted together that winter in Detroit were concerned, Christian charity did not extend as far as accepting Indians as equals.

Hannah learned to block out the women's contempt. Soon she had Daniel to care for when Tecumseh was away. Tecumseh had beheld his son and had loved him. Love. They had loved each other, Hannah and Tecumseh. For too brief a period.

After his death in battle, Hannah and her infant son returned to Cincinnati. Her period of mourning ended when Hannah married Micah MacGowan, a former suitor.

A Scots parson educated in London, MacGowan had dedicated his life to serving men and women on the frontiers of America rather than returning to a parish post in England. A year after Micah and Hannah married, MacGowan left his church, leaving behind also the scandal of having joined himself to the former wife of an Indian and her half-breed child, and took his wife and the child further west.

"We settled in Saint Louis because your uncle Harmon and aunt Isabella were already here," Hannah said.

Molly had gotten up and begun dressing while her mother talked. Now she perched on the foot of the bed, gazing out the window, entranced, seeing in her mind's eye the young family trekking from Cincinnati to this city, where she was born, on the Mississippi River.

"They had put down roots. Saint Louis was a prospering community. Over the years, Harmon and your other uncles built Roebuck Trading Company into what it is today."

"Pretty big."

"Pretty big. And then, eventually, Alissa and then you came along as sisters for Daniel."

Molly sighed, feeling somehow complete again. "I wish I'd known your Tecumseh, Ma."

A warm light entered Hannah's eyes. "I have never forgotten him, and I never will." She cautioned her daughter, "Not that I don't love your father."

Molly nodded. "But it was something special, wasn't it?" she said dreamily.

"Yes. It was something special."

Hannah rose. "Molly. . . ."

"Hm?"

"You won't ever do anything without telling me first, will you?"

"Do anything?"

"Or—go anywhere? Away?"

Molly felt a great rush of love for her mother. "Oh, Mama. I couldn't hurt you like that."

A fountain of relief spilled over Hannah. "Thank you."

After her mother left, Molly pulled on her stockings and shoes, her thoughts returning again to Alissa riding horseback in a split riding skirt. What fun it must be! And she had to wear a million petticoats and hitch up the trap just to get to town! Suddenly Molly felt charged with energy.

Half an hour later she was snapping the reins over the back of the dapple gray. Her mother had not been afraid to live, to follow her dreams. She had not let other people's conventions stop her when she knew what was in her own heart. *And in my heart,* thought Molly, *I want to go to California!* She'd go to California and surprise Lansford. Not that he'd be surprised. Of course not! He knew she was coming. It was their secret. Oh, Lansford! It *would* be different in California.

Molly spurred the gray to a smart trot, hoping to find Jared McCloud at the Roebuck Trading docks.

She found him working on a dock, several feet below the pier, off-loading crates from a trader. His sleeves were rolled over his muscular biceps, his legs braced against a sluggish current that moved the dock lazily under foot.

"Jared! Jared!"

At the sound of her voice he shaded his eyes and stared up against the sun. Above him, on the wharf, he saw the young woman whose red hair was famous in Saint Louis.

"Hello, Molly!"

"Well, finally! May I come down?"

"You'll get your pretty dress dirty. Stay there!"

Jared bounded up the suspended wooden stairway two steps at a time. Molly was as pretty as could be in the peach colored dress that somehow seemed only a shade paler than her hair. The dress was Jared's favorite. A frosting of white lace covered the gently swelling bosom. Her hands, protected in the whitest of gloves, tipped her parasol to and fro, as though she could barely contain her excitement. Her face beamed. "Guess what!"

Jared stared at her. He stuck a finger in his ear and waggled it.

"Oh, quit. I've decided to go with you!"

"Yeow!" Jared yelled. "You're going to marry me after all!"

"No, no," Molly cried, waving her hands frantically. "That isn't what I meant. I'm going to be on that wagon train, too."

Jared's face fell.

"Oh, Jared, I'm sorry." Contritely, Molly clasped her hands together over the handle of the parasol.

Jared scuffed at the dirt in embarrassment. "Well, uh, that's real great. I didn't think your pa would let you go."

Her lips came together stubbornly. "I'm just as old as Alissa was. Almost. And you'd be there to protect me. Not that I'd need any protection."

Jared's dark eyes were bleak with sadness. "You want to go, but you don't want to marry me."

Molly sighed with impatience. "Why do things have to get so complicated? You're going. We're almost the same age. Why should I not be allowed to go, too?"

"It ain't proper, and you know it, Molly MacGowan. I'm gonna march right over to your pa's and tell him so."

"Don't." Molly looked at her shoes. "Pa didn't say I could go. I just thought that if you'd tell him you'd look out for me, he'd—he'd—" She stole a glance at Jared, through a thick fringe of lashes. Jared was shaking his head.

"No way. I got to get back to work." Jared turned away.

"Wait!"

"Well?" The day was cool and dry, but Jared's shirt clung to his skin. Sweat trickled down his sunburned face and plastered his thick black hair to his forehead.

Molly looked at him as if seeing him for the first time. "Nothing," she said softly. "Will I see you tonight?"

"Do you want to?"

"I think yes."

"Come on, I'll walk you back to the trap."

Molly allowed him to escort her back to the light buggy a dozen yards away.

Jared pulled out a red kerchief and wiped his face. With his fingers he combed his hair. "You know what everyone says? That it's only a matter of time till our country takes California away from Mexico. I'm going to have me a piece o' that land." He lifted his face like a bloodhound sniffing the wind.

"I always thought you liked working for the company."

"I do, but it's just a job. I'm going to be my own man, Molly! You'll see!"

Hannah knew as soon as Molly came in with Jared in tow that evening what her daughter had in mind. Her heart sank. Molly, her youngest. Was God destining her and Micah to be a childless couple in their last years? Her heart felt as if it would break.

26

Micah crossed the front hall from his study to the quiet parlor and paused at the open door. A pool of sunlight spilled on the flowered carpet. Hannah was perched gracefully on the edge of the settee, forgotten needlework in hand, gazing out into the lace-worked rhythms of a cottonwood shading the window.

She made such a beautiful picture that he hesitated to break the spell. When was the last time he'd told his wife how much he loved her? A lump lodged in his throat, and he cleared it away.

She looked up, paused a moment as though her thoughts had to fly a great distance back before she could say, "Are you finished with your sermon?"

He shook his head. "It can wait." He meandered into the parlor. "Still thinking about Molly and Jared?"

Hannah forced a quick smile. "It was a lovely wedding, wasn't it?"

Half the town of Saint Louis had turned out for the marriage of the daughter of Pastor and Mrs. Micah MacGowan, four weeks ago. But it was neither the generous outpouring of handmade gifts for the young couple so shortly to start their life together with a physical journey nor the festivities at the house afterward that dwelled in Hannah's mind.

Over and over she saw the same tableau: the young couple kneeling before the altar of Micah's church. Molly's face, upturned toward her father as

Micah in his black robes asked the implacable questions that ended "till death do ye part?" Molly's face had blanched with fright. Her response had been so faint that Hannah, only a few feet away, could scarcely hear it. Micah had lifted the hands of the young couple and placed them together. "What God hath joined, let no man put asunder. . . . " Hannah would have sworn that at that moment Molly shuddered.

The scene faded. Hannah glanced at her husband. For a moment she was tempted to share her fears. But Micah would not have understood. To him, things were either black or white. She realized for the first time that Micah was wearing his frock coat and holding his top hat. "Where are you going?"

"Do you remember meeting the scout who took Daniel to Texas?"

Hannah nodded.

"I have a note from Harmon that one of his men saw him in town."

"Oh!" Hannah dropped her needlework on the settee and sucked at her finger. "He is back? After all these years?"

"Yes, he's back. Here, let me see." Tenderly he took his wife's hand. The stern face softened, and he kissed her finger where she had pricked it with the needle. "I am making no headway on my sermon, so I thought to call on him."

"Micah, I'd like to come."

An edge of caution stole into the flinty blue eyes. "Perhaps you should wait. This man is a rough individual, not at all the sort you are used to meeting."

"Don't try to protect me, Micah. There isn't anything he might tell us that could be worse than what I have already imagined."

He stared at her in astonishment. "You always said you knew God was taking care of Daniel."

"God's ways are not our ways," she said.

The trapper was lodged in a rooming house near the wharf. Hannah waited in the lobby while Micah went upstairs to seek him.

He was as lean as whipcord, as stringy and tough as harness leather, as grayed out as an uprooted mesquite rotting in the desert. And he remembered them. "Ain't hard to remember people when you on'y see two dozen a year." The slitted eyes disappeared completely as a smile wrung a thousand creases in his face. "Sure I 'member Daniel! Smartest kid I ever knew. Yeah. . . . I wanted him and me to be partners, young as he was. Never saw a kid could track like him. He could read and cipher, too. He could do anything. On'y had to show him once."

Hannah heard the soft clink of silverware on a tablecloth and glanced through a fringed archway. "Would you like some breakfast, Mr. Gunn?"

"Sure 'nuf." Gunn got promptly to his feet and headed for the dining room, thumbs adjusting his wide suspenders as he went. Micah and Hannah hastened after him.

Gunn packed away enough porridge, ham, and biscuits with honey to hibernate for a month. Between mouthfuls, he told them that Daniel stayed with him until one year an army scout and mapmaker by the name of Frémont had come through Texas and gotten Daniel to sign on with him because the youth could speak so many tongues.

"Frémont! John Frémont?"

"Yeah, that's the one." Gunn fetched a bit of lumber from his vest pocket and waved it at Hannah and Micah. "Ain't never run across another body seed young Daniel scouting or trapping anywheres, so army's pro'ly where he's still at." He began to pick his teeth.

Hannah glanced at Micah. "Frémont! Isn't he the one who caused such a fuss when he married Senator Benton's daughter a few years ago? His name is still in the newspaper."

Micah nodded. "Yes, and I think he is with the army yet. He's been to California half a dozen times."

"If Daniel is still with him, why hasn't he been back?" cried Hannah. "At least for a visit?"

Gunn watched them with seeming unconcern, one hand placidly coddling his full belly, the other rolling his toothpick.

Micah pushed away from the table and held his wife's chair. "Mr. Gunn, thank you for your information. If you should hear any more about our son, will you send word?" He fished in his pocket for his coin purse.

Gunn waved it away. "You folks don't owe me any more'n you give me a'ready. Thanks fer the grub. I'll keep a eye an' ear out for ye."

As they left the rooming house, Hannah said, "If Daniel was working for the army, they would have records, wouldn't they, Micah? And if something had happened to him, they would have let us know!"

"Yes, they would," agreed Micah. "Mr. Gunn has given us something to work on. I'll write to the department of the army in Washington."

"*I'll* write, Micah. You finish your sermon."

He chuckled and drew her arm into the crook of his sleeve. "I confess I hadn't planned to write the letter today."

"But *I* do!"

27

The man moved with grace and familiarity through the timbered woods, his beige buckskins blending with the dappled shade. He was tall, powerfully built, with braided black hair, pewter gray eyes, and tobacco gold skin. He stopped and listened, shook his head slightly, and walked on. His wife was bearing his son. He wanted to be there, with his wife, his Lark. For the sake of his men, he was not.

Che-Muc-Tah had caused them to be confused once already this season by unstrapping Lark's burden from her back when she was growing big with child. She was not to carry heavy things.

Pity stirred in his breast for the women of the tribes. Many were treated no better than slaves. It was their lot to carry everything but their man's bow and arrow—or his rifle, if he were fortunate enough to possess one—to erect and take down shelter, to clean and cook the catch, to make the clothing, and rear the young. In some respects, the women were better off at the missions.

He stopped again and listened to the silence. She knew, Lark did, that each cry from her lips would reflect on him. It was bad medicine to sour a camp with cries of pain. Che-Muc-Tah covered his eyes and prayed for Lark, for the baby. It was good to pray. A leader must have a Leader. Che-Muc-Tah had not wanted to be a leader like his father was. He had fought against being a leader. Yet he was.

The man thought of his mother, living so far away it was like another life, a life that a boy, Daniel, had once lived; Daniel, son of Hannah and foster son of Micah MacGowan. Now he was Che-Muc-Tah, son of Tecumseh the Shawnee. *God, protect my wife and babe!*

Che-Muc-Tah gazed down into the peaceful mountain valley sloping down the western side of the Sierras range. He could see the conical shelters of the Chumash, who had welcomed him into their camp over two years ago.

The cone-shaped shelters were constructed of flat bark slabs and a few animal hides, tied together with rags. From his vantage point he could see plainly the charred rings of bark around the smoke hole topping each cone. In one hut lay his wife. Several of his own men squatted in a circle nearby, throwing sets of bones and betting on the throws. Their laughter drifted upward to him, dissolving like smoke. He walked on.

As a scout for Gunn, the Texan, Daniel at fourteen had received his first dose of respect for a skill that he possessed beyond the ability of other men. It was a way of knowing. That was the closest he had been able to come in trying to explain to Gunn how it was that he could track when no one else could find anything to track, how he could find a trail, a waterhole, a man lost in the desert. At fourteen he found value as a man and never looked back.

The early years of his boyhood taught him who his people were; the years with Gunn taught him who he was. In 1840 he met John C. Frémont. Frémont opened up to him who he could be.

Daniel had felt at home in the hot, arid reaches of Texas with the genial Mexican people. As he traveled west with Frémont, he grew fascinated by the Indian tribes of the Southwest, whose lands they traversed. Their lives were utterly unlike his boyhood imaginings of the mighty Shawnee race. His people had once dominated the forests and rivers of the Ohio Territory. These tribes did not dominate so much as adapt to the excesses and frugalities of desert life.

Captain Frémont was with the army engineers. With Daniel his chief scout, and accompanied by cartographers, surveyors, and a detachment of soldiers, Frémont had marched into California near the Sonora border. The first night, they had camped in an area of aged boulders and rolling, watered foothills. Hot springs burbled up in pools. After months of desert travel, the oak-forested hills seemed like a sanctuary in paradise. The area abounded in deer, bear, antelope, fowl of every description, more wildlife than Daniel had seen since leaving Missouri. Nor were signs of native tribal life absent, especially near the plunging streams. Daniel wondered that he had not caught a glimpse of anyone.

The second day, while the mapmakers were busy charting their explorations, Daniel wandered again to the streams, drawn by some inner urge to the sounds of clear rushing water, the cool feel of a fern glade. He ran lightly up the tilted granite face of a huge boulder jutting over the stream. He thought he heard an unfamiliar sound. When he reached the crest, he discovered an abandoned stone pestle. He hefted it. It would fit a smaller hand. Nearby was a basket of acorns. Several fist-size depressions were worn in the rounded rock face. In one of the depressions he spied a handful of partially ground acorns. A gathering place, then, for the women to ease the monotony of hours of grinding meal.

Daniel smiled. Poised on the rock, he let his eyes and ears probe both sides of the brook. A flick of leaf and a jay took off. A squirrel scampered up a trunk. Two chipmunks fought a neighborhood quarrel. He heard a small laugh. He ran down the rock and leaped across the stream.

The girl barely reached his shoulder. She was wearing a cotton shift that appeared to have been dyed with deep red berries. Her cheeks were round and the same berry red. Her eyes snapped with fun. She clutched a tree trunk, darted a look at him, and dashed away.

Daniel laughed aloud and trotted after her.

He could not speak her dialect. But her name was Lark, from the meadowlark that filled the twilight with song, and he could not tell her he was Daniel. The name that leaped to his lips was Che-Muc-Tah, from a distant memory, the name of someone who had known his real father, who had come to see him when he was very young and still living near the Ohio. He never learned the meaning of the name, but now it belonged to him.

Che-Muc-Tah met Lark's people, the Luisenos, and learned the reason why few of them allowed themselves to be seen. One night they took him to see how the Indians lived with the strange holy men who wore heavy, dark robes and rang the beautiful bells. Their brethren lived in stick huts, raised wheat, and herded sheep and cattle. They worked from morning until night, tilling, cobbling, tanning, weaving, their lives ordered by the ringing of the bells.

There was a graveyard into which the Luisenos crept before dawn one morning, taking Che-Muc-Tah to see. He found wooden markers bearing symbols that meant nothing to his new friends but which Che-Muc-Tah recognized as Catholic.

Still he did not understand why the Luisenos hid.

Because those who go to the missions can never leave again. The holy ones practice witchcraft. The Indians living at the missions are taught that if they leave they will burn forever in someplace hotter than the desert, for a day and a night that are without end.

This, gradually, he came to understand, and at last Che-Muc-Tah knew who he was.

Captain Frémont beat the dust out of his blue uniform and polished his buttons. He performed a civil marriage ceremony for Daniel and Lark. Daniel's closest friend, a big Texan called Cooper, stood as his best man. Cooper had been the first to welcome Daniel into Frémont's company, with the blunt words, "How'd a Injun like you get to be called Dan'l?" Cooper was strong as a bull buffalo, had long, coarse blond hair tied carelessly back in a thong, and a big, open face.

After the wedding, Daniel formally resigned from the company, promising at Frémont's insistence to come to his aid if he should be needed. Cooper's bear hug was a final farewell to army life.

Then Lark and Che-Muc-Tah were married again by the shaman, at Lark's insistence.

Many in Lark's tribe had friends or family who had gone to the mission, usually during a season of drought or disease, only to later want to return home. Those who once accepted the faith and later escaped were hunted down and brought back. Sometimes they were punished. Sometimes the women were made to go with *el cholo,* the government soldier.

In the ensuing seasons, Che-Muc-Tah discovered that the dialects of the tribes he came to know were linked. Once he had mastered his wife's speech, he could converse with little difficulty with the Dieguenos, the Gabrielinos, and even the Chumash.

"It is not bad to live at such beautiful missions," Che-Muc-Tah told them. "It is only bad to live there when you do not want to stay."

"But Che-Muc-Tah, you do not know these holy men. They *know* things."

"I have a father who also knows things," Che-Muc-Tah insisted. "And his Father is the same Father whom your holy men know. And He is the same Father whom your shaman blesses for the good things for your tribe."

"Who is He?"

"He is the Father of all people. He is called God. My father knows him, and I know him. And I know that your friends will not burn in a land hotter than the desert if they leave the holy ones at the mission. The holy ones know God, but they are not the only ones who know God."

"Then Che-Muc-Tah! We will get word to them. We will tell them this. And you will help them escape."

"Yes. . . . Yes."

Che-Muc-Tah and Lark lived with the Luisenos for three years. Che-Muc-Tah kept a journal. It was the one aspect of his life as a boy that he could not part with. Lark teased him about shaping his thoughts into black lines. She was there. Couldn't he tell her? And she would remember and tell their children. What need did he have to trap his story inside a *jour-nal?*

One day a rider from another tribe came seeking him. He spoke a dialect of the Chumash and told them he lived many days north, in mountains that were much higher, that were covered with snow for a long season each year. He had heard of Che-Muc-Tah. He wanted the Shawnee to come with him.

He had once lived at a mission, he told them. He showed them his back, where he had been whipped. He told tales that horrified the Luisenos, tales of rape and beatings that ended in death, of their former leader who had led an escape of 500 men, 1,000 horses, and 200 women from the convent. Later he returned to raid the mission stores. He had been tracked down in the Sierras by soldiers and beheaded. His head had been brought back and put atop a pole at the mission, as a warning to others.

Lark begged Che-Muc-Tah not to go with him. But Che-Muc-Tah knew in his heart that this was what he must do. His name, his habits and his whereabouts were too well-known anyway. Even the *rancheros,* normally a peaceable lot, did not wish to defy their padre. If they found him, they would be obliged to report him. And he had done what he felt his Father had wanted of him here: He had convinced the Indians who had wanted to leave the missions that they might and had helped them to do so. He taught them that their lives were still held in God's hand.

Ten of the younger, more adventurous men of the Luisenos chose to accompany Che-Muc-Tah and Lark on their journey northward. Six of these had formerly belonged to a mission. This made them particularly valuable, as they spoke with the authority of experience and not only their native dialect but some Spanish.

The camps in the Sierras were equally as beautiful as the Luiseno camps. In winter they dwelled in the foothills. Men hunted and fished. A few of the more ambitious ones trapped and sold pelts. In summer they moved to higher ground, out of reach of the occasional farmer or Mexican trapper.

It was because of the death of their former leader that the Chumash had sent for Che-Muc-Tah. They had foreseen continual rescue raids on the mission, but in fact in the two years he had lived with them, few mission Indians had sent word they wanted to escape. The soldiers' final barbarous act had cowed them completely. Occasionally the Chumash stole a few horses or cattle, justifiable in their eyes, since it was their brethren who tended the flocks and herds.

Che-Muc-Tah's gaze was arrested by some movement at the entrance of one of the conical huts, bringing his attention sharply back to the present. Two women filed out and spoke to the men playing games. One man sprang to his feet. He heard their voices. The day was waning. Che-Muc-Tah had waited the day away since Lark's pains first began and she had sent him out of the camp. He did not hear the traditional shout accompanying news of the birth of a son. A pang of fear darted at his belly. He dismissed it and headed toward the camp at a run.

Inside, the hut was roomy and warm. Woven baskets suspended from the willow wall supports contained root vegetables and early fruit. A clay jug stood within reach on the packed earth floor, with a tin cup and baskets of nuts and dried grasshopper cakes.

Che-Muc-Tah felt a rush of gratitude and love as he squatted beside his wife's bed. He feasted his eyes on the sight of his newborn daughter groping at Lark's mocha breast.

"If I could, I would let my mother know that she has a beautiful granddaughter, a princess among women."

Lark smiled from her bed of red-fox furs. "Why can't you?"

Che-Muc-Tah shook his head.

"But you are an American citizen, Che-Muc-Tah."

"This is not America. I belong to my people here more than to the Americans."

"Then you will have to write your thoughts in your jour-nal." Her soft brown eyes lingered on his face. "What will happen?"

"When?"

She shrugged.

"Che-Muc-Tah," said a low voice from the other side of the bark wall.

Che-Muc-Tah exchanged a glance with Lark. Leaning over her pallet, he kissed her lips tenderly, then the warm red face with the damp shock of obsidian hair peeking out from the fur.

As he was leaving, Lark said, "What shall we call your daughter?"

Without hesitation, he answered, "Hannah."

"*Ana?*"

"*Han-nah.*"

"Han-nah. Han-nah." Lark smiled, revealing small, perfect teeth. "What a strange name. What does it mean?"

"It is my mother's name. It means nothing in Shawnee, but in the Bible of our Christian God, it means '*the gracious one.*'"

Lark appeared mystified. "I would feel better if she had a practical name."

Che-Muc-Tah smiled. "Like Lark?"

"Yes."

"Then, what?"

Lark's brow puckered in concentration. Her eyes fell on the basket of grasshopper cakes. "*Grasshopper.* That she might be agile and quick and able to vanish from sight as if by magic."

Che-Muc-Tah laughed. "It is a good name. My mother would approve."

Lark smiled proudly.

28

"Sir?"

Harmon Roebuck looked up as his clerk popped his head in the door of his office.

"Somebody here to see you."

A tall, well-dressed young man with dark, curling hair brushed by the clerk.

"Stephen!" Harmon strode around the desk and pumped the young man's hand.

Gratitude and relief mixed in Stephen Davis's stance. Impulsively he dropped the older man's hand and hugged him.

"Sit down, my boy." Harmon grasped the carved arms of two captain's chairs and tugged them closer together.

"I wasn't certain what kind of welcome I would receive, sir. You know that I—that we—that Alissa and I. . . ."

Harmon's stern gaze did not let him off. "Well, then, how is Alissa?"

"She . . . is well," he said reluctantly.

Roebuck's eyebrows shot up.

Unwillingly, Stephen's eyes met Roebuck's. "She is properly cared for as a young lady of good breeding should be. She is in Monterey now, a guest of the American consul and his wife. She is well," he repeated. "Oh, blazes, Mr. Roebuck, the whole mess is my fault! Whatever she wrote to you, it's true. A man I considered a true friend, Ramon Antonio Bandini-Warner, has fallen in love with her."

"*Who?*"

"Hm? Oh. I'll tell you all about him."

"Does Alissa love him?"

Stephen shrugged. "He was there when she needed someone." He gazed out the windows. The docks shimmered in a blue haze of summer heat. He sighed. "I was headed for the MacGowans', but I couldn't face them yet. The reverend would be right to call for a horsewhipping."

"He did have the idea when we first heard about the split, but he's probably cooled by now."

Stephen turned his bleak gaze on Roebuck, as if it didn't matter one way or the other.

"Would you like me to accompany you?"

Stephen shook his head.

"Then, as long as you are here, do you want to give me a status report?"

"Yes, sir. Copies of the bills of lading are at the hotel. I brought the *New Horizons* into Boston with a full cargo. . . . " As Stephen spoke his eyes gradually cleared and his voice became animated. He talked the morning away, giving Harmon not only a complete report but lacing it with astute anecdotes on the political climate in California.

"I must say," said Harmon, who had sat reflectively, his hands steepled, immersed in Stephen's words for the better part of an hour. "You gave me a far better picture of California than Mr. Hastings did."

"*Who?*"

"Your friend, Lansford Hastings."

"My friend!" The blood drained from Stephen's face. "O God, I wish I'd never heard of the man!"

"What's the matter?"

Stephen shook his head. "Too—too blasted ambitious. I should have known better. I told myself it was all for Alissa. She saw through it, I believed it!"

"Pull yourself together, Davis," said Roebuck sharply. "What about Hastings? Why are you now disavowing your friendship?"

"I met him in Santa Barbara. He told me about a cache of furs—"

"The furs you sent east last year?"

Stephen nodded. "We got the furs out of the Sierras. Hastings said they had been abandoned." He glanced at Roebuck, his tone full of scathing self-hatred. "As if anyone would just abandon a cache of furs worth thousands! But no one was there, true enough. They were done up with deerskin thongs, but no marks of identification that I recognized. I didn't ask any more questions. We hauled them out by mule. You can get a ship halfway to Sacramento through the bay at San Francisco. I brought the *New Horizons* in, and we got them aboard with no one the wiser."

"Didn't you wonder at the time why all this secrecy was necessary?"

Stephen shook his head. "Hastings said it was to avoid paying duties. We all do that." He couldn't look at Harmon. He heard him rise and walk to the window.

"So you were a party to possible thievery. Anything else?"

"I agreed to factor them for Hastings in return for a fifty-fifty split on the profits."

"What changed your mind?"

"Nothing, then. I still have my share of the money. But later I learned that someone had shot up a tribe of Indians in the Sierras. The men were known to be trappers. Larkin believes Hastings led the massacre just for sport. *Sport!* Then he probably stumbled on the cache after he'd driven the rest of the tribe away. But I didn't know about this, Mr. Roebuck, I swear I didn't! If I ever see him again—"

"He was here last fall, you know. And again this spring."

"Here!"

"He said you asked him to look in on Alissa's family."

"Yes, but that was before—"

"And that you endorsed his leadership of a wagon train."

"What?" Stephen said in a shocked voice. "Is he still here?"

Harmon shook his head. "He persuaded eighty people to pay him to lead them across the continent. Another trainful of emigrants left a week later—two months ago—to meet him halfway across. Including Alissa's sister, Molly."

Stephen sank back in his chair, his face ashen. "This is terrible," he croaked. "This is terrible. A couple hundred people in the hands of a completely amoral scoundrel. If those folks get into any trouble, he'd just go off and leave them, I know he would."

Harmon reached for his beaver and his cane. "Come. We'd better go up to the house."

Stephen rose, moving like a sleepwalker in a nightmare. "They should be all right," he said, as if trying to convince himself. "Wagon trains come through all the time."

"Through the Sierras? I thought most of them used the Oregon route."

"Through Oregon. Yes, you might be right. The Sierras are not the Appalachians. I must talk to Reverend MacGowan!"

Hastings again. A devil-spawned man if there ever was one.

The white knuckles of the hands clasped together like two mismatched halves of a gourd, the hands of the elder MacGowans, clenched on the sofa between them.

"We will go to California," Micah decided. "God forgive me that I ever gave Alissa permission to leave unmarried."

Stephen hung his head.

"Stephen came back, Micah," said Hannah. "He's here to help us now."

"In any way I can," promised Stephen. "The *New Horizons* is in Boston. But there is a nearer way, by clipper ship from New York. We hailed one going out. He had made his last run in under one hundred days. Sixteen thousand miles from New York to San Francisco in three months!"

"By the grace of God, that's practically flying," said Harmon Roebuck.

"We could be in California by October," Hannah said tremulously. "And see our girls again."

"We should arrive just about the time the wagon train does," added Micah. The proud old man cleared his throat and glanced at the others. "Well. I shall have to see about finding someone to lead my congregation while we are gone. I believe I shall study that right now, if you will excuse me."

He rose and strode into his study, looking neither left nor right, and closed the door softly behind.

"You'll go back with us, won't you, Stephen?" asked Hannah.

"If you will allow me," Stephen said. He glanced at Harmon. "I won't expect to be on the payroll for this trip, Mr. Roebuck. But it will be a good opportunity to study the clippers with an eye to our future trade."

Roebuck laughed. "A businessman through and through."

Stephen threw him a peculiar glance. "Someone else said that to me."

Hannah laid a hand on her brother's arm. "We received a letter from army headquarters about Captain Frémont's men."

"You did! Have they located Daniel?" asked Harmon.

Hannah smiled uncertainly. "Yes and no. He did work for Captain Frémont. The paymaster has receipts that he drew regular wages up until six years ago. Then his name cropped up again in 1843, three years ago, when Captain Frémont was last in California. Oh, Harmon! Could the Lord have in mind to deliver all of our children to us in that land?"

29

"Sh-h!" commanded Molly.

"What?" Jared whispered.

"You're making too much noise!"

Jared and then Molly started to giggle. They wriggled deeper into the toasty mound of quilts in the back of their wagon to smother the sounds of their love-making.

"Honey?"

"Hmm?"

"Tell me if this feels good. . . ."

Six weeks had passed since the forty-odd wagons led by the Donners departed from Saint Louis. At first Molly and Jared McCloud were known simply as the newlyweds. But as the days passed, an awareness of the magnitude of their great adventure captured the immigrants. Individual backgrounds dropped away, and the most important things became one's ability to deal with day-to-day crises and the humor and fortitude to stave off boredom.

Day by day they penetrated deeper into buffalo country. For city dwellers like Molly and Jared, the differences were stunning. Long, empty days, sounds that had to be redefined. The *thuck* of wooden buckets hitting the wooden sides of the wagon, the dry clunk of harness and axle, the quiet, rhythmic clops of patient ox teams, a bird sweetly calling its mate.

The grass was coarse and tough, high enough to hide a calf. The Sioux called it buffalo grass. Trail herds thrived on it. Often they recognized the wheel tracks and campsites of trains that were days or weeks ahead of them. One lazy afternoon Molly imagined Lansford sitting next to a campfire, telling tales while others hung on his words. When she realized the dangerous drift of her thoughts, she grew furious with herself and spent the rest of the day tatting lace to use someday in her new house.

The days passed with monotonous regularity. A morning's trek could be four miles or it could be seven. At the nooning, children had a chance to run and work off energy, men to grease the wheels and sometimes do a little hunting or exploring, women to find others to share recipes and remedies, exchanged with pleasant small talk, while their hands never stopped working. Sometimes, if the trek had been grueling, the morning oxen were turned out with the common herd and relief teams were hitched to wagons. Each family, though seldom out of sound and sight of the others, maintained an illusion of privacy. One did not enter another's wagon without first knocking on the rear panel.

One nooning Jared and Molly saddled their horses for a brief ride ahead of the train. It had been Jared's idea. Molly had seemed restless and discontented lately. He hoped a ride away, just the two of them, would improve her spirits. The morning had begun with low clouds mounding in the western sky. As the day progressed, the clouds moved steadily forward to meet them. As they loped up to a high tableland, they were met by a fresh, cool wind.

"Looks like we're in for a summer storm," Jared commented.

"Good," was Molly's only comment.

Jared studied his wife. To combat the drying winds and hordes of insects, Molly and most of the other women wore long-sleeved, high-necked dresses. The dress she had chosen today, a serviceable maroon cotton, did nothing for her red hair and fair complexion. Her girlish figure sat the horse with an un-customary stiffness, anger bristling from every pore.

"Bored, ain't you?" he finally said. "Not like you thought it would be. You sorry you came?" When Molly didn't answer, Jared looked away.

The panorama of miles of grass-covered plains sweeping away in all directions thrilled him. The mottled clouds produced a quilt of greens as changing as the sea. He spotted a distant herd of buffalo moving like a gigantic, oozing mud slick across the prairie and pointed it out to Molly. "There, I'm going to have a herd big as that," he announced.

"You've said that for weeks," said Molly, slapping at a mosquito whining past her ear. "Can't you talk about anything else?" In spite of wearing a huge, white sunbonnet, Molly's face had bloomed with hundreds of freckles. She took such teasing from the Donner children that sometimes she just had to escape for a while.

"If you didn't want company, all you had to do was say so," said Jared.

A gust of wind bent the brim of her sunbonnet against her face. She sighed and squinted up at her husband. "Sorry. Maybe it's the weather. Storms seem to press down on me. . . ." Suddenly she lifted her face. "Phew! What is that odor?"

They stared into the wind. In the distance they saw what appeared to be mounds of freshly plowed earth, dark birds circling overhead.

"If it's animals, they are not moving." They crossed the high mesa and started down the far slope. Suddenly Jared uttered an oath. "It's buffalo, and I think they are dead." They trotted on and soon found themselves in a sea of rotting carcasses. Buzzards sailed on the wind and screeched outrage at the human intrusion.

"There must be hundreds of them, Jared!"

"By thunder! Wonder what's killin' them?" Jared spurred over to a carcass and swung out of the saddle. His face was intent as he leaned over the huge fly-ridden, dust-covered mound.

Molly hung back, having no desire to get closer to the gruesome sight. "Don't touch it, Jared, you might catch something," she called.

Jared ignored her. He poked at the carcass for some minutes before wiping his hands on the grass and coming back to her. "It ain't catching," he said grimly. "It's been shot."

"Shot!"

"I'm going to see Elliott."

Milt Elliott was George Donner's head teamster.

" 'Twasn't Sioux," Elliot declared when Jared and Molly found him changing a wheel on one of the Donner wagons. The big, rugged man was dressed in a heavy red wool shirt, with the neck of his long johns exposed underneath and well-worn buffalo hide chaps over his jeans. "Most likely it was some trigger-happy fool on one of the trains ahead of us. Indians won't kill more'n they need. Hides to trade. Enough meat to jerk. Robes and things for winter. Heck, some of 'em even worship the buffalo."

"Worship the buffalo?" said Molly incredulously.

"Makes sense," Jared said, as much to get back at her for her meanness as to defend the teamster, Molly suspected. "If something gave you almost everything you needed to live, you might worship it, too."

"I don't suppose Indians have souls anyway," said Elliott.

"They do too have souls!" said Molly. "They have souls just like anybody else!"

Milt Elliott's eyebrows shot up in surprise. He laughed uncomfortably and said to Jared, "Your missus is got a red-haired temper."

"You can say that again," Jared nodded. Suddenly the billowy clouds flattened out. A peal of thunder shook the ground, and forks of lightning threatened to crack open the sky.

Elliott looked up in alarm. "The herd! A storm like this could spook 'em good!"

"Give Elliott your horse and get to the wagon, Molly!"

Molly jumped down. "I'll see if anyone needs help."

In one swift move Elliott was on the horse's back, leaving the new wheel propped ajar on the axle. "Come on, McCloud, you kin help!"

Jared tore out after Elliott.

The train was strung out half a mile. Again and again the thunder crashed. Torrential rains whipped by screaming winds pelted Molly as she ran. She flung an arm up across her eyes. She saw Tamsen Donner ahead of her, running through the high grass, calling her children. The two Donner brothers and their wives had close to a dozen children between them. Molly helped her collect and get them under canvas.

Later, peering out the rear of her own wagon, Molly felt small and lost on the vast, gray prairie. One wagon she could see had had its white canvas top torn nearly off by the wind. The rain had gentled into a steady downpour. The herd must be secured, for she saw men drifting silently and soaked back to their own wagons. Maybe Jared was right. What was she doing here? Back in Saint Louis, crossing the prairie in a covered wagon had sounded so romantic! Something to tell Alissa that would be as exciting as her sailing to California on a trader.

But it wasn't romantic. Being married to Jared wasn't romantic. She thought again about Lansford Hastings, somewhere ahead of them on the trail, and this time did not check her rebellious thoughts.

One evening a scout came by and informed them that they were less than a day from Fort Laramie. So eager were the pioneers to reach the outpost that they skipped breakfast and were on the road by four the next morning. Other wagon trains were pouring onto the Oregon Trail now, and frequent bands of Indians as well.

A tribe of Pawnee closed in from a side trail, fierce-looking warriors with heads shaved except for a thick strip of hair running from forehead to nape. Proud in their brilliant garb, the men were mounted and carried rifles. Their women and children followed on foot, as plain as peahens.

Molly was sitting on the driver's seat beside Jared as the Pawnee streamed by their wagon. As they came abreast, one brave looked at her and unexpectedly giggled. He nudged the man beside him and pointed. Molly shrank against Jared.

Jared grinned. "It's your hair, honey. Don't be afraid. They probably never seen white folks before, and nobody with red hair."

Milt Elliott rode up on Jared's other side. "They's 'sposed to be friendlies, but they give the herd a good look, movin' up. Probably got every horse spotted. Keep a eye out."

Jared nodded and Milt moved on to the next wagon. The wagon train slowed and then stopped, without any obvious signal from anyone. The Pawnee women surged up, milling around the wagons, laughing and chatting. They were dressed in faded cotton calicos with many beads. At least one little Pawnee child was completely naked.

Just ahead, Molly saw Tamsen Donner looking out the back of her wagon. She waved brightly at Molly, looking as though she were enjoying herself immensely. Tamsen was a small, neat woman, unafraid to speak her mind. She planned to establish a school when they reached California. When Tamsen spied the naked child, she disappeared into the wagon for a moment, reappearing with a pair of trousers.

She climbed over the tailgate and was immediately engulfed by the strange-looking women and their children. Alarmed, Molly jumped over the wheel. As she pushed through to Tamsen's side, she, too, was surrounded by a chattering horde that fingered her blue linsey dress, fought to touch her white skin and red hair. An unexpected wave of panic swept over her. She glanced back at Jared, but Jared was keeping an eye elsewhere.

By signing, Tamsen showed the child's mother how the trousers went on the child. With shy delight, his mother accepted them, pulling them on the boy with the buttons at the rear and happily showing him off to her friends. Tamsen broke into laughter, and Molly with her, her fear draining away. From every wagon women now began to bring extra or outgrown trousers for the other children.

Suddenly a painted horse cut Molly off from the rest of the women. She looked up into the most ferocious face she'd ever seen. The warrior stared down at her with the arrogance of authority. Copper loops with beads hung from his ears. Both sides of his head were shaved.

"Jared!" she screamed.

Jared sprang to the seat of the wagon, a whip in one hand, his rifle in the other. Milt Elliott appeared out of nowhere. Laughing and joking, more braves crowded in beside the wagon. George Donner and some of the other men pressed in. "What's he want?" Jared demanded.

Milt got the warrior's attention. He tried some signs, coupled with a few words. The brave pointed to Molly, then himself. His followers laughed and nodded agreeably. Milt shook his head adamantly. He pointed to Jared and pounded his chest with a closed fist.

Still watching the warrior, Milt said, "He wants to buy Molly off you, McCloud."

Molly gasped.

Jared threw her a reassuring glance. "Tell him I thank him for the honor but that she is my wife forever."

The warrior thought this over. He stared at Molly for long seconds, then reached down with one bronze finger and touched her hair. There was a wistfulness to his voice as he spoke again. The he rode peaceably on.

Jared jumped down from the wagon and threw an arm around her. "Are you all right?"

She swallowed and nodded, keeping her lips firmly together.

"What did he say, Milt?" asked Jared.

"We'll never know."

The Pawnee tribe moved on. Many of the emigrant women now wore strings of beads, gifts exchanged for clothing. As the crowd broke up, Jared quietly watched his wife. She was shrinking against the wagon wheel as if fighting against life itself. It seemed to Jared that she was becoming more distant as each day passed. "Ready to go, Molly?"

She nodded, and he helped her up to the seat.

By late afternoon Fort Laramie came into view. Built at the eastern base of Mount Laramie, the fort was so solidly built that it had never been molested by the tribes. Around its outside perimeter were permanent Indian lodges, testament to the peaceful lives of both peoples. The train drove right inside the gates, which were buttressed by adobe walls two feet thick and twice as high as a man. Log cabins with common walls were constructed against the inside walls of the fort. Here, Molly supposed, lived the people who worked on the post.

Molly squinted against the glare of the sun on bare earth. Her first impression was one of disappointment.

"Well? You gonna get down or set up there all day?"

She hadn't noticed that Jared had left her side. "I'm coming."

Together they went into the trading post just as Tamsen Donner was coming out, shaking her head.

"They want too much!" she said in an outraged tone. Molly and Jared stopped. "The trader is asking forty dollars a barrel for flour and a dollar and fifty cents for a pound of sugar! It isn't right. He *knows* there is nowhere else we can provision up." She pulled her shawl firmly about her shoulders.

That night an angry bunch of immigrants gathered around the campfires, all complaining about the high prices and scarcity of supplies. Most of the men and women drifted to George Donner's.

"Mr. Hastings didn't say anything about larceny!"

"That's not something he can control," said Donner. "And we don't really need much now, anyway. We got plenty of meat."

"Still an' all, it ain't Christian."

"It'll be better at the rendezvous, won't it, George?"

"Bound to be," Jared answered for him. "Hastings said."

Folks from other parts of the States drove in that day and next, most headed for the Oregon Territory, a few bound, like themselves, for the Mexican province of California. Donner said mildly that they should be on their way at dawn, but under a storm of protests quickly withdrew the suggestion.

"We ain't exactly sick of our own company, but it sure is nice to talk to folks from other parts o' the country," drawled one old lady, a farmwife from Springfield at least ten years older than Molly's parents. "I'm having the time of my life! You got to let me enjoy it."

"Are we halfway yet?" Molly asked in a plaintive voice.

The men looked at one another. No one seemed to know.

The wagon train rested up at Fort Laramie not one extra day but three. It was July. The sun was hot and dry, spirits were high, and it seemed that summer would last forever.

30

West of Fort Laramie they left the flat plains behind and entered a region broken by shallow ravines and rocky outcroppings. One morning they had been underway about an hour when Donner signaled a halt. Jared had gone forward to scout with Milt Elliott. Molly pulled up the wagon. She jumped down, wriggling her fingers out of the heavy driving gloves as she went forward. A lone rider pulled up beside George Donner's wagon.

"He's from the West," Tamsen said. "He has a message for us."

"Howdy, friends!" The rider was lean and deeply tanned. His horse carried a large pack and three canteens, suggesting provisions for a long trek either before him or behind. "You all on your way to California?"

"Yes," said Donner. "Care to join us? Always room."

The stranger laughed. "Thankee, but I'm heading East to bring my family. I got a letter for you!"

He reached into a saddlebag and gave Donner a folded paper.

Donner opened it and read: "At the headwaters of the Sweetwater. To all California emigrants on the road—" He glanced at the bottom of the paper. "This is signed Lansford W. Hastings."

"It is!" Molly crowded forward eagerly. "May I see it, Mr. Donner?"

Tamsen Donner glanced at her quickly, a question in her eyes.

Molly avoided Tamsen's eyes and feasted on the black flourishes of Lansford's handwriting. "He is at Fort Bridger, waiting to guide us himself down his shortcut," she said in a lilting tone. "Just like he said he would!"

"What do you know about this shortcut?" Donner asked the rider, taking the letter back.

"Not much. Ain't never been that way myself. But Hastings got a large party he's aiming to take, and 'way he tells it, it ought to take off a bit of travel time. Don't know as it's rightly four hundred miles, like he claims, but pretty close."

"Sir—," Tamsen, sitting next to her husband, rose from the wagon seat. "Our friends from Saint Louis told us that Mr. Hastings collected a dollar apiece from those of his train."

"That's customary, ma'am, when you hire a guide. I take it you folks don't have a guide."

"We've just been following the Oregon Trail," said Donner.

"We've already been traveling for over two months," Tamsen persisted. "If we join Mr. Hastings at Fort Bridger for the shortcut, he should not require the full amount. That is a dear price."

"Well, ma'am, you can argue with him when you get there."

"*If* we decide to hire him," Tamsen said tartly.

"But we don't go to Fort Bridger," objected one of the men. "In a few days we reach the Green River rendezvous. From there we turn north to Fort Hall, ain't that right, George?"

"So they told us back at Laramie," Donner acknowledged.

"So we are going to have to make a decision before we ever talk to Hastings. Once we go on to Bridger's, we're committed."

Jared and Milt Elliott rode up during this interchange. Jared quickly sought out Molly's face in the crowd. *I missed you,* his eyes telegraphed.

"Hello," Molly said indifferently.

"What's going on?" asked Milt.

"He brought a letter from Hastings," Donner said, briefly filling them in.

"What kind of shortcut is it?" asked Jared. "Mr. Hastings wasn't too specific back in Saint Louis."

Eyes went from Donner's face to Jared's. Though young, his steady good sense and willingness to help made others look up to him.

Donner consulted the letter. "Well, he says if we take this cutoff we don't need to go to Fort Hall. We go to Fort Bridger and then around the south side of Great Salt Lake. Then he says there's a two-day drive through the desert till we reach water, but he'll be with us every step of the way."

"We're nearly out of flour again. My missus planned to provision up at Fort Hall," said one of the other men.

"And I need some fixings for one of my wagons," added Donner.

"You ought to be able to get everything at Fort Bridger you can at Fort Hall," said the rider. "It's a company store."

"And there is bound to be a lot of trading going on at the rendezvous," added Molly.

"We have till then to make our decision," said Tamsen.

"That's right, you do," agreed the man. His horse danced in a tight circle as if the rider had communicated an impatience to be off.

"Sure you can't join us?" asked Donner.

"Got to be on my way. You want to give me that letter?"

"I thought you said it was for us."

"It's for all the trains coming through."

George Donner surrendered the letter, and the rider turned away. Jared called after him, "What if everybody signs up? How can one man take that many people?"

"That's his problem," the rider called back blithely.

Molly started for the wagon.

Jared caught up to her and dismounted, walking his horse beside her. "Remember what Hastings said that day at your folks' house, Molly? He wouldn't wait for the Donners, because he said it was better to take smaller groups so that there would be plenty of grazing for all the herds."

"He must have a reason," said Molly. "Maybe it's different where he's taking us. Maybe there's so much grass there's plenty for everyone."

"Whoa! We haven't even decided to go with him. Personally, I think we'd be better to go slow."

"Four hundred miles is four hundred miles!" retorted Molly. She turned hostile blue eyes on him. "Even on our best days Mr. Elliott says we don't cover over twenty miles. That's twenty days, Jared! Twenty days we wouldn't have to worry about running out of provisions or finding good water or grass." She looked back along the string of wagons, feeling hot and dusty, thinking what pleasure it would be just to sit in a real chair again, in a real room, with pictures on the wall and curtains on the windows. Windows! There was a forlorn catch in her voice as she added, "Twenty days sooner we'd be in California."

And what would Lansford do when he found out she was married? It was different in California, he had said.

"Molly—," Jared caught her hand. "Look at me. I feel so bad when you are unhappy. I love you. I'd hitch your wagon to the moon, if I could. Did I do something?"

She looked up at him and thought, *You're not Lansford.* "It's nothing you did," she said in a flat voice. "Do you want to drive, or shall I?"

Molly and Jared walked over after supper that night to be with the Donners. All the campfires were burning late, she noticed. Everyone seemed to be debating the cutoff. She didn't see why there should be any fuss and bother, it just made good sense to *do* it. The two brothers, their wives, the older children, and a smattering of teamsters sat on campstools, logs, or blankets. The McClouds were greeted as they joined the circle.

"Fort Hall is a safe way," Tamsen Donner was saying. "We have friends in California, who used to live in Springfield, who came that way with no trouble."

"That's not to say the cutoff *isn't* safe. . . ."

"Men who live around the rendezvous ought to know something about this cutoff," suggested Jared.

" . . . I think it's plumb asking for trouble. . . ."

"One thing," said George Donner, "is time. Now I know winter is three months away, but we lost half a day to that bad storm back along the Little Blue, we spent two extra days at Fort Laramie, and we halted a day to celebrate Independence Day. It is nearly August. We got to think about getting over the Sierra Nevadas before the snow."

Tamsen rose and wrapped her apron around the handle of a blue enamel coffeepot that was sitting on a flat rock next to the fire. "There isn't much coffee left, but may I pour some for anyone?"

"I have some left in the pot, too," said Molly. "I'll get it."

"I'll walk over with you," said Tamsen as she dispensed the last of hers.

A barrage of crickets entertained them as Molly matched her long-legged stride to that of the smaller woman. Molly admired Tamsen greatly. Though in her forties, Tamsen Donner never seemed to lack for energy or ever had an unkind thing to say.

"I found some watercress today, Tamsen," Molly said. "I don't know how it got overlooked," she added as an afterthought.

Since they had left Laramie, the trail showed increasing use. Scouts had to go as far as two days ahead to find campsites that still offered good forage for the herds. Wildlife, though, was abundant, and cookpots rarely lacked for a joint of buffalo or occasionally venison, wildfowl, or a hare or two.

"I've been meaning to tell you how much I appreciate your help with the children," Tamsen said.

"I like kids. And it gives me something to do."

"You behave as if you are just a wee bit homesick, Molly. It is hard enough to start a trip like this when one has all of one's family around. Tell me about your family in Saint Louis."

For a while the loneliness eased as Molly told Tamsen about Daniel and Alissa and her father's church. Tamsen waited while she fetched her reserved coffee from the wagon.

"Where did you meet Jared?" Tamsen wanted to know as they started back.

"I've known him all my life," Molly said simply.

"Childhood sweethearts, how wonderful!"

Molly glanced at Tamsen, choosing her words carefully. "No . . . , he was just *there.*"

"And you became sweethearts."

Molly smiled ruefully. "I guess so."

"He loves you very much. I was watching him when he rode in today. His face lighted up so, it was just full of love."

Molly stopped on the trail and sighed deeply. "Tamsen, may I ask you something?"

"Of course you may."

"When you don't feel romantic about a person, does that mean you don't love him? I mean, I like Jared, but, you know, when you grow up with somebody, well, I mean, he's just like a brother. Even when—when—you know—it's almost as if we were two kids being naughty. I don't feel *married!* I don't feel swept off my feet, like when—"

"Like when you met Mr. Hastings?"

Molly gasped. "How did you know?"

Molly could feel the burning directness of Tamsen's gaze through the darkness. "You have talked about him a lot since we've gotten to know each other. And I watched you this morning. You had to see the letter for yourself when George said it was from Mr. Hastings. You defended him when you have no way of knowing any better than the rest of us if his cutoff is a good one. Your face looked as bright as Jared's did when he was looking at you a few minutes later."

Suddenly Molly's shoulders began to shake. Muffled sobs tore out of her throat.

Tamsen took the cold coffeepot from her hands and led her out a way from the wagons. She caressed Molly's shoulder. "We like to think marriage will make everything perfect. Sometimes it doesn't. But it can get better, Molly. Why, the way Jared loves you, it can get to be about as good as you want it to. He's a good man, Molly. Trust the Lord that he delivered you in the hands of the right man."

Molly stood before Tamsen like a penitent.

"I'm going to pray for you every night from now on, both of you. Will you do the same?"

Molly nodded. "I'll try. And I'll pray for you and George, too."

"Thank you, dear. Lord knows, after twenty years, a marriage needs even more strengthening than when it began. . . . Shall we go back?"

"Yes. Thank you, Tamsen."

"I love you, honey. Everything will be all right, you'll see."

31

Molly woke suddenly, senses alert. She had slept deeply. The smell of sage hung in the dry, cold air. Unwilling to leave her warm bedroll, she stared up into the indistinct gray white canvas. The voice of the night sentry came through the blurred light as he awakened the camp.

She glanced at Jared. His finely chiseled jaw bristled with whiskers. His cheeks were a healthy red. His heavy lashes rested against them without moving. She leaned over to kiss his cheek, then changed her mind, and inched out of the bedroll. She climbed over the bedding, propped her arms on the back of the wagon, and peered outside. The horizon was graying into pink. Somewhere she heard the low call of a quail and wondered where it could possibly nest on this treeless plain.

Suddenly she remembered: Today was the day they would reach the rendezvous. She crawled back to Jared. "Jared!" she hissed softly. "Wake up! Today's the day!"

A spurt of excitement ran through the camp. The swarms of children flew about their chores with unusual cooperation. Cows were milked, breakfast plates washed and repacked, fires quickly choked with dirt and stamped down. By the time George Donner called, "Chain up! Chain up!" most wagons were already chained up and maneuvering in line.

From the moment they started, Molly found herself craning ahead for her first glimpse of the fabled rendezvous. Like others dotting the Rocky Mountains, each spring and fall the Green River rendezvous drew Indians from many tribes, English, French, and American mountain men, emigrants in trains, and soldiers.

After an hour's drive up a long, low slope, the train topped a rise. Hundreds of tepees unfolded before her eyes on the open plain below as thick as mounds of a prairie-dog town. Beyond the tepees she saw a few flat-roofed log outbuildings. She let out a moan of disappointment.

"What's the matter, honey?"

"It's not even as big as Fort Laramie."

"Well, it ain't a fort, it's just a meeting place. Okay?" he smiled anxiously. She smiled. "Okay."

As the lead wagon passed through the tepee village, hundreds of Sioux streamed out, calling to them, running alongside with hands out in gestures of friendship.

Elliott trotted up, and Molly realized with a shock of amusement that except at mealtimes, she never saw the teamster off his horse. As if he were growing roots to the saddle. And she also never saw him out of that red wool shirt.

"Morning, folks. Jared, could use an extra hand. We got to put up some sort of rope corral for the herd. Then we'll swing the wagons 'round th'outside." He massaged his heavy jowls and stole a glance at Molly. He had been timid with his words to her since the time she had jumped all over him for saying Indians didn't have souls.

"Good morning, Milt. Go ahead, Jared, I can get the team in place."

"Good girl."

To her surprise, Molly found another wagon train already in place. By the lines of wash strung between the wagons, they had been there for at least a day. What if Lansford was their guide, too? Skillfully Molly guided the wagon to her place in the circle, maneuvering the team at a right angle so that when she unhitched them they would join the cattle in the inner corral.

That done, she climbed into the back of the wagon, humming to herself. She took the pins out of her strawberry-red hair, brushed it, and rewound it into a bun. She tied her sunbonnet on and looked at herself this way and that, trying to get the effect from a tiny square of mirror. All she could see was millions of freckles. She pulled out wisps of hair to frame and soften her face. Now she looked as if she were all huge blue eyes.

Molly MacGowan McCloud. The voice was so distinct that she jumped. *You are not prettying yourself up for Jared, are you?* "Yes, I am!" She jumped lightly from the back of the wagon and spotted Tamsen.

Tamsen was tucking hair back into her bun, pulling her shawl neatly over her shoulders. She was surrounded by a swarm of children. She waved at Molly. "Do you have your list?"

"Oh, no. Wait for me!" Hastily Molly reentered the wagon, found their money pouch, and mentally reviewed what supplies she and Jared were lacking. The children ran on ahead, Tamsen and Molly following. They skirted an anthill swarming with giant red ants. Lizards skittered here and there, off their warm rocks and under sage brushes and greasewood.

"Look, children!" cried Molly, shading her eyes.

A magnificent brown bird hovered high above them. The sun glinted streaks of gold on its head and neck. Its outstretched wings looked as long as a man.

"An eagle, a golden eagle!" They watched the eagle glide and dip. Suddenly it swooped to the plains. Its high, piercing scream split the air. In an instant the bird was skyward again, in its beak a writhing rattlesnake. Molly stared in astonishment, awed by its strength and beauty. Winter seemed far away in the strong August sunshine.

Eagerly the women passed through the post gates. Braves bartered behind heaps of furs spread on the ground. Squaws clustered in vivid, chattering knots. Red brown children darted in and out among the throngs. The Donners and other children from the trains hung near their parents, suddenly quieted by the sight of un-self-conscious nakedness of the smaller children of the plains.

The American women were joined by their menfolk as they reached the verandah of the trading post. Molly flashed Jared a look of relief, clinging gratefully to his arm. The post was as crowded as a Saturday afternoon in Saint Louis. Fierce-eyed trappers passed in and out, as craggy as the mountains they came from. Milling among them were Sioux warriors in full regalia and men in the dress of a dozen different tribes. On the plains they might be enemies, Molly realized; at the post they were not. The coming of winter brought all tribes into alliance as each traded and provisioned against the common enemy.

Provisioning was ample, though expensive. Every square inch of wall space was covered with wares for trade. Big pots with wire handles, ladles, grills, tar buckets, tin and pewter mugs and plates, ropes of varying length and thickness, bridles, and even an old saddle. One counter seemed to draw most of the young boys. Here were half a dozen rifles, powder, and bullets. Ropes of tobacco hung drying from a hook in the ceiling, and on the counter a glass jar of hoarhound drops. Molly and Jared quickly finished their purchases and strolled outside.

To their surprise, mild-mannered George Donner was engaged in a shouting match with a man who towered over him. Narrow braids ran down each side of his tawny, shoulder-length hair. His buckskins were heavily decorated in beadwork of the kind squaws did for their men, with an added fringe of porcupine quills decorating the outside seams of his trousers.

Jared and Molly moved closer. Donner's face was red with anger. "There is a nigher route, Jim Clyman, and it is no use to take such a roundabout course." He hefted a book under the mountain man's nose. "It says so right here!" He flipped open the book and read what Hastings had written about his cutoff.

"Hastings could charm the skin off a snake," the giant drawled. "You folks try to take his way, you'll end up your bones bleachin' the desert."

"Why should we take your word over his?"

Jared stepped forward. In a friendly voice he said, "Clyman, is it? I'm Jared McCloud, this here's my wife, Molly." The men shook hands. "Come, you don't believe what the man's written? Is that your train, the one we pulled in next to?"

"Dang right it is. Look, it don't make me no mind which way you folks get to California. Most folks go the way we're goin', Fort Hall, Fort Bidwell, followin' the Oregon Trail. From Oregon you can slide into California easylike. You don't have them Sierras to battle."

"We'll be over the Sierras before the snows, if we take Hastings's cutoff," said Donner. "Even if it only saves us three hundred miles, that's two weeks of good time—and provision."

"You from around here, Mr. Clyman?" asked Jared.

"Son, I been here as long as the grizzlies. If they was a quicker way, don't you reckon I'd a found it? If Hastings's way is the one I'm thinkin', it ain't even a right trail. I'd sooner let the Sioux tie me over a anthill than take wagons through the Wasatch."

"But Mr. Hastings wrote a book . . . ," said Molly.

Clyman regarded her sourly. "Meanin' no disrespect, gal, you got a lot to learn. I hope you live that long."

"How much are the folks in your train paying you to guide them to Oregon?" Molly asked tartly.

Clyman smiled and shook his head. "Dollar a family."

Jared looked uneasily at George Donner and Molly. "Mebbe we ought to think hard on it."

"Yeah, well you think hard on it, and pray mightily to be shown the way, Son, because the way you're headed sure ain't it!"

A meeting was held that evening with all families of the Donner party. George Donner outlined in impartial detail what the rough-spoken mountain man had said at the post.

"The other train is taking the northern route to Fort Hall tomorrow," he finished. "Clyman's leading it. Now there are not going to be any bad feelings for any who want to go with him."

For a long moment no one spoke. Then a timid voice piped up, "You think the other train will take us on?"

"Clyman said they would. My family is taking the cutoff. Mr. Hastings has promised to meet us at Bridger's post and guide us the rest of the way, and I believe him."

Molly heard a gasp from Tamsen. "Oh, Mr. Donner! Oh, please! We should pray on it!"

The fear in Tamsen's voice caught Molly by surprise. Instinctively she put her arm over Tamsen's shoulders and shot Jared a look of wonder. Who would have expected Tamsen to be so untrusting?

Jared frowned, as if torn in both directions. At last he said, "Molly and I'll stay with the Donners."

One by one the men voted. When it was over, twenty-three wagon families were remaining. The others would turn north. Reluctantly the camp broke up. Good-byes were said. Families who had never laid eyes on each other before last May now clung to each other, weeping. Amid promises of, "We'll see you in California!" they disappeared through the darkness to their own wagons.

Tamsen seemed to have shrunk as she waited by the fire with Molly, while George, Milt Elliot, and Jared made arrangements to separate the herd at dawn.

"Why are you so upset, Tamsen?" said Molly.

"I must abide by my husband's decision," she said in a troubled voice. She clutched her shawl to her breast. "But I feel Mr. Hastings is not to be trusted."

"Not to be trusted! Tamsen Donner, and you a schoolteacher."

"Oh, dear Molly. Books do not always tell the truth."

"Things will look different in the morning," Molly consoled her. "Come, let me walk you back to your wagon. Everything is going to be just fine."

Molly smiled to herself in the darkness. And in a few days she would see Lansford again.

32

Padre Gonzalez Rubio was standing near the open gates at the Santa Clara Mission. A smile wreathed his seamed, ruddy face as he watched the slow progress of his old friend Padre Muro from Mission San Jose. Once each summer the two priests managed a few days' visit together. Both their missions were falling into decay, and few were the pleasures left to them, which made their visits all the more precious.

Muro's procession drew close: three horses, the second bearing a native attendant, the third bundled with goods. Moments later the two priests embraced and set off to stroll in the courtyard rose garden so that Padre Muro could walk off the aches and cramps of miles and hours passed in the saddle. The roses were in their last summer bloom, their scent already whispery of dried petals and fine dust.

Rubio dug deep in the pocket of his robe. "Look here, my friend, what one of my children found today."

Muro stopped and chose one of the nuggets with long, slender fingers. "Humph! Gold." Dropping it back in Rubio's hand, he started forward again.

Rubio replaced it in his pocket.

"What are you going to do about it?"

"I thought nothing. In the last year, I have seen more Americans than ever before crossing over the Sierra Nevadas. They care nothing for the church."

"Or the Indians," remarked Muro. "They will interfere with the work of the missions. Is it at last too late to keep them out? I have the letter you sent."

The letter Muro referred to was one that Rubio had received from the Colegio de Zacateca, which in years past had sent the missions money to keep the structures in repair. In the past they had also supplied fresh, younger priests to carry out the work. Rubio's mind was heavy with the knowledge that there would be no more money, no books, and no young priest.

"Mexico has abandoned us," said Gonzalez Rubio. "Our church has abandoned us."

Muro shook his head in sorrow. "Who will Christianize the Indians and teach them Catholic ways?" He looked up bleakly at Rubio.

"While I am alive, I will stay with my children. They will have to carry me out." Rubio clasped Muro's shoulder with a reassuring hand. "And I will not hasten that day by letting the government *or* the Americans know that there is gold in our streams."

Muro nodded.

A steady thrum of busy insects filled the air. Rubio batted at a swarm of gnats and breathed in the dry August heat. "It is a beautiful day, is it not?"

On his own land Captain Johannes Sutter prided himself that he was a benevolent despot who rightly demanded obedience and meted out his own order of justice. Thus, on this day he was particularly outraged. It was the time of the wheat harvest. Eighteen forty-six had been a propitious year for wheat, with good early rains and a hot, dry summer. Fifteen days ago he had hired a work force of two hundred Chumash Indians to harvest his grain and sent them to work in Grass Valley. Yesterday the captain of his army had reported that over half the Indians had taken their first week's pay and returned to their own tribes.

His soldiers refused to do Indian labor, and Sutter was faced with loss of a valuable crop. Within an hour he was on his way to the Santa Clara Mission at the southern tip of the bay of San Francisco. He arrived at the mission many hours later. Ignoring his own exhaustion, he demanded immediate audience with Padre Rubio.

It was the third day of Padre Muro's visit. The two men were dining when the Indian servant brought word that Sutter was waiting. The priest's face settled into lines of forebearance as he wondered at the purpose of this visit. Surely not for confession, although he did not doubt confession would be a blessing to such a driven man. He had always felt uncomfortable in his presence. So with a sigh for his dinner, which would grow cold, and a wry face for Muro, he left the dining room. Tucking his hands in the sleeves of his robe, his sandals making a gentle slap on the well-worn tile, he made his way to the door of the vestry.

Sutter turned away from the tiny square that emitted light in the thick adobe wall. Powerfully built, with a wiry, fair beard and the reputation for a ferocious disposition, Sutter was a man not often crossed. The heavy blond brows knit together. No glimmer of warmth invaded the blue eyes as he said by way of greeting, "Huh. Got a problem, padre."

"Greetings, my son. We are just having our dinner. Come and join us."

Sutter shook his head. "I am up to my neck in my wheat harvest, padre. And I got to tell you, I am sick of using the hostiles to harvest my crops. I tried, God knows. I *wanted* to hire them."

Rubio waved Sutter to a seat, which he declined. Rubio slid behind a well-used table. "Tell me about the hostiles," he said. Sutter stalked impatiently around the cramped vestry Rubio used as an office. The priest watched his guest with a closed face.

"The locals. You know, the Diggers," he said, using the contemptuous epithet. Rubio remained expressionless. "The Chumash that are not missionized. They have been stealing horses from me for years. Only to eat, so I don't bother sending my men out to punish them. But even when they work, padre, they work for a day or a week, then they want to take what they have earned and spend it."

"Buy liquor, you mean."

Sutter nodded. "They come back, some of them. Too late! They do not give a thought to my harvest! Rotting wheat? Means nothing to them! They are ignorant, lazy, stupid. . . ." Sutter planted his palms on the padre's table and leaned over him. "I have come to hire your men, padre. They are trained. They are obedient. Any workers would be better than this crew of layabouts."

"Captain Sutter! My Indians are not slaves."

"I'll pay them. Or pay you, that way you can husband the money and see that it is spent wisely." The heavy eyebrows raised and piercing blue eyes fixed on Rubio. "From the looks of this place, you're none too prosperous," he added bluntly. He shoved himself away from the table.

"It is true that the church fathers have limited our funds—"

"And a lot of them come that's down-and-out, too, isn't that right? And squaws that some Mexes got big with babes, and the tribes turn them out. I can't see you turning them away, padre. You must have heavy expenses for food and medicine."

"We have always had plenty of food and clothing, my son." Rubio did not want to discuss the affairs of his mission with this man.

"And money to fix up the place?"

Rubio shrugged.

Sutter nodded. "Everyone has to fight for what he wants in this world."

Rubio left the table and stared out the cell-like window. He thought of the gold nuggets his Indians brought in from time to time. If there were enough gold pieces, it could make a difference at the mission. Perhaps he could pay the government the gold and buy the mission himself!

But as always, he returned to his belief that the mission would prosper only until word leaked out. Then he would have no peace until he revealed where the nuggets came from. And gone would be his mission, overrun, and the quiet, peaceful life he enjoyed here with God's children in his charge. He turned back and contemplated the man before him. What would a man like Sutter do if he knew about the nuggets?

"Not all that much to think about, padre. You need the money here. You'll do it, right?"

Rubio sighed. "I shall ask my children. Only those who want to work for you will go."

Sutter shook his head. "I need two hundred, and I need them now. You just tell them they will be working for me for the month. They'll come. Dawn tomorrow we leave. And you be sure to tell 'em my men'll shoot them if they try to leave before the harvest is in!" Sutter paused for his words to sink in. "A thousand *reals* in gold, padre. Or part of it in medicines or supplies. I'll feed them well and not neglect their health. I'll even throw in fifty *arrobas* of wheat, free, if they get the harvest in safe. I believe in paying for what I get."

"You have made your point, Captain Sutter. You may have your men. And none of the money shall be spent for ought but the good of the men and their families."

Sutter's grin widened. "Of course, padre. One more thing: Round up a dozen or so women for them."

Rubio felt the blood draining from his face. "What did you say?"

"Insurance. Keep 'em happy so they don't want to run away."

The priest began to shake with anger. "No, Captain Sutter. God forbid that I should even hear such evil. Take yourself out of my sight! I will tell my servants to prepare food and a bed for you—"

"Whoa!" Sutter snorted. "Easy, easy. Have it your way. I can always get the women."

"Have you no regard for the spiritual lives of these people?" Rubio cried passionately.

Sutter heaved a sigh and planted massive hands on his hips. "Let's face the truth, padre. I am a businessman. I look at your mission and the other ones here in California, and I see that you have had fifty years or more to civilize these poor souls in a good Catholic image. How well have you done? A businessman would've looked over this proposition years ago and seen that the missions were fine places to raise cattle and plant crops to benefit the church. With a free source of labor. As a plan to convert a race of hostiles to Christianity it's been a first-class failure."

"The salvation of souls is not a 'business proposition,' " Rubio said bitterly.

"That is true. But if the salvation of souls was a losing proposition, it wouldn't still be around after thousands of years. Therefore, padre, the problem is not in the salvation but in the method. Your Indians are no more Christian than they were before you came."

The merciless words bit like fangs. "You are a cruel man, Sutter. And you're wrong. My children love their God."

"All right. All right. You'll still lend me your Indians?"

"Yes. The men."

"I don't wish you evil, padre. I wish I could help you, but I don't see any way out. Good luck to you."

Rubio struggled with himself. After a minute he was able to master his emotions and ask, "Do you want to be confessed before you leave?"

"Me? What for?" Sutter was laughing when he left.

Padre Rubio remained at the narrow window for a long time after Sutter left. The valley before him was so beautiful. He could see several of the bark huts where his children lived, men and their wives who had grown up on mission lands. Their children were a new generation of Chumash Indian Christians, baptized into the Faith at birth.

Jesus had directed them to carry the Word to the corners of the world. Where had they gone wrong, if they had gone wrong? Surely the sweet faith and the simple, pleasant lives of his children meant more than the scorn of a man like Captain Sutter.

The bell tolled evening prayer. His dinner and Padre Muro forgotten, Rubio hastened eagerly to meet his flock at the sanctuary.

33

"Back home Ma and Lavinia and I would be putting up vegetables, and we'd be thinking about harvesting the corn," said Molly. She and Jared were walking beside the wagon.

"I could do with some fresh greens, how 'bout you?"

Molly nodded. "Or some roasting ears."

Jared ran his hand down the flank of the lead ox. He could feel the ribs through the stringy layers of muscle. "Some grain for the team would be good, too." The McClouds had only one team for their wagon, which was smaller and lighter than most others. Over a hundred beasts remained in the herd belonging to the emigrants following Hastings's route, including the milch cows, relief teams for some of the wagons, and some horses.

From the rendezvous the twenty-three wagons left in Donner's charge had headed southwest along the Green River toward Bridger's post. The first day and a half passed pleasantly as they went through groves of aspen and greasewood and moss-pale willow. The second day they left the Green. The lush shade paled into leathery swells of tableland dotted with blue lupine. Topping a butte, Molly and Jared could see snow-capped mountains far to the west and south.

Molly gave an appreciative sigh and smiled up at her husband as they walked.

"Sure beautiful, ain't it?" Jared said awkwardly. "Molly . . . , you like being here with me a little better now?"

Molly nodded, but looked away. She couldn't get thoughts of Lansford out of her head, and she tried, she really did. Unfair comparisons deviled her mind. Jared was handsome, but in such a rugged way next to Lansford's smooth manner. Lansford dressed so elegantly. Even the day his train left Saint Louis, he looked like a fashion plate. He had a way with words, he—

"What are you thinking, Molly?"

Jared had such an anxious look on his face that Molly couldn't help giving his arm an affectionate squeeze. "Nothing important, honey."

Patches of white appeared on the trail. Jared leaned down to pinch and taste it. "Alkali. Hope there isn't much of it."

But as the day wore on, the patches of alkali thickened and overlapped until the train could no longer skirt it. The emigrants, most of whom had been walking, clambered back on their wagons. As hooves and wheels crushed through the crust a thick, choking dust deviled them. Soon everyone was coughing. Molly and Jared tied bandannas over their mouths and noses and worried about the team.

Through watering eyes Molly glanced at Jared. His eyes were so encrusted they looked frosted. She could barely see the wagons before and behind.

"Get in the back," Jared said. "It won't be so bad there."

"It's just as hard on you."

"Please."

Reluctantly Molly climbed inside. She peered out the rear of the wagon as she felt the wheels grind through a rocky stream. The water was mustard yellow and foul smelling.

By midafternoon they were through the alkali flats. By evening, the extra team for one of the Donner wagons was bellowing in misery.

"What's the matter with them?" Jared asked Milt as the teamster tramped into camp. He looked like a refugee from an Indian ghost dance. His face was streaked rust and white with iron dust and alkali. "They must have drunk from one of the alkali streams. They got the bloat."

The agonized cries of the animals rang through the evening. Finally Donner eased to his feet. "No help for it, Milt. Put 'em out of their misery. We'll dress 'em out and take the meat with us."

"I'll help," said Jared, automatically rising to his feet. Molly watched his retreating back with grudging admiration.

While children gathered wood for fires, Molly and a few of the other women pitched in to help Tamsen cut the butchered meat into strips. They would smoke as much of it as possible through the night and carry it with them.

By the next morning Molly's arms ached from struggling with the heavy meat. Her pride would not let her complain when none of the others did.

Late that afternoon the train pulled into an area laid out by Milt and Jared about a quarter mile from Bridger's fort. As Molly was preparing their supper, Jared came back to the wagon with a worried look in his eyes. "I haven't seen hide nor hair of Hastings's people."

Molly felt an unformed mass of fear gathering in her stomach. "Maybe they've got a spot on the other side of the fort."

Jared shook his head. "I doubt it, but come on."

The Donner brothers were at Bridger's ahead of them. The fort was no more than a log building with cabins on either side, built in an ell shape, with a fence running from building to building and enclosing a small corral behind. The post was nearly deserted. Molly could hear an unfamiliar voice raised before they entered. The trader was shoving money back at George Donner. "Senor, your money is no good. We have a contract with Hudson's. They ship us goods out of Saint Louis. Now if we do not keep enough supplies for their trappers, it is our necks, yes?"

"But—but we were promised—"

"The trappers expect us to have the kettles, the salt, the tobacco, the corn, the flour, the beans—," the trader slapped Donner's list. "Everything *you* want! Now you folks are welcome to stop here and rest awhile and fix your wagons. That's just fine! Only I can't let you have all our supplies."

Donner seemed to falter.

Jared stepped up beside him. The trader was a small man with olive skin and close-set eyes. "Are you Jim Bridger?"

"Yessir. I been trying to tell your friend here, the last train took all we had extra."

"Hastings's train?"

"Yessir."

"Where is he? He was supposed to meet us here."

"He hung around till a couple days ago. Had sixty-six wagons. He was holding meetings for days, signing up folks left and right. Finally he said he couldn't wait no more."

"Couldn't wait no more!" Jared exploded. "He *promised* us he'd wait. Way back in Saint Louis he promised. And that rider that came out to meet us when we were just clear of Fort Laramie—he had a letter signed by Hastings!"

Bridger's eyes narrowed. "That ain't no business of mine."

Molly pushed her way up to the counter. "There must be some mistake, Mr. Bridger." This couldn't be happening. Lansford wouldn't let it happen!

"Just what the devil are we supposed to do now?" demanded Jared. "How are we going to get through with no guide and no extra supplies?"

Bridger stepped back, his hands up. "Hold it, hold it. Look, I can't help it, it's been a good season, I sold all my goods. I'm sorry." He shrugged his shoulders in a gesture of dismissal, but threw an uneasy glance at the four angry faces. "Hastings did say if any more was to come this way, he'd come back and guide 'em through the Wasatch once he gets his own people through."

"I wouldn't believe him now if my life depended on it!" declared Jared. He threw an angry glance at Molly.

"I think we should turn back," she said in a small voice.

"Hastings said he'd mark the trail for you," supplied Bridger.

Jared glanced at George Donner. "What about it, George? You think we can get through the Wasatch?"

George looked helplessly at Jared and then at the trader. "I lost a team in the alkali flats. . . ."

"I can let you have a team. Took in four oxen a couple days ago."

"Where is the next post?" asked Molly.

"Sacramento."

"That's in California, isn't it?"

"You're two-thirds the way there." Seeing their desolate faces, Bridger relented. "Well, look, I got some dried beans and corn left. You folks are coming through pretty late, not much chance there's any more behind you. I'll sell you whatever I can spare."

In the corral behind the post were the four oxen. "A pretty sorry lot," said Donner, when Bridger showed them.

"I'll bet he took them in from some poor traveler who was down on his luck," murmured Molly to Jared.

Bridger watched as the disheartened emigrants led the oxen toward the campground. When he had built his post a few years ago, he had plenty of trade from trappers working for Hudson's. Then the demand for beaver hats slumped, fur prices went down, and trapping fell to a trickle.

"I wouldn't take a train through the Wasatch," said his partner, coming out on the veranda and interrupting his thoughts. "Bad enough on horseback."

"If Hastings makes it, they can."

The other man spat. "They ain't got a guide with them. That ain't all. I happen to know Hastings ain't never been that way himself. He got his maps from someone in California, who made it through by horse. And that was *with* a guide."

Bridger didn't answer.

"By the way."

"Now what?"

"United States is at war with Mexico."

"What?"

"Over Texas. She wants to be part of the U.S. of A."

The train spent three days at Bridger's post. Wheels were replaced, axles greased, the herd moved from one graze to another, eating steadily. Without supplies to see them through, edible roots were scoured from the ground, and every hand good with a gun went out after game. The smoke fires remained lit the whole three days.

At last they set off, on a perfect August day when the hills were ripe with weeds. Patches of red and orange dotted the slopes. Here and there a stand of small pine wove its rich green into the wild tapestry. Elk, antelope, foxes, birds—the countryside abounded with life.

As the foothills of the Wasatch Mountains grew steeper, the teams again began to lose weight. Pasturage was lush but never seemed enough. Each day the struggle grew harder. The beauty of the mountains, the rushing waters, the abundance of life gradually formed a living nightmare, taunting with its beauty while disguising its near impenetrability. The train dogged the trail of the sixty-six wagons Hastings was guiding somewhere ahead of them.

"If they can make it, so can we!" George Donner stoutly insisted.

His encouragement kept their spirits up. Not one word of reproach did Molly hear Tamsen utter as the folly of their decision began to impress itself on them. Some slopes were so steep the wagons had to be unhitched and raised by rope winches to a new level. The wagons took a continuous beating. Wheels reset at Bridger's were already shaking loose from their iron tires. Each day they expected to sight Hastings.

On the fourth day in the Wasatch, they entered a steep-walled canyon. Sounds of the wagon wheels clattering on bald rock reverberated up and down the canyon. Here they found a river flowing northwest, so rich in iron it looked bloody. Donner dispatched Elliot to scout ahead.

"It's the Red Fork of the Weber," Milt Elliott reported and then rode with the news to the following wagons. "Clyman told us it goes up into the Great Salt Lake."

"We're in good shape then, aren't we, Jared?" said Molly, glancing to Milt for confirmation.

"Looks like it. Hastings's tracks go on for miles ahead. Funny we ain't spotted them yet."

Jared gazed across the Red Fork to the western range of the Wasatch. "I've been watching those mountains. They looked even meaner than the ones we just crossed," he said. "I sure thank the Lord that we don't have to get through those."

Two days later word came back that Donner was stopping the wagons.

"There's still two hours of daylight" said Molly. "I hope nothing is wrong."

"He can't make camp here, that's for sure," said Jared. "The grazing's all chewed over." He jumped over the wheel and gave Molly a hand down. They joined the rest of the train heading for Donner's wagon.

"What's the trouble?" Jared asked.

From the seat of the wagon, Tamsen Donner was staring rigidly into the distance. Donner was standing with his back to the wagon, his face in a state of shock. In his hand was a scrap of paper. "My girl found this," he croaked when they were all gathered around. "It's from Hastings. It was stuck in a bush downriver. He says the route is bad. Our wagons can't make it."

A frightened silence descended on the emigrants.

"It's your fault, George Donner!" a man yelled.

"Hush! It ain't," said the man's wife. "He di'n' make no one come!"

"O dear God," whispered Molly.

Jared put an arm around her. "How did he get his wagons over?"

Donner looked at the scrap in his hand. "No telling how long this has been out here. He could 'a come this way and seen it wasn't fit and gone back days ago."

"You mean we've been following his tracks *backward?*" Milt Elliott was incredulous.

"He ain't just leaving us here!" exclaimed another teamster.

Donner shook his head. "He wants us to go back to the fork of the Weber and the Red and make camp and send someone down this canyon to overtake him. A horseman can make it through."

Ominous quiet greeted his words.

"He says he will come back and guide us over the mountains by a better way."

Tamsen could keep still no longer. "Oh," she cried. "Let us not do that, Mr. Donner! That man has deceived us every step of the way. I beg you, in the name of the Lord who loves us, lead us back to the rendezvous. This shortcut is a shortcut of the devil. Take us back to the Oregon Trail."

"What kind of a man would deliberately lead us astray?" wailed one of the women.

No one had an answer. Donner looked around with a heavy heart. "My friends, if someone else wants to lead. . . ."

"I don't think I could face going back the way we come," muttered one of the men. No one opposed this.

Jared spoke up. "I'll go after Hastings. I know the man."

"You know he ain't gonna honor his word," said a teamster.

"Put a bullet through him, if he gives you any trouble," suggested Milt.

"I'll go, too. I know him better than any of you," Molly said with dignity. "He was a guest in our home. If anyone can persuade him to come back for us, with God's help, I think I can."

Jared started to protest, but Tamsen burst out, "Yes, Molly, oh, bless you!"

"You go, too, Milt," ordered Donner.

At dawn the three rode out of the camp on the Weber while the rest prepared to go back to the fork. Molly's brain was in turmoil. *He must have a good reason, he must! He isn't like that!* she told herself.

Three days later the trail slipped out of the mountains. There, on the Great Salt Plain below them, was the huge encampment of Lansford W. Hastings. As they rode down the slope, Molly's heart began to beat wildly.

"Look, I believe that is him coming to meet us! I *knew* he wouldn't desert us, Jared, I knew it!"

Jared didn't answer. His mouth set in a grim line, he rode steadily to meet Hastings. The man was on foot, as slender and dapper as ever. His pencil moustache was neatly trimmed as always. His thumbs were hooked in his flowered waistcoat, his walk jouncy. Behind him, a stream of emigrants flowed out of the camp to meet them.

Jared recognized one man from Saint Louis. There wasn't a smile among them. Jared glanced at the rifle in his saddle holster and then at Milt. Milt caught his meaning.

Hastings threw his arms wide. "Molly! Molly, darling girl! I didn't know you were coming. Welcome, welcome, friends. Here I am, right where I said I'd be! We are not far now! Two months, and it's California!" He took a deep breath and struck his solar plexus. "Ah! I can almost smell the ocean air of that sweet, gentle Pacific. Molly, did I tell you that the Pacific was named for—?"

With an oath Jared leaped off his horse and seized the flowered waistcoat. "I've had all I can take from you, Hastings. Get your horse. We've twenty-three wagons stalled in the Wasatch, just waiting for a man to honor his word."

"Get away, get away from me!" Hastings slapped at Jared's hands. "How dare you?"

Suddenly they were facing a line of rifles. Jared stepped back. Molly gasped. "Lansford . . . , you promised."

For a moment a look of frustrated regret entered Hastings's eyes. He shook his head with the barest movement.

One of the men with Hastings said, "Look, mister, you ain't comin' here threatenin' us. We paid Mr. Hastings to guide us to California, and we ain't lettin' him out of our sight."

"Did you pay him a dollar a head, like the folks who signed on in Saint Louis?" demanded Jared. A light dawned in his eyes. "I'll bet Bridger paid you, too, to bring folks past his trading post!" Suddenly Jared rushed Hastings and shoved him to the ground. Two of Hasting's men leaped forward.

Milt whipped out his rifle. "You touch him, and your leader is dead," he roared. "Then he won't do nobody no good. Or no more harm."

"You ought to be horsewhipped," yelled Jared. "It was you that got us into that hellhole. You ain't never been this way before, have you?"

"Well, no, I—I've studied the trails a good deal, maps and—and I've been up that Fort Hall road." Hastings glanced up at Molly, a pleading look in his eyes. "Why, that road isn't much better, Molly."

Milt's eyes swept the desperate army behind Hastings. "We can't force him, Jared."

The man Jared had recognized from Saint Louis stepped forward. "Maybe we could wait here until they catch up—"

"We can't do that," said another. "We got our own provisions to worry about."

"Before God, Lansford," begged Molly, "you must help us!"

Hastings shook his head in distress. "Stay with me, Molly. Join us. I'll pay—"

"O God!" Molly cried. She clenched her fists. "How could I have believed you?"

"Please, don't cry! I'll—I'll come back part way with you—to the top of the mountain—and point the way. My friends will come, too," he added hastily.

At first Hastings had attempted to ride beside Molly. She refused to have anything to do with him. The rebuff didn't seem to faze him for long. He prattled on like a tour guide for hours. By dusk, the riders had reached a lonely pinnacle. Now they were fanned out, eight horses in a line, gazing silently eastward. Somewhere, not far as the crow flies, but days away, twenty-three wagons waited to be released from their rock-walled prison.

The three from Donner's party listened gravely as Hastings pointed out landmarks to the passes and ravines they must follow to get through the mountains.

Hastings and his bodyguards left. The trio kept their eyes eastward.

"We can do it," Jared said quietly. He smiled warmly at Molly and Milt. "Come on. We *will* make it."

Two more weeks the train fought through the Wasatch Mountains. The fourth day they again lost Hastings's trail. The struggle took its toll on humans and animals alike. Each day a different teamster took the lead, forcing his oxen to break ground, hacking away with pick, shovel, and ax over bushes and small trees and around rocks. Sometimes the sweating men had to fill ravines with boulders to widen them sufficiently for wagons to cross.

Finally, as they descended to the edge of the salt plain where Elliott and the McClouds had found Hastings two weeks earlier, they stopped to figure the price of Hastings's shortcut: thirty-six miles in twenty-one days. Twenty-one precious days, and now it was August twenty-seventh, and somewhere ahead of them, the salt desert and then the Sierras waited.

34

"His name is Salvador, and he is from Captain Sutter's fort in Sacramento." Che-Muc-Tah's lieutenant had come to speak to him while he sat in the long grass, playing with Hannah Grasshopper. Lark lay nearby, her head propped on one loosely coiled fist. Her glossy hair spilled over her shoulder.

His lieutenant dropped to his haunches and explained patiently, "We did not want to bother you. Salvador came to us a week ago because he quarreled with Captain Sutter about some Indians who came from the mission to work in the wheat fields. Now he wants to go back to Captain Sutter's. He does not like our food. He misses his woman."

Che-Muc-Tah nodded. "I will speak to him."

The lieutenant motioned to a muscular, anxious-looking Indian standing apart from the other men in camp.

Most of the Indians who found their way to the Chumash tribe living in the Sierras wore loincloths of buckskin, but Salvador wore the white cotton pants and shirt that announced his status as a servant in the household of Johannes Sutter.

"I do not like the food, and I miss my bed," Salvador blurted in Spanish. "Captain Sutter allowed me to have a glass of wine with him sometimes. Here I am nothing. I am treated like a—a Digger!" he spat. "I want to go home."

A handful of Che-Muc-Tah's men, those who had been with him since the years in the south, understood Spanish. They glanced at him uneasily. Salvador could not go home, their eyes told him. They were safe only as long as the government soldiers and Sutter's mercenaries did not know where to find their camp.

Che-Muc-Tah's gray eyes regarded the wretched man. He shook his head. "You cannot go back, Salvador. Perhaps sometime. A year or two."

Salvador's jaw worked. His voice wavered between tears and bluster. "I am going. You have to let me go!"

"No. Be warned."

Suddenly Salvador's manner changed. "I will not tell," he pleaded. "No one. Not anyone where you are! I swear by the virgin! I have a wife at Captain Sutter's." His moist eyes darted to the naked, plump infant waving her tiny fists in the air. "I have a baby, too."

Hannah Grasshopper burbled a cooing sound on her blanket of fur. Che-Muc-Tah leaned over her with a delighted smile.

"In God's holy name . . . *please.*"

Che-Muc-Tah sighed and rolled on his back. He sat up and clasped his knees with his arms. "Sit down, Salvador."

As swift as a hare, Salvador dropped, cross-legged, to the grass.

"How is it that you did not think of this before you ran off?" he inquired. "How are we to know that Captain Sutter did not promise you the moon and the sun if you would report where we were?"

"No, no, I swear! Captain Sutter has all the men he needs now. He does not want any of the hostiles—ever—to work for him again. He says you—," Salvador frowned and placed a finger at his temple. "He says a free Indian does not know what it is to save up for a rainy day."

Che-Muc-Tah laughed. This Sutter sounded not unlike the men of Saint Louis, Missouri. "Tell me more about Captain Sutter. And remember it is a sin to lie!"

Meekly Salvador bowed his head. "Yes, O Che-Muc-Tah. Captain Sutter is a good man sometimes and a bad man sometimes. When he is good, he is good to all of us. That is when he allows me a glass of wine, too. When he drinks too much, it makes him angry, and we must tremble in fear, because he will beat us."

"Has he beaten you?"

". . . Yes."

"What? Speak up!"

"Yes! One night by mistake I left open the door to the smokehouse, and bears carried off some of his meat. Nothing makes Captain Sutter angrier than to lose something that is his. He beat me so badly I could not leave my bed for a week."

"What will happen to you if you go back?"

Hope leaped into Salvador's eyes. "He will beat me. But not so hard that I could not work. He will be glad that I have not deserted my wife and babe."

Che-Muc-Tah glanced toward his men, observing that they had moved near enough to hear the interchange. Their faces were carefully blank.

"Salvador will not stay with us willingly," he announced. "We will have to kill him or at least cut his hamstrings."

Salvador blanched.

Che-Muc-Tah continued to gaze at his men. "Well? Who will do it?"

The Luisenos glanced at each other. "It is up to the Chumash," said Che-Muc-Tah's lieutenant. "He is one of them."

In rapid dialect the state of Salvador's health flew about the camp. Che-Muc-Tah stole a glance at Lark. Her eyes danced at her husband's cleverness.

Salvador jumped to his feet. "Wait! I must tell you something more! When Captain Sutter came back from the mission, I heard him say that the old governor is gone. His soldiers are gone! They got on a ship and sailed away. You do not have to fear him anymore!"

Finally the lieutenant spoke in Spanish again. "We have decided, Che-Muc-Tah, that if you are willing, Salvador may go back to his wife and his home. But he must promise never to tell Captain Sutter where he found us. If he goes back on his word, we will cut every tendon in his body and let him live."

A tremor passed through Salvador's body. Then he threw out his chest. "You have my word. I am a man of honor. I swear by my honor and by the virgin. Bless you, Che-Muc-Tah! Bless you and your wife and your babe!"

As if fearing that someone might change his mind, Salvador charged out of the camp.

The Luiseno lieutenant dropped beside his chief. "I hope we do not regret our clemency."

"I have a feeling we will not," said the new father, getting to his feet.

"Where are you going, my love?" asked Lark.

"To see why the soldiers have left. I will return in a few days."

Salvador raced down the low hills toward his home. Free! He was free! As he ran he prayed mightily that God would make Captain Sutter so good-humored this day that Salvador would escape any beating at all. "I pray for a surpassing wheat harvest," he panted, "I pray for the grapes—for the wine—for the sheep herds—and the cattle, too!"

An hour later he loped through the gates of the fort. The German guards were laughing and talking, a relaxing of discipline Sutter *never* permitted. They ignored Salvador completely. The dusty courtyard was filled with horses. He slowed to a walk, mystified by all the activity. Now he could hear laughter and

music. He examined the horses more closely. Horses with tooled Mexican saddles and sheepskin pads; horses with uniform saddles, gray wool blankets, and
bridles that had a foreign, military look.

He proceeded more cautiously in the direction of the cookhouse.

"Salvador!" The head of the servant staff, an efficient, nervous Frenchman,
called to him irritably in his whiny accent. "I don't know where you have been,
but I need you right now!"

"Yes, sir!" said Salvador. "What is going on?"

"Hah!" said the Frenchman. "All Californians are crazy. Some American
soldiers who call themselves Bear Flaggers took a Mexican general and his men
prisoner. They brought them to Captain Sutter—"

"Frenchy! What's keeping you?" Captain Sutter's voice bellowed from the
house. "Bring more brandy! More wine!"

Frenchy glanced in the direction of the command with supreme disdain.
"And now they are all getting drunk together, the Americans, the general's
party, and Captain Sutter. Here. Take the key. Bring up three bottles of brandy
and a dozen of burgundy. And be sure to lock the door!"

"Yes, sir. Yes, sir!" Happily, Salvador sped away. He was home.

35

The remorseless sun ate the chill off Molly's back. The miracle of frost on
the sage became dew and then dried. They had been walking through this
desert forever.

"He told us *two days*," said Jared in a bitter, raspy voice. "He said once we
got through the Wasatch, a hard two-day drive would carry us through the
Great Salt Plain."

"And today makes two. . . ."

"He lied, may God damn his soul!"

Molly nodded, saving her strength. In the blistering heat their voices and the
movements of the wagons and animals rang with an odd sound, both sharp and
hollow. Donner had split the day's drive into two parts. They drove late afternoon to midnight, then dawn till noon. In the worst of the heat and cold they
slept and tried not to move, not to need extra water.

Molly's lips grew chapped and cracked. The leather of her shoes cracked. On and on they went, through heat shimmering off the desert floor like wraiths. Through the shimmers she saw something moving. She nudged Jared, walking ahead, like her with one hand on the side of the wagon, crowding into the thinning line of shade.

"It must be Lansford. We caught them," she rasped.

The train appeared to be forward and off to the south. All morning their train trailed the other, never coming closer. She stared with mystical concentration.

"Why can't we hear them, Jared?"

"Look," said Jared. Before their eyes the other train wavered, grew thin, and with excruciating slowness disappeared. "It ain't real."

A ghost train. . . . They walked on.

The third morning Jared and Molly thought they could see foothills and patches of dusty green.

A sob broke through her voice. "Is that real!?"

"Real and coming closer."

Water! By noon it was upon them. Shouts of joy and laughter rang out. Children, men, and women waded into the springlike streams. Sat in it, clothes and all, dunked their heads, praised God.

"This can't be the Humboldt," said Jared, rearing up in the water and sweeping his wet hair back with his hands. "Up, lady, and cook your man a decent meal!" He pulled Molly out of the water. Her soggy skirts clung to her with delicious coolness.

"Yes, lord and master," she said. She felt miraculously revived. "Where are you going?"

"Take a look over the foothills. The Humboldt must be on the other side."

"We just got here! Think of the poor horse if not yourself. Wait till after lunch." The animals had waded in downstream and were drinking and standing contentedly.

"All right." Jared smiled and took her in his arms. The water flowed around their knees. "Think of the stories we're going to have to tell our grandchildren."

After lunch Molly and Jared saddled up and rode into the low foothills. Molly reached the top first. "Oh," she cried out. "Jared, oh!"

Jared spurred to her side. They gazed in horror at the scene before them. The afternoon sun glittered on a sheet of pure white.

"It looks like milk glass," breathed Molly. Slowly she shook her head. "Jared, we can never cross it. We can't do it. Somewhere, we must have gone wrong. It just goes on and on. . . ."

"I've never seen anything like it," Jared said. "It's a world of pure salt."

Back at the camp, Jared asked George to call a meeting and reported on what they had seen.

Someone began to sob quietly as the truth sank in. Tamsen left Molly's side and went back to comfort the woman.

"We'll face it as best we can," said Donner. "You folks run your wagons in the water, let the wheels tighten up to the rim again. We'll retar all the buckets and fill 'em with water." His gaze burned with compassion for the dozens of children scattered among the men and women. "You children got to help your parents. Get all the grass you can and tie it into bundles. Fill the wagons with it, because we don't know how soon our animals will get to graze again."

"Yes, Papa," said a small voice just behind his shoulder.

George leaned down and picked up his youngest daughter. "That's good, honey. You are Papa's good little soldier." He glanced around. "Hunting don't look promising, but if any of you's a mind. . . ."

Not a squirrel or a rabbit was to be found. One man brought down a strange white bird that someone believed was a sea gull.

Molly dug down into her cornmeal barrel. Only eight inches of cornmeal remained, and three eggs. She had about two pounds of rice, a sack of dried beans, and the flour was almost gone. Jared tossed in some final bundles of grass and climbed in after it. He found her sitting in the midst of her stores.

She forced a smile. "Our diet won't be exactly varied for the next few days."

"I don't mind," he said gently. "George thinks we ought to start about four. We're going to break up the herd. Each of us will be responsible for our own animals. Strange. When we left home, I felt bad I could only afford to buy a team and two horses and the cow. Now I'm glad that's all we got. Let's get some sleep."

They snuggled down together in the bedding.

"Jared?"

"Hm?"

"I think you're the best and bravest man I know."

"I think you are, too."

"Man?"

"Best and bravest, dummy. Come here. . . ."

An hour before dawn they gathered to pray, entrusting their lives in God's hands. Then the twenty-three wagons with eighty-seven men, women, and children crawled around the foothills and onto the edge of the Great Salt Lake Desert.

The sun rose and beat on the glittering salt sheet. Wheels crunched through the crust. The teamsters fanned their wagons out across the desert in an effort to find new crust to drive on. Once the crust was crushed through, it became impossible to drive the wagons through. In places the salt was as thick as a man's hand. The wheels mushed into it. The oxen strained and panted.

A headache pounded behind Molly's eyes as she squinted to reduce the glare. The sweltering sea of salt stretched before them like an endless lake. The metal wheels became too hot to touch. Finally the horses' reins were too hot to handle, and even Elliott dismounted and tied his horse behind George Donner's wagon.

By the second day the herd began to rebel. The boys baited them with occasional bits of grass from the wagons. Only the oxen in the yokes got water, a quart apiece.

By nightfall the second day the surface of the dry lake became like a sheet of fire.

To endure, that was all. Molly no longer thought where she was going or why. *Just a screen door between us and hell.* The next step was the only one to worry about. Jared picked up a couple of pebbles and gave one to Molly to suck on.

"So you won't feel so thirsty," he said.

By noon the third day people were close to despair. Children began to whimper as some of the wagons ran out of water. Now there were no pebbles to pick up and suck, and some began to suck on flattened bullets instead.

The train descended slowly into the center of a strange, gigantic sinkhole. The sloping salt crust looked like cracked plates curled around the edges. It was so brittle the animals' hooves broke through, and they sank inches into a salty brine that oozed up between the cracks.

In midafternoon, one of the McCloud's oxen lay down in the yoke, forcing the other to its knees. Molly ran forward. "Get up, get up. Jared!"

Jared began to unbuckle the yoke.

"What are you doing?"

"Trying to save their lives. Molly, we're going to have to drive the animals ahead. They're goners if they don't get water soon."

Molly looked at him with wide, stricken eyes. Jared's dark eyes burned like coals in his leathered face.

"We got to, honey. Come on. We'll come back for the wagon."

Scattered across the salt, they could see several other wagons in the same predicament. One and then another unbuckled the teams, abandoning the wagons, hoping that water was near enough to save them all.

Molly filled their canteens, and Jared gave the four animals the last of the grass and water from the buckets. She loosened her clothing and her sunbonnet and took the horses' leads in hand. As a last thought she filled the pockets of her dress with cold biscuits.

Jared brought up the oxen and watched with a wry smile. "Try swallering one of those with no water. Ready?"

They walked until time had no meaning. At night it was freezing. They kept on walking. About two or three in the morning, Molly's arms ached so they felt they would drop off. Numbly she clung to the horse's tail and let it pull her along.

At last they reached the willows beside the springs at the western edge of the desert.

They had lost thirty-six head of cattle and four wagons.

"At least," said George Donner, calling them together, "we can thank our Lord that we'll never be thirsty again. Clyman told me that once we crossed the desert he was pretty sure we could follow rivers clear into California. Now what could be as bad as what we just went through? Some of you lost teams, and others lost stock, but among us we still have enough teams for all the wagons that are left. We just need to do some shifting around."

"We can take a couple of folks to ride and eat with us, can't we, Molly?" asked Jared.

"Of course, but—"

George Donner looked at her expectantly.

"We don't have enough provision to get to Sacramento, Mr. Donner," she said apologetically, "even if our wagon will make it."

Several discouraged nods acknowledged this fact.

"I been thinking a couple of us ought to go on ahead to Sutter's Fort and bring back enough to see us over the Sierras."

"I'll go," Milt Elliott volunteered.

Donner shook his head. "I need you to drive a wagon."

A small man with a pipe in one hand got quietly to his feet. "I don't have a wagon." Frank Stanton, bachelor, had paid to use part of another's wagon to store his food and a small personal trunk. Affable and well liked, Stanton said, "I'll go."

Jared glanced at Molly. "Molly can handle the team as well as I can. I'll go with you, Stanton."

Molly bit back a protest, hoping his offer would be turned down.

A German immigrant with a bristling beard and a stout trunk began to mutter under his breath.

"What is it, Mr. Keseberg?" said Donner, somewhat startled. Keseberg, a man of about sixty, traveled with a wife who spoke no English and another recent immigrant from Germany by name of Hardcoop. Why Hardcoop, who was older than his hosts, had paid to be carried to California was the subject of much speculation and no enlightenment, since Hardcoop also spoke no English and Keseberg usually kept to himself.

Keseberg lumbered to his feet. "I say yah that's a good idea send McCloud. He got a wife. He come back. Others maybe not."

"No—," said Molly.

"I think we ought to send only single men," said Elliott. "Jared can drive for Donner, Molly can handle their team, and I'll go with Stanton."

Donner nodded. "One man shouldn't go alone. We are back in Indian country."

Another driver got to his feet. "I got little ones, Mr. Donner, or else I'd volunteer. But Jared's a better shot than Milt—beggin' your pardon, Milt—and he'd stand a better chance of getting there and back. I'll be happy to give Mrs. McCloud a hand when she needs it."

"We'll all pitch in," another voice said.

"No!" Molly cried passionately. "I can drive and ride as well as Jared. I want to go with him!"

"Can you shoot, girl?" said Donner in a gentle voice.

"I—," Molly compressed her lips in a silent scream. He was really going. He was going without her! Molly rose, filled with fury, and ran out of the meeting. She climbed up into the back of her wagon and began to sob.

Jared came a few minutes later. He tried to take her in his arms. She beat him off with a clenched fist and refused to look up. "Honey, it's for you and all the others. You wouldn't want any of the men with children to go, now would you?"

"But Jared, there were other men who could have—"

"But they didn't." He smiled. His dark head bent closer. He tipped up her chin. "What you got to do is more important than what I got to do. You got to help folks not be afraid. When they see you, just a slip of a thing, managing the team and carrying on just fine, they are gonna be ashamed not to do as well."

Gradually Molly's tears stopped. "Oh, Jared, why can't I just run away and meet you down the trail somewhere? I don't give two crackers for the team or the wagon. I just want to be with you!"

Jared laughed and cradled her in his arms. "Honey, if you was with me, I don't know if I could *make* myself come back!"

36

"My eyes! Isn't she a clipper? See how she throws up the suds for'ard!" Lieutenant Osborn, United States Navy, stood on the docks at Monterey in October 1846 and watched the approach of the first clipper ship he had ever seen. The beautiful symmetry of her spars, sails, and rigging, the elegance of her hull, her trim appearance, her skysails and man-of-war semblance brought the young lieutenant and his company crowding forward in awe.

At last she dropped anchor. Osborn watched a man, whom he took to be the captain, help a lady and two men down a Jacob's ladder into a rowboat manned by a half-dozen sailors; then he descended to join them. When they reached the dock where Osborn waited, he was surprised to see that the graceful lady was actually well along in years, as was the erect gentleman at her side. The other passenger, a dark-haired young man, was commendably solicitous of the elders. All three were impeccably dressed.

As the captain strode up the gangplank behind his passengers, Osborn stepped forward and snapped a salute. "How do you do, captain, madam, gentlemen. Lieutenant Osborn, United States Navy. Welcome to California!"

"How do you do, sir," beamed the captain. "May I introduce—"

"Sir, I am obliged to commandeer your vessel." Osborn grinned. "And may I say she is a beauty!"

Hannah gasped.

"Just a moment, Lieutenant Osborn!" said Stephen. "This is a privately owned vessel. You have no authority—"

The grin fell away, and the officer said, "I am sorry, sir. You may not be aware that Mexico and the United States are officially at war. I am acting under orders from Commodore Stockton to do whatever is necessary to advance the cause of the war effort." He tucked his cap under his arm and reached into his blouse pocket. "Here are my orders."

As the captain accepted the papers Stephen said, "You'll be leaving American citizens stranded!"

"You will be safe here. Monterey and San Francisco are in the hands of the Americans. We need this ship to convoy troops to Los Angeles."

"Where my ship goes, I go!" said the captain.

Osborn nodded. "Good, we can use you."

"How will we get home again?" said Micah MacGowan.

"It will not be for long—"

"What is going on down there?" Stephen demanded.

"Please," said Lieutenant Osborn. "The American consul is in residence here. He is responsible—"

"Yes, yes, I know him—"

"Good," said Osborn imperturbably. "He will see to your comfort and your questions."

"How are you, my boy?" said Larkin, pumping Stephen's hand vigorously. "Have you really been to the East Coast and back in this short time?"

"Yes, sir."

"I understand they took your ship."

"Not a company ship, a clipper." Stephen grinned with relish. "You ought to see her, Larkin! We made it from New York to Monterey in only three months' time! Trade will soar."

"I'm sorry the navy had to borrow her. They are commandeering all vessels."

He turned to the MacGowans, seated in his office. "The last time I saw Stephen was ten months ago, right here. I have not had the opportunity to thank him in person for rescuing a friend of ours."

"Who is that?" Micah asked.

"Ramon Antonio Bandini-Warner."

An awkward silence momentarily stopped them. Larkin glanced from one to the other. "Well, Stephen and I can talk about this later."

"Mr. Larkin," said Micah, "we have come all this way hoping that God will reunite us with our children. Stephen told us that our daughter Alissa was staying with you."

Larkin smiled. "Indeed she was! She is a lovely, courageous girl. You should be proud of her."

"Isn't she with you now?" said Hannah anxiously.

"She's not at the Warner rancho!" Stephen said in alarm.

"No." Larkin's eyes flashed him a reassuring message. "She is in San Francisco, staying with friends there, waiting to meet an officer of Colonel Frémont's company. This gentleman knew her brother when he scouted for Colonel Frémont."

"Daniel!" cried Hannah. "Oh, praise, praise the Lord. Is our Daniel here? After all this time!" Suddenly her voice broke. "We've come so far." She turned to the reassuring comfort of her husband's arms.

"He *may* be," Larkin cautioned. "This is not the best of times to seek him. As soon as the war is over, I'll have staff available to help you."

"I want to go to San Francisco," said Hannah.

Larkin chuckled. "Don't you want to rest a few days?"

Hannah's lips turned up in a determined smile. "No. Plenty of time for that after I am dead."

"Just a moment, dear," said MacGowan. "Mr. Larkin, has Mr. Lansford Hastings brought a wagon train through recently?"

Larkin's affable face drew into a frown. "I didn't know he was bringing another train west. Frankly—well, no, I have not heard. Is there some reason you ask?"

"A train left Saint Louis in May and was supposed to hook up with a train Hastings formed up a month earlier," Stephen supplied.

"They were supposed to reach California some time this month," said Mac-Gowan anxiously.

Larkin nodded. "Well, they'll be along. Plenty of good weather for a couple months yet. Who knows, the war may be over by then!"

"But our other daughter and her husband are on the second train," insisted Micah.

Larkin nodded. "Keep in touch with me. I'll let you know as soon as I hear from them."

"Please, Mr. Larkin. Just one moment."

The agitation in Micah's voice finally arrested Larkin's whole attention. "Yes?"

"Isn't it customary to have some sort of schedule, so that folks know when a train is due or overdue?"

"Why, no, I am afraid it isn't," admitted Larkin. "Wagon trains are mostly private endeavors."

"Then if a train runs into trouble, how is one to know?"

"In the summer months the wagon trails are filled with emigrants. If your daughter's train were experiencing difficulties, someone would cotton on to it. We'd hear, reverend. You can count on it."

Micah frowned. "I suppose I shall have to take your word on it."

Larkin smiled. "Thank you. I hope you will do me the honor of staying at my home until we can arrange transportation to San Francisco."

"By ship will be the best," said Stephen.

"No ships, remember? And the roads are no more than trails. I may be able to secure a cart. It will be a rough journey." Larkin turned to the others. "Mr. and Mrs. McGowan, why don't you send Alissa word of your arrival? I can have a horseman there and back in three days. You will be much more comfortable here."

Micah glanced at Hannah. "Thank you, Mr. Larkin. I believe we should abide by your advice. The important thing is that Alissa is safe and that she'll know we are here."

"Very well, Micah," said Hannah.

"Good!" nodded Larkin. "It's settled then."

Larkin insisted upon escorting them to his home personally. As the McGowans descended the stairs from the office, Stephen held back. "May I have a word with you, sir?"

"Of course, Stephen."

"Lieutenant Osborn said there is fighting down south."

"Yes, it's the vigilantes," said Larkin.

"The rancho owners and their vaqueros trying to protect their property."

Larkin nodded. "First it was the cholos running like renegades, and now it's American freebooters. I've reports that the southern missions are being looted of everything. I'm not proud to be an American at this moment. 'Victory spoilt before it's well begun.' "

"What about the Bandini-Warners?" said Stephen.

"I'm sure they are in the thick of it. Ramon said before he left that you had warned him—"

"I'm sorry it's come to this," said Stephen. "Mexico should have sent an army to protect them. She has sold them like so many sheep."

"That's true," said Larkin. "The Californians feel they have to make a show of defense. The vigilantes can't win, of course. But their pride is at stake."

Stephen pounded a fist into his palm.

"What is it?"

"I should be down there with them. The Bandini-Warners are my friends. But I've got Alissa's parents in my care."

"They are perfectly safe here, Stephen. Nothing you can do for them at the moment, unless you particularly wanted to go to San Francisco. . . ."

Stephen's dark eyes met Larkin's candid gaze. "I don't expect Alissa wants to see me."

"How do you feel about her?"

"I don't know, Larkin. When I thought she was in love with Ramon, I could have killed them both." He gave a self-conscious laugh and added lightly, "I'm unused to baring my soul." His expression grew thoughtful. "No way Mexico can keep this territory, is there?"

"No."

"Then if Lieutenant Osborn will permit, I'll sail back to Los Angeles with him."

Larkin smiled. "I'm glad to hear you say that, my boy. I must confess that when I first met you I was a little put off by, shall we say, your devotion to profit, but I can see a change, and I approve. What is it you have in mind?"

"I am a lawyer. I speak both languages. I have—ah—a sum of money that must be used for good cause. It's a foregone conclusion that the Bandini-Warners and the other owners are going to have the devil of a time defending the titles to their lands. I propose to work in their behalf."

Larkin's eyes glistened. He held out his hand. Solemnly they shook. "I hope California draws many more like you, Stephen Davis."

"Thank you, sir."

Thomas Larkin had found Alissa and Guadelupe a respectable boarding house in San Francisco in the spring of 1846. It was a move Alissa had insisted upon when the consul told her that Lieutenant Colonel John C. Frémont and his Mounted Rifle Regiment were expected there sometime during the summer. The sudden eruption of the war intervened in all their plans, and after Larkin returned to Monterey, Alissa quickly found herself caught up in the struggles of the American colony.

The clothing she had adopted with so much enthusiasm while living at the rancho remained packed in tissue at the bottom of her trunk. By day she lived in proper but impractical long dresses with many petticoats, enduring splintery boardwalks that snagged her hems and dirt streets that by day's end either weighted her skirts with caked mud or embedded them with dust. She wondered how she had ever thought such clothing comfortable.

By night she kept her journal or wrote letters to the family in Saint Louis and to the Bandini-Warners. Often her thoughts flew to those living on the isolated rancho. She missed all of them: Arcadia and Juan Julian, Mariana and Ramon. Even Ben Gee. Their lives seemed like a dream to her now, surrounded as she was by a medley of American accents, by rough, noisy city life. She rarely thought of Stephen, except to wonder whether he were still in California.

Eventually her path recrossed that of Parson Finnegan, the garrulous circuit-riding preacher whom Stephen had brought to the Bandini-Warner rancho a year ago last spring. Finnegan introduced her to a group of American ladies from Oregon who founded and ran the missionary society. In a modest hall, the society fed and clothed newly arrived immigrants and women who had no other shelter.

When Finnegan was in town, he conducted nondenominational religious services at the hall. His thunderous sermons could be counted on to bring spectacular contributions when the hat was passed. Other times, the ladies provided religious guidance themselves, even affording temporary sanctuary for Chinese and Jewish emigrants to set up altars where they might worship in their own faiths.

Interlarded with their "good works of the spirit" as the ladies liked to phrase the distinction, was much vigorous "elbow grease," such as airing the bedding, a task in which Alissa and Guadelupe were engaged one hot October afternoon.

"You look mighty uncomfortable, ma'am, snugged up in that there wool dress." The voice was deep, with a Texas drawl.

Alissa turned around and pushed back the damp blond strands from her perspiring brow. Her eyes met a wide pair of shoulders filling out a homespun cotton shirt with lacings at the throat. A rock-bleached white shirt against the sun-tanned throat. Further up, a rugged, good-humored face and a mane of coarse blond hair.

"Were you addressing me, sir?"

"Reckon I was." The man's big hands gentled the brim of his hat, pulling it through his fingers. "They said a gel with yaller hair, dressed like winter's comin'."

Alissa burst out laughing. "Who said *that?*" She glanced around his shoulder.

Her merriment brought a grin of enjoyment that enlivened his light blue eyes. The Texan gestured with his hat. "Them ladies, ones inside. My name is Baylor C. Cooper, ma'am. I'm a surveyor attached to Colonel Frémont's mounted rifles."

The heavy quilt in her arms fell to the ground. "Mr. Cooper, oh, I'm so glad to meet you, sir!"

Cooper scooped up the quilt in one paw, like a bear swiping salmon out of a river. He spied Guadelupe. Without a word he thrust the quilt at her, then took Alissa's arm. "Might we talk, ma'am?"

"Yes! Come inside, please." Alissa's heart pounded. Cooper might hold a life-or-death verdict. Did she want to know? What if Daniel was.... Nervously she escorted him to a windowed corner with two needlepointed chairs and a threadbare Oriental rug, which the ladies called their parlor. Use of that corner was reserved for privacy and never invaded otherwise. "Please sit down. I'll get you a drink of water."

"Obliged."

Cooper balanced the tumbler on the knee of his dark brown twill pants. His high brown laced boots were polished to a satin finish. She felt his eyes on her while she pulled her chair close to his and arranged her skirts. When she looked at him at last, she was startled by the empathy of his expression. She gave a tremulous smile. "I'm trying to find out something about my brother, Daniel."

A lopsided grin found a comfortable home on the sunburned face. "No foolin'! You don't look like Daniel. 'Course he didn't look like a Daniel, neither." He studied her face with frank curiosity. "You part Indian, ma'am?"

She shook her head. "Same mother, different fathers. My mother's first husband was Shawnee." She drew in a deep breath. It didn't help. Her heart was still pounding like a steam engine.

"Rest easy, ma'am. I'm sure he's all right. You got a name?"

"Alissa. Alissa MacGowan."

"Well, Missus MacGowan. . . . ," he paused, a tease in his eye.

"*Miss* MacGowan. . . ."

The tease became a grin. "Last I knew, ol' Daniel got himself a Luiseno wife and was livin' with her tribe in them hills in southern California right near the pass that comes in from the Arizona Territory."

Alissa's jaw dropped. "A wife! An Indian wife! Why didn't he let us know? Oh, I wish— Is that near the Bandini-Warner rancho?"

Cooper scrubbed under his chin with the back of a fist. "Few leagues, I reckon. How come you to know that place—you been there?"

She nodded. "Just last year. Was he there last year?"

Cooper shrugged. "Couldn't say. He mustered out, and we moved on. Been five years or so."

"Mr. Cooper—"

"You could call me Cooper, everyone does."

"I'd be proud to call you Cooper. I know there's fighting. Would Colonel Frémont permit you to look for Daniel?"

Cooper chuckled. "It ain't likely he'd think that was of passing importance. But we're headed down south day after tomorrow. If there's a way, I'll surely visit his wife's tribe, and if Daniel's there, I'll let him know you're lookin' for him."

Tears filled her eyes. "You are very kind, Mr. Cooper. Cooper."

Cooper sighed and rested his gaze upon her for a few moments. "You're mighty pretty, Miss MacGowan. Wish I was going to be around a spell. Say, you ain't free tomorrow, are you?"

"Yes," she replied without hesitation.

"Hills are awful brown this time o' year, but pretty. You care to take a picnic?"

"I'd love it! But I haven't a horse."

Cooper's face brightened. "You ride, Miss MacGowan?"

"The Bandini-Warners taught me."

"I'll bring you a good horse. One with good manners."

She laughed. "That will be much appreciated. And I'll bring the picnic!"

After Cooper left, Alissa sent Guadelupe on a berry-picking expedition. Berries were still plentiful. The women stayed late at the missionary-society hall to use their oven to bake raspberry tarts. The aroma filled the hall, and they decided to bake several pans of tarts so that all the ladies could share it the next day.

The following morning, as she and Guadelupe were preparing to leave the boarding house for the missionary society, Alissa flew at the last moment back into her bedroom and unearthed her riding costume, the polished black boots, split skirt, white ruffled blouse, and form-fitting jacket. It slipped on as easily as a well-worn glove. She perched the flat-brimmed hat at a jaunty angle over her smooth hair.

The costume created a sensation as the two women walked the short distance to the society hall. Alissa could not have cared less. It felt wonderful!

Cooper appeared at high noon leading a beautiful mare whose brown coat had been curried to a silken sheen. He was dressed identically to yesterday but wore a fresh shirt.

Alissa saw him through the window and carried the heavy picnic basket to the door. She set it down on the doorsill. "Good morning! I hope you are hungry."

Cooper stared at her. "Ma'am, Miss MacGowan, by thunder you look like a high-born California lady! If that ain't—if you aren't—if you aren't something!"

Alissa grinned. Cooper caught the sense of mischief and jumped down to take the basket. "Feels like enough food for a regiment. What you got?" he asked as he lashed the basket behind his bedroll.

"Baked grouse, peaches, tomatoes, and corn bread. And fresh raspberry tarts. My mother's recipe. I haven't made them since I've been in California. I hope they are good."

"I am honored, Miss MacGowan." Cooper's glance kept returning to her as he tied the basket. "You look pretty enough to eat."

As they rode out of Monterey into the hills, Alissa asked, "What does a surveyor do?"

"Studies the lay of the land. Makes maps. Figures out the best way to lay roads. Me and Daniel. . . ." And for the next hour Cooper drew Alissa into a world she could only imagine, stories of the year Daniel rode with Frémont's men from Texas to California. Generously Cooper made Daniel the hero of every story. He pointed out what a surveyor looks for: How contours of hills gave clues to the types of rock formation beneath the smooth grasses. He showed her likely ground for water when choosing campsites.

After two hours' ride they paused upon a high hill, gazing eastward. "Now here," she said. "This is the kind of land where I would like to build a house."

Cooper's eyes kindled with interest. He hooked a leg over the saddlehorn. "Why?"

She smiled. Her arm swept in a broad arc over the valley. "Several kinds of trees—hardwoods for furniture, pine for the house and fences—a good-sized stream where that band of bushes follows the bend in the hill—"

She shot him a glance. He was listening intently. "Of course the stream would have to have sufficient water for irrigation, perhaps even for a mill. Land flat enough for wheat fields. And the house—," she lifted her eyes to the distant blue of the Sierras, spreading grandly north to south as far as the eye could see. Their crowns gleamed with snow. "The house would face east, toward the morning. Toward those beautiful mountains."

Alissa glanced swiftly at Cooper. "Being in the army, a man probably doesn't think of houses that don't pack up and fold away."

He laughed. "That's a right neat turn of phrase. But it don't fit me. I don't plan to stay with Frémont after this here war is cleaned up. That looks like a likely place to picnic, Miss MacGowan."

Slowly they walked the horses toward a copse of willows hanging over a small stream. Cooper went on, "I been in Texas, New Mexico, Sonora, up and down and around these here Sierras, and it's time to hang up my spurs and put down roots." He helped her down and unrolled his bedroll to use as a table-cloth.

She untied the picnic basket, knelt, and opened it on the blanket.

"You know what you forgot?" he said.

"Oh! The salt?"

"About this here land. Game. A body'd never starve, even in a bad year. Fur trapping. For a little extra money whilst you were getting started. Fish. I had me some dandy meals out of streams no bigger'n this puddle jumper."

She gazed up at him. His strong legs straddled the land. His fists rested loosely on his hips. He glanced down, a look that took in all of her. "This here land, a woman like you . . . a woman not afraid to work with that outfit the missionary society, proud enough to love a half-breed brother and want to find him, not afraid to be different . . . ," Cooper reached down and pulled her to her feet beside him.

"A man would have to be a fool to stay in the army." Slowly he drew her into his arms.

Alissa's hands grasped the strong biceps. Her fingers slid up his shoulders, up into the warm hair behind his ears. He felt as if her arms had known him for years.

"Alissa. . . ."

37

Milt Elliott rode by Molly's wagon. "You okay there, Miz McCloud?"
"Yes. Certainly!" Her spine stiffened. She snapped the reins with authority. Her anger lay like a fire within her with nowhere to go. Jared and Frank Stanton had left an hour ago. Donner's familiar call had rung out, and her team had pulled the wagon into place behind the Donner wagons.

"Anytime you want a relief, you just holler, hear?"

She relented slightly. "Yes. Thank you."

For three days they followed the southwest edge of the foothills, rounding the southern edge of the hills in the direction Jared and Stanton had taken, and turned north again along a river which as near as they could figure was the South Fork of the Humboldt. The trail was suddenly easier, and Molly began to repent her self-enforced loneliness. Since Jared had gone, she had pleaded tiredness and refused to join the Donners at evening campfire, despite Tamsen's efforts.

Each day became like the rest, as they had crossing the buffalo plains ages ago in this interminable summer. At last they rejoined the main southern route of the Oregon Trail, and now the train surged steadily forward at a pace Elliott said must be twenty miles a day.

In the second week of October the Humboldt River, which had become an uncertain stream in the past few days, disappeared completely in the sand. From talk back at the rendezvous, they knew this was Humboldt Sink, unpleasant in passing but not impossible, so they did not panic. Two days later, a broad, sparkling river greeted them.

At the nooning Molly and Tamsen wandered through the thick grass by the river.

"It's heaven!" yelled one of Tamsen's daughters as she raced past them to the river's edge.

Molly permitted a smile. "None of the children seem the worse from the desert drive, do they?"

"No," said Tamsen, "In fact, there has been remarkable little illness on the train. What stories *they'll* have for their grandchildren!"

"Jared said the same thing."

"Mama! Elitha found something!" Leanna Donner galloped through the grass toward them, followed by a smaller girl.

Prancing after her sister, her brown hands holding aloft a goose feather and a paper, Elitha delivered them to her mother as if they were priceless treasures. "The paper was stuck with the feather. We found it in a bush right beside the trail!" Elitha rolled her eyes and pounded on her chest. "I was the one found it!"

"I helped," insisted Leanna.

Tamsen laughed. "You're good girls, and Mama's proud of you." She opened the paper. "Why it's from Jared! Here, Molly, you read it."

Molly took the paper with trembling fingers. The writing was faded. "It says he's going straight to Sutter's for horses and mule loads of good things for us." Her eyes filled with tears. Her voice quavered as she contemplated Elitha's goosefeather and said, "At least he's eating well."

"Mama, may we tell?"

"Of course!" Tamsen laughed.

The girls raced on to carry the news. Tamsen peered up solicitously into Molly's face. "Molly, dear, is something the matter?"

Molly shook her head and stumbled a few paces ahead.

Tamsen caught up with her and found her hand. "Let me be your friend, child. The Lord's asking a lot of you, to bring this wagon through by yourself, with Jared gone."

"I've been so angry at him, Tamsen, for leaving me! And for being right about Lansford Hastings. I think if I hadn't talked about him so much, Jared wouldn't have felt obliged to vote for that horrible cutoff. He was mainly showing he had faith in me. And then we wouldn't be short of provisions now, and Jared wouldn't 've had to—"

"Whoa!" said Tamsen. "Molly, Molly! Jared's an independent young man. I doubt that you talked him into anything he didn't believe was right himself."

"But Tamsen, you didn't want to take the cutoff either, but you didn't take it out on poor Mr. Donner! I just feel so *mean!*"

They walked on, and Tamsen kept silent. When Molly spoke again, her voice was quieter.

"And now I'm frightened, Tamsen. I feel the Lord will surely punish me for—for wickedness. For wicked thoughts. Oh, Tamsen, I don't deserve to have Jared!"

Tamsen paused and took both of Molly's hands. They had reached a small glade. The sounds of the river and the voices of children filtered through to them.

"Then I'll tell you what we'll do. We'll stop right here, and you can pray it all out. Just to yourself. And I'll pray, too. Because you and I both know our Lord is never stone earry, and when we come in true repentance, he hears us."

Together the women knelt under a canopy of alders, Molly's bright red hair tumbling about her cheeks. When she rose, she felt at peace with herself. She smiled at Tamsen's kindly face. "Thank you."

Tamsen returned the smile. "Well now, since we're here, shall we gather some cress for supper?"

Supper that night was a feast of fish, rabbit, a bit of rice, and the cress the women had found growing in the shallows of the Truckee River. One of the men broke out a harmonica, and the poignant notes blended with their voices.

Molly took a long drink of the fresh water, the first water from the Sierras. "How good and cold it is," she said. She cocked her head wistfully. "It's been a month. . . . I wonder if the men are in California yet?"

For three days the procession of wagons snaked up Truckee Canyon, the music of the rushing river always in their ears. Travel was easy, water and game plentiful, and spirits high. On the fourth day some men and beasts appeared around a bend ahead.

A shout went up from the lead wagon. "It's Stanton and McCloud! It's Stanton and McCloud!" Word raced back along the wagons.

Molly halted the team and vaulted out of the wagon. Picking up her skirts, she dashed ahead. Stanton was there, but the other man in trousers and shirt was an Indian as was a third man who wore only a breechclout. Where was Jared?

Pipe in hand, his face red with delight, Stanton opened both arms to greet the rush of children followed by their parents. "Hello, hello, my friends! You all look well. Lost a couple wagons, eh? How's the cattle column, lads? Captain Sutter is a generous man. He's sent everything we need to complete our journey. What's the matter, little ones? Oh, my Indian friends?" Stanton laughed heartily. "These two are California Indians. This one is Salvador and this is José. They won't hurt you. They work for Captain Sutter. They came along to guide us." His eyes danced as he added, "Also to see that Sutter gets his mules back."

"Mr. Stanton!" Molly had stood by, fighting down her fear, craning for a glimpse of her husband. Surely he'd be here in just another minute!

Stanton's expression changed. He reached through the crowd and took her hand. "Now, Miz McCloud, I don't want you to feel upset—"

"Jared!"

"Jared's all right, he just wasn't fit to travel yet. He took sick at Sutter's, a fever of some sort."

"Oh, no! Is he going to get better?"

" 'Course he is! You'll see him yourself in a few weeks. Now don't you fret. I promised him I'd see you through."

Sutter's seven mules were laden with provisions. As Stanton passed out jerked beef and flour to all the families he kept up a stream of talk. "We had to wait out an early snowstorm, or we would have been here sooner."

With new energy the train forged on, by nightfall reaching Truckee Meadows. After supper Molly sat before the fire, hugging her knees, so worried about Jared that she gave scarcely a thought to her own situation. He would not have stayed back for a simple fever. He'd have to drop before he'd stay away! Unless he took her anger to mean she did not want him back. That could make a person sick, too. *O Lord,* she thought miserably. *Give me back my Jared, and I'll be a better wife, I promise!*

She lifted her head as Stanton scrambled to his feet and stood in the light of the campfire. "Folks, if you want to give me an ear. . . . We can make Truckee Lake with three days' good travel. The pass is only a day above that. We get over that, and we're in California. The hills are rugged, but the worst will be behind us."

A full moon had risen, and by its glow they could see the dark mass brooding above them, west of Truckee Meadows. "Is that the pass, Frank?" came a voice out of the dark.

"That's it."

"Oughten we rest our oxen down here a whiles, where there's good grazing?"

"No." Stanton stared in the direction of the voice. "There's a'ready been one snow on the pass, two weeks ago. Hastings barely got his train through. Over in California folks say most storms ain't too bad this time o' year. It melts in between, up to mid-November."

"I'm ready to go tomorrow," Molly said resolutely.

Gentle laughter greeted her words. "I guess you are, " Frank Stanton sympathized.

"That gives us nigh a month to get over the pass," said one of the teamsters, ignoring Molly's remark. "I didn't come this far to kill my teams on the last stretch."

There was a general murmur of assent.

Stanton glanced in the direction of Sutter's Indians. They had declined his invitation to sit by the campfire and squatted over a small fire of their own. "I should tell you Sutter's boys say it's going to be an early winter."

"What's the difference if we start up the mountain with half-starved oxen and get caught in a storm or rest here a couple days and then go? At least our teams will be stronger."

Keseberg stepped out of the shadows. "Vy kill ourselfs going now? I say ve vait, ve eat, sleep a bit, the teams eat, sleep a bit, ve all feel better."

"Mr. Donner?"

George, sitting with Tamsen and their children, smiled up at Stanton. "Whatever the majority want, Frank."

"Well, I guess we rest a couple days then."

Gradually their voices hushed. Someone threw more logs on the fires. Sitting all around Molly, with the huge campfire pushing back the frosty night, the emigrants began to sing hymns and praise God for delivering them from the worst of their journey, for provisions that had come in time, and for the safety of their brave men. Their voices rang into the night. Molly gazed upward at the glittering bowl of heaven and fancied that Jared was looking at the stars and thinking of her, too.

The day or two layover stretched into five. On the morning of the fifth day, they started upward. Soon the wagons were strung out over a mile, those with the strongest teams forging ahead. Stanton rode up beside Molly.

"Hi!" he called cheerily. "Want me to take a shift?"

"Doing fine, Mr. Stanton," she called back.

"Then I'll ride ahead and keep everyone on the best path. Godspeed!"

Most of the wagons were ahead of Molly's. At midmorning she passed George Donner's wagon, pulled off at a wide spot in the trail. Tamsen and George were standing beside the wagon, Tamsen wrapping a bandage around her husband's hand.

"What happened?" Molly called.

"We broke an axle, and Mr. Donner cut his hand with an awl, fixing it," Tamsen replied. "We shall be along in good time."

"Shall I stay and help?"

"No need," Tamsen laughed. "George loves to be babied, but only by me."

"Hey, it's snowing," cried Leanna. She started whirling in a circle, palms up. "Elitha, come out, it's snowing!"

Molly left the Donner girls clambering out of the wagon and concentrated on keeping her team out of the way of rocks.

The snow began to tint the greens and ochers with shades of gray. Worriedly, Molly kept glancing behind for the Donner wagons. Word was that all five had stopped when George and Tamsen did. When she unhitched the team, they still had not appeared. The oxen, her cow, and the horse had to nose through the soft snow for their dinner. After sharing supper regularly with the Donners, Molly prepared to eat alone. When she saw Stanton ride by, she invited him to eat with her.

"I'm worried about the Donners," she said as she made coffee.

"I'm sure they are all right," said Frank. "Between you and me, I'm more worried about the weather. You got enough blankets? Likely to be real cold tonight."

"I'm fine," she assured him. When Frank left, Molly put out the fire and carried her coffee into the wagon. Setting her lamp and coffeepot carefully on the food chest, she secured front and rear flaps and tightened all the lacings holding the canvas to the sides. If a wind came up, she did not want it blowing snow through and soaking the bedding. At last she reached for her writing folder and a pen. *Dear Jared. . . .*

Molly awoke to absolute stillness the next dawn. Quickly she wriggled out of her bedroll and into her warmest clothing. Throwing a shawl over her head and shoulders, she unfastened the back flap and climbed outside. Her boots sank through four inches of snow. She caught her breath. Down in the valley they had climbed through yesterday, the pines resembled a million frosted tepees.

She tramped around the side of the wagon. Her jaw dropped. Before her eyes rose sheer walls of gray, pierced by tall, gaunt pines and laced with belts of snow. How could anyone get through that?

"Quite a sight, isn't it, Miz McCloud?"

Molly turned around. Stanton's pipe made a frosty wreath around his head. His cheeks were bright red.

"Good morning, Mr. Stanton. It's hard to believe there's any trail at all!"

"Oh, it's there. The sun will melt this in no time."

"Did the Donners catch up?"

Stanton hesitated, then said, "No, but it probably took them the rest of the day to get the axle fixed. I expect they are already on the trail this morning."

Fingers stiff with cold despite heavy woolen gloves, Molly fed her animals the last of the grass gathered at Truckee Meadows. Then she hitched the team to the wagon and tied her cow and horse behind. All morning she followed the wagons ahead in a steady climb. By noon, dark clouds were mushrooming over the mountaintops, and a stillness descended so tangible it seemed all the earth was trembling in wait.

"We'll go on," was Stanton's stolid reply to all questions.

Five days after leaving Truckee Meadows, the forward wagons descended to the north shore of a lake nestled like a deep blue jewel set in prongs of pine. The black clouds that had covered the skies for four days rolled into ponderous balloons, and between them shone the sun. How blue and deep the sky seemed in the thin air!

"Truckee Lake!" Stanton's voice rang back along the trail. "Only a few miles to the pass. Tonight we'll be camping on the summit!"

As they rounded the lake, the lower clouds parted to reveal the pass, rising incredibly steep before them, an unbroken wall of snow and granite.

"Merciful Lord, I can't believe it," Molly whispered in awe.

Stanton pulled up alongside her wagon. "Miz McCloud, m'girl, you look as if you'd seen a ghost."

She shook her head and mustered a laugh. "You must have eyes that can see through rock."

"Don't worry, there's a way through."

"Did it look like this before?"

"No, but the trail is there, under the snow. I'm going up with our guides this morning. Salvador's mule has a nose for trail breaking. You all keep going, hear? And pray it doesn't snow any more till we are over the top."

Molly nodded, afraid to speak and betray her fear. The Donner wagons had not caught up with them. No one had gone back to discover the reason. She drove the team steadily upward. Once in a while she caught a glimpse of Stanton and the guides, their mules plunging through snow almost to their backs.

Stanton had cautioned that the stop for the nooning should be brief, just long enough to cut pine boughs for the stock. As she carried her bundle back to the team she noticed several families gathering by the first wagon. She checked her water supply, then fetched up some jerky and biscuits from her stores to gnaw on while she drove. Settling on the springboard, Molly realized that most of the others were still afoot. And Stanton was returning. Good. Some of the families had become fractious with the passing days.

Molly swung down and tramped over to hear his report.

"How well you did!" said Stanton.

"It ain't no use!" complained a widow traveling with her son and his family. "We're plumb tuckered. All this snow. . . ."

"We can't stop here." Anxiously Stanton gazed upward. Thunderheads were unrolling again, threatening to eclipse the sun.

"You said there'd be clearing between storms," her son accused Stanton.

"Well, it's clearing. Maybe the sun'll be out full this afternoon. In the morning we can top the pass."

"In the morning," echoed the mother, her chin puckering and unpuckering. "Half the day's gone now. Ain't no sense to go for a few hours and have to camp short of the pass."

"That's right!" nodded Keseberg, who had tramped up to discover the delay. "You vant to kill us?"

"There's no guarantee another storm isn't right behind," Stanton replied.

"Heck sakes, it ain't even November till termorry," piped up another. "They's lots o' time. This is hard climbing, Stanton. I'm winded myself."

"We chose Mr. Stanton to lead us," said Molly. "Mr. Donner isn't here. We must do what Mr. Stanton thinks is best."

Stanton shot her an appreciative glance.

"That's right," another voice agreed.

The widow crossed her arms and thrust out her lower lip. "I'm staying."

Molly held her breath. She had a feeling the old lady had gotten her way many a time with just such behavior.

Stanton gazed at the woman in silence. Then he said, "We must go forward, madam." As he turned to roust the rest of the wagons, a few snowflakes drifted lazily down.

A farmer behind Molly muttered, "We best hurry on."

Quickly the emigrants dispersed to their wagons. Snow began falling softly. A vague uneasiness settled over them. Suddenly everyone found the energy to get going. Anxious glances lifted skyward. Molly felt a sense of time slipping from her grasp. The sky grew darker. The snowflakes grew larger, like moth holes in a blanket.

Now the trail itself was gray. Gone was the gay sparkle of sun on snow. Ahead it looked only blacker. Snow began to fall thicker and faster. Molly reached into the wagon behind her and pulled up a quilt, settling it over herself like a tent. The wind began to moan softly in the treetops.

It became like trying to run in a dream. Behind Stanton's lead mules Molly saw the wagons disappear one after the other between two gateposts of rock. Thicker and faster fell the snow. The occasional barking of pet dogs, the creaking of the wagons, the pull of teams grew strangely muffled in the snow.

Now she gained the granite boulders herself. The first wagons had disappeared nearly an hour ago. *I haven't covered more than half a mile since the nooning!* Molly thought with despair. She strained to see. An even steeper grade rose ahead. On that grade, like beetles on the skin of a gigantic beast, Stanton and the guides crawled forward with excruciating slowness.

The sky grew blacker. Needles of sleet began to sting her face like angry bees. At each step it seemed the animals were plunging deeper. The wheels of the wagon became encased in ice, and Molly beat at them with an empty bucket to break the crust. The oxen blew great puffs of steam. Their sides were heaving and shuddering.

Tears caused by the force of the wind froze in her eyelashes. Her cheeks grew numb. She wiggled her toes inside her boots and was grateful to feel them. Gray blackness covered everything. She lost all feeling of time. Time was forever, time was following the ruts of the wagon ahead. Not much farther to the top. . . . *Jesus loves me! this I know,* she hummed. How could the guides read this trail? An object loomed before her. The wagon ahead had stopped.

Then Stanton was beside her wagon. "We have to halt! The Indians have lost the trail! They are afraid to take Captain Sutter's mules any farther. They believe he will kill them if they lose his mules."

"Can't we go without them?" Molly shouted.

Stanton shook his head.

Molly felt the white wall close around them. They'd never get the wagons over now.

Part III

Hannah's Daughters

38

Jared McCloud leaned weakly against the doorjamb of the cabin, bundled against the cold. Through the huge open gates of Sutter's Fort he could see the golden stubble of wheat fields. It seemed to roll on for miles. Haymows dotted the fields in an irregular pattern. He heard the quarrelsome caw of a couple crows, and moments later a covey of pheasant took wing from the field.

Jared had always prided himself on his constitution. To be felled by something as soft as a fever . . . not even shot . . . or taking an arrow. . . . He was dressed for the first time in weeks. If it hadn't been for his suspenders, his trousers would have had a battle to stay hitched. The lost heft had sharpened the planes of his face, the chiseled nose, the fine cheekbones. The fingers he thrust through the thick black hair were white and chilled easily.

Jared pulled the heavy coat closer about his throat as the cold wind churned up dust pods in the yard inside the gates.

"Mr. McCloud! Good to see you on your feet, lad," said Captain Sutter in a brisk voice. Sutter had a seaman's cap pulled down over his bristly blond hair. "Your party ought to be coming out of them hills any day now. You care to look at this?"

Jared glanced indifferently at a paper resembling a bill of lading in Sutter's hand.

"Want you to see that it is all right and proper," Sutter said. His sharp blue eyes watched Jared closely.

"What is it?"

"Well! Let's see. . . ." Sutter examined the paper as if reading it for the first time. "Seven mules, no charge unless any of them are lost or injured. Two Indian guides, dollar a week apiece. Hundred weight of flour, fifty of sugar—"

Jared took the bill out of his hands with a careless swipe. "It'll be taken care of, you got my word. Can't say when, you know most folks on that train ain't got a lot o' ready cash." Jared frowned. "We passed Hastings's train this side of the summit. His party come through here?"

"Over a week ago, all hale and hearty. You were feeling middling bad, probably don't remember."

Jared uttered a curse.

Sutter threw him a passionless glance. "You ain't forgive him yet, that it?"
"Not till my wife and everyone else is here safe. Mebbe not even then."

Alissa felt new life singing in her veins. *Go carefully,* an inner voice cautioned. But she couldn't. She was in love! She felt like a giddy girl again. As she flew about her chores at the missionary society hall, her thoughts were filled with Cooper. He was gentle yet spirited like Ramon. He was not oblivious to good business, but it did not overwhelm his thoughts as it had with Stephen. She prayed lustily that this was the man God intended for her.

Don't be silly, her cautious nature said. *No one falls in love in two days!*

Why not? her other half said, throwing caution out the door.

Somehow, *somehow,* she was certain that Baylor Cooper would find Daniel. Cooper had left San Francisco for Los Angeles with Frémont's regiment the day after their picnic. He promised he would get in touch with her within the month, even if just to report no news.

When a messenger came a week later, he was not from Cooper but from Larkin in Monterey, with the unbelievable news that her parents were there, waiting to see her. With a whoop of joy she pressed Guadelupe and a well-armed volunteer from the missionary society to accompany her and the messenger on horseback for the two-day ride. Not even a rainstorm, which had drizzled its dreary way through the week, could dampen her enthusiasm. Donning her split-skirt riding costume under a heavy wool cloak, she dressed Guadelupe in boots, a pair of men's woolen trousers, and a heavy shirt. "Can't have you getting a chill," she told her, bundling her up like a child.

Thomas Larkin had also written that Stephen had gone to join Ramon in order to render assistance. Along with a prayer for their safety, she sent up another of gratitude that the two would once again be friends. Perhaps she, too, could someday be their friend without pain.

Guessing her parents would be housed at Thomas Larkin's residence, Alissa rode straight there, arriving about midafternoon of the second day. Gratefully she dismounted and sloshed through the mud to the adobe brick walk. As she strode up the walk, her heart was pounding. It had been nearly three years since she had seen her parents.

Larkin's servant gaped in astonishment when he opened the door.

"Good afternoon, Farley! Are the Reverend and Mrs. MacGowan here?"

"Yes, miss, you are all wet—" Farley glanced past her to the female in men's clothing and two gentleman tying their horses to the hitching rail at the edge of the yard.

"Shall we come through the back? We're muddy and wet."

"Oh, no, Miss MacGowan, come in! Come in, all of you." Alissa pulled off her hat. She shook out her blond hair, darkened by rain. Unobtrusively the servant shepherded Guadelupe and the two men in the direction of the kitchen.

"Alissa! Oh, darling!" Hannah MacGowan flew down the stairs with a radiant smile, her walnut brown silk dress rustling, and threw herself into Alissa's arms.

"Mother!" Alissa was crying and laughing at the same time. "Careful, I'm soaked!" Her mother, here in her arms at last, smelling wonderfully sweet and clean. The scent of her face powder filled Alissa with a rush of memories and aching homesickness. "Oh, you are so beautiful, Mama. Your hair is simply elegant. Where is Father? And Molly, is Molly here? What a wonderful surprise."

"Your father is napping. I'll call him." Tears sparkled like a thousand diamonds in Hannah's warm brown eyes. "You look wonderful, Alissa! You've changed. You've—you're different. I used to think you were my reserved daughter. And I believe you are taller!" Hannah laughed with a giddiness that sounded not unlike Alissa's. "And this—what do you call it, is it a dress? It is what you wrote Molly about."

"There are so few carriages, this is the most practical thing to wear sometimes."

Hannah nodded with approval. "Have you come far?"

"Two days on horseback," Alissa replied carelessly.

"How I admire you," Hannah laughed. "I must waken Micah." She placed a foot on a stair. *Beautiful calfskin shoe,* Alissa noticed. *Couldn't find a pair like that out here.* Hannah came back with a smile and took her hand. "You come with me. What a blessing you are to my sight!"

Arm in arm, the women ascended the stairs.

The blissful, giddy exuberance of Alissa's reunion with her parents was made sweeter when she learned that Molly would arrive any day (with a *husband! Molly?*). In turn she imparted her own revelation of Daniel's marriage to a native and that even now a wonderful new friend who knew Daniel had promised to find him.

The week of rain ended on a beautiful sun-washed November Saturday. The Larkins and the MacGowans decided to breakfast in town at the new hotel.

Monterey did not seem like a city at war. Aside from occasional detachments in khaki passing through with rifles holstered in their saddles and led by stiff-backed officers in blouses of various colors, life went on as before. Even the prominent Mexican citizens seemed less perturbed by the passing of their city from the hands of one government into another's than by the specter of business reverses. Reports of sporadic fighting near Los Angeles were posted about town. Confrontational raids with few casualties seemed to be the gist. A token resistance, Larkin had assured them.

Alissa was first out of the carriage at the hotel. As she waited on the board-walk for the others to alight, she noticed a colorfully dressed man on a superb horse. He rode toward the hotel as if leading a parade, although conducting a contingent of but five riders.

His high-pitched voice reached the boardwalk clearly. "This will be the capi-tal after California becomes a state, mark me," he proclaimed. "Anyone who invests in land now will make a fortune. A fortune! In five years a city lot will be worth hundreds. Look at New York. Look at New Orleans."

Alissa smiled. The hawkers were out. A sure sign the war was almost over. Suddenly she heard her mother say, "Micah! That's him! That's Mr. Hastings."

The outrage in Hannah's voice caught Alissa by surprise. Her mother was actually *pointing* at the stranger on horseback. She'd never seen her do such an unladylike thing in her life!

The man on the horse spied them and appeared to recognize them. Alissa fancied he would have bolted if he could.

Thomas Larkin, soul of dignity, ran into the muddy street and seized the stranger's reins. "Lansford Hastings, get down from that horse!" As well-known as Larkin was, it was only minutes before several citizens came vigor-ously to his aid. Hastings found himself off the horse and on the sidewalk, con-fronting the MacGowans. His companions remained on their horses.

Micah MacGowan fixed them with a stentorian pulpit voice: "Are you men from this rascal's wagon party?"

"No, sir, we are not. We are newly arrived from Oregon. This gentleman was showing us some real estate."

"Don't buy the time of day from this wretch!" advised Micah.

"No, sir." Hastily the men conferred and as inconspicuously as possible took themselves out of the scene.

Micah turned his attention to Hastings. "Well, Mr. Hastings, how long have you been in Monterey?"

"Just got here, sir." Hastings pulled out a gold watch and examined it. "I had an appointment—"

"Where is the wagon train?"

Hastings looked at him politely, as if faced with a man making no sense whatever.

"Wagon train?"

Micah took a step toward him.

"I brought my wagon folk through safely weeks ago."

"Weeks ago!" cried Hannah. "Then where is Molly? Where is Jared?"

"Jared's at Sutter's Fort, ma'am, 'bout, oh, hundred and thirty miles as the crow flies. Unless he went back."

"Where is Molly?" repeated Micah.

"Molly!" Alissa cried.

Micah backed Hastings against the clapboard wall of the hotel. Hannah clutched Alissa's arm. Alissa could feel her mother's fear.

"You have some explaining to do, Hastings," said Larkin grimly.

Surrounded by a sea of faces, some unfriendly, some merely curious, Hastings threw up well-manicured hands. "Please, please, let us not forget we are all gentlemen here. And ladies, mustn't forget the ladies—"

"Hastings!" snapped MacGowan.

"Molly's train never caught up with us!" Hastings cried. His glance slid from the red-faced preacher and stared past the shoulders.

"But you said you've been in California for weeks. If they didn't catch up to you, what happened?" implored Hannah.

"How do you know Jared is at Sutter's Fort?" Micah demanded.

"Please! Give a man a little room!" The MacGowans and Larkin backed a half step, and Hastings grasped the lapels of his coat and tugged it to his satisfaction. Alissa pictured the man's brain churning at a furious pace. Whatever he said, she would be disposed not to believe him.

"I—my party—came through Sutter's Fort late in September. Jared and another man from his party had been there provisioning. Their folks had somehow run short of food—"

Hannah uttered a cry.

Hastings didn't look at her. "Jared was fevered, and by the time my party broke up and folks went their own ways, he was still too sick to go back. It was my understanding that Sutter lent the other gentleman a couple guides to take back with him."

"And food? Did he give them food?"

"Of course. Seven mules' worth!" he said disdainfully to Micah. "It's not my fault if they didn't know what they were doing."

With a cry of rage Micah seized him by the throat and dragged him to the ground. He scrambled on top of Hastings, grabbed his hair with one hand and began pounding his face with the other. "That—is—my—daughter—you abandoned! You wretch! You coward!"

Hastings screamed and tried to protect his face. He did not try to get up.

"You knew they were in trouble and you walked away! You wouldn't have told a soul—"

"I—I was on my way. . . ."

"You *belong* in hell, Hastings!" Micah panted. Then he hit him as hard as he could.

Hastings screamed again.

"Micah, let him go!" cried Hannah.

Micah rolled off, exhausted. Hastings lurched to his feet, his face bloody.

"If I had any authority, you'd be in jail!" swore Larkin. "You'd better hope and pray that those folks are all right."

"I haven't done anything—"

With a cry of disgust Micah went for him again. Hannah and Alissa stopped him.

Hastings danced out of the way. "All right, I'm going. It's all just a mistake." He stopped to scoop up his hat from the gutter and plunged across the street.

They watched him go, Micah having difficulty getting his breath.

"Let's go inside," said Larkin. "Are you all right, Reverend MacGowan? I wish there was a way to make him pay for his misdeeds. You can wash up, and then we'll eat. Good decisions are rarely made on empty stomachs."

"We should go after the wagon party," Micah insisted.

"Where is Captain Sutter's?" Hannah wanted to know.

"He has a rancho at the base of the Sierra Nevada Mountains," Alissa told her mother. "It's right on the path of the wagon trains."

"Then we should go there," said Micah. "If Jared is still there, he can help us find Molly and her party."

"Excuse me, Reverend MacGowan," said Thomas Larkin. "What you are suggesting is right, but it presents some problems. The first is the fact that we are still at war. The journey to Sutter's is no picnic in the best of times. By land one must go by cart or horseback and with ample protection against the Indians. One may go by river, but all the boats of any size have been conscripted for the war effort. There may still be some fighting between Mexican and American troops in that area, I don't know. And if I may add, sir, and please do not take this amiss, you and Mrs. MacGowan should delegate the search party to hands that are more familiar with the area."

The long, gaunt form of Micah MacGowan straightened. "I can take care of myself."

Larkin nodded emphatically. "Indeed you can, sir. But rest easy. As soon as the military can free up some extra men, I'll see that they are sent out to check on your daughter's party."

39

For three days and nights the storm raged. The wagon families, strung out along the trail between the lake and the pass, blanched under its fury like abused children.

On the morning of the fourth day, Molly awoke to an unearthly stillness. She eased outside. The wagons were snowed in to the canvas. They looked like cotton wool cocoons scattered on the snow. She caught a glimpse of Stanton's red plaid mackinaw. Good. Somebody was out. She climbed over the tailgate and fell waist deep in snow. Her surprised cry brought Stanton thrashing toward her.

"I'm all right," she called. "Good morning!"

"Nice to see daylight," answered Stanton. His cheeks were as ruddy from the cold as his mackinaw. "I'm looking for the stock."

"The team!" said Molly in shock. "The storm was so bad I didn't think to hobble them."

"I can hear them."

Molly flailed in Stanton's direction. Their voices brought others popping out of their wagons. Soon came the relieved cry, "We found them!"

The animals had instinctively sought the protection of the trees. Cattle, mules, and horses had walked circles under the huge pines, pounding the snow into windproof shelters. Not an animal was missing. Gratefully Molly shook snow from the more tender boughs and cut them for her hungry team and the horse and cow. As she worked, she glanced anxiously at the sky and then at Stanton, working near her.

"Can we try for the pass this morning?" she asked.

Stanton gritted his teeth on his pipe. "Not with the wagons. We might strip them and load the mules." Under his heavy black eyebrows he glanced at the other emigrants. Some were feeding animals, some shaking out bedding. "This bunch ain't really a *team*, Molly. Getting 'em to agree on a single direction might take more than you and I can do."

"God will help us," she said confidently. She wished Jared were here. Or her father. She gazed for a long moment in the direction of the Donner clan. The younger ones were running around working off pent up energies with the other children. Neither George nor Tamsen was visible. "Mr. Donner doesn't seem to *know* what to do. I'll support whatever you think is the best course."

Stanton gave her an approving nod. "You're a fine young woman, Molly. Jared'll be right proud of you."

But four days snowbound had chastened the wilder spirits and fused the wagon party with a single-minded determination to conquer the pass. They readily agreed when Stanton directed them to strip the wagons and load the mules. With few possessions of his own, Stanton lent Molly a hand.

"Oh, it's just *criminal* to leave anything!" she cried as she knelt in the wagon bed among all the things that had been destined to give Jared and her a start in life. Here were her wedding gifts, painstakingly stitched linens, irreplaceable cooking utensils, precious packets of flower and vegetable seeds for her garden. Each one evoked a memory of a happy, loving face of family or friend. And Jared's tools for the farm. . . .

Stanton leaned over the tailgate, his arms crossed. "They're just things, girl. Warm clothes, blankets, food, and a cookpot, that's what you got to have."

Something in his tone sent a shiver through Molly. "You're right," she said. "I'll have it sorted in a minute."

Seven pack mules did not hold much provision for sixty people. Some of the families refused to leave anything behind and shifted the spillover of clothing, bedding, and household goods to their oxen and horses. Trained to work in yoke together, the oxen promptly headed for the trees and rubbed the packs against the bark until they sagged and pitched at impossible angles.

Salvador and the other guide stood off to one side and laughed at the amateur attempts to turn oxen into pack mules.

"There's a trick to everything, I swear," muttered Milt Elliott.

Eventually all the animals were packed to Stanton's satisfaction, and he gave the order to go. They struggled valiantly upward with the loaded beasts, but the snow was deeper with each step. Finally it was deeper than the tallest man. The truth had to be faced.

Stanton turned to those struggling behind and shouted for attention. "We ain't going nowhere today, folks. We'll have to make camp this side of the summit."

A groan went up.

"We got this far, let's camp right here."

"No, no, not here," objected another, "we'd die if a storm caught us here."

"It's back to the lake for us!" cried a man with wife and seven children. "The snow isn't near as deep. There be a stream we can fish."

"If we go back, it won't be for long, will it, Mr. Stanton?" asked Molly.

"It *will* melt before spring, won't it, Stanton?" added Milt Elliott.

"Good chance," Stanton answered. "Winter isn't hardly started yet. There's bound to be some warm weather left."

Slowly they turned about and started back down the trail. They halted by the wagons to strip off the canvas, then retraced their trail of four days ago. On descent, nothing appeared the same to Molly. Wind had driven the snow into grotesque shapes over bushes and rocks and small trees. A little stream feeding into the lake was still unfrozen.

"There's only a couple inches of snow here!" said Molly. "This isn't bad at all!"

George and Tamsen Donner offered Molly shelter with them, which viewing practically, she accepted. The emigrants set to work cutting logs for cabins. Over window and door openings they nailed canvas and hides. They laid green poles flat across the tops of cabins for roofs and piled over this all the spare canvas, tents, and hides that were available.

By the end of the following night, the little clearing beside the lake resembled a peaceful village. The stock and Sutter's mules grazed near the cabins, nosing through the light snow, and drank at the stream.

"There we are!" said Tamsen, coming to find Molly as she gazed out over the frozen lake. "Quite comfortable. A roaring fire inside, plenty of beef on the hoof to carry us over. We will be all right till help comes. If I know your Jared, he is already halfway up the other side of the mountain."

Molly gazed down at the determinedly cheerful face. She smiled. "Tamsen, can you keep a secret?"

"Of course."

"I am expecting a child."

"Praise the Lord," said Tamsen delightedly. "If Jared knew that, it would take the devil himself to slow him down."

That night, a storm worse than any of them had ever experienced broke over their heads. The wind rose to a screaming gale. Snow and sleet battered the snug cabins, sealing windows and doors with drifts. It was the first of many storms they had to wait out through the month of November, each lasting three to six days, with warm spells between. Sometimes it rained, melting the snow into muddy slush in their clearing.

The men hunted at each opportunity, but the frozen mountains yielded nothing. The lake remained unfrozen, but the fish didn't bite.

"I can see fish down there," complained Milt. "But they ain't interested in eating."

The Donners slaughtered the last of their cattle. Finally Molly reached the decision that they must slaughter hers, too. She told Tamsen what she had decided. "We have been nearly a week without meat in our soup. It isn't enough for the children."

They stacked the meat next to the cabin. It would be stiff by nightfall. Not even the wolves would fight over it frozen.

That night they celebrated the slaughter by roasting the rib bones over the fire as they had done back on the prairie when buffalo was so plentiful. The delicious aroma of roasting meat filled the cabin as it sputtered and crackled, its juices dripping into the fire. The Donner children hovered about the fire as if afraid the meat might suddenly disappear.

"Oh, Mama, please, can't we eat?" begged Leanna.

Molly swallowed hungrily.

"Yes." Tamsen laughed. "Now we can eat. Wait! First we'll have the blessing. Mr. Donner?"

George Donner's hand had never healed from the wound suffered at the time his axle broke. Now he propped his swollen hand and arm in his lap and glanced with a smile over the ring of hungry faces. He began, "We trust in thee, Lord, and in the strength and resourcefulness thou has given us. Bless this food. . . ."

After the meal, the bones were collected. With a few dried beans and a handful of rice, this would be their soup stock for many more days. Each day Molly and Tamsen hacked off a small piece of frozen beef to add to the water.

One morning as the women went outside, Tamsen drew Molly out of hearing of the rest of her family. Both women were bundled to their ears, with the scarves knotted loosely over their mouths and noses.

"Has Mr. Stanton said any more about crossing the pass?"

"Not to me." Molly gazed closely at her. She could see that Tamsen was deeply worried.

"If he does try again, promise me that you will go with him."

"I can't do that, Tamsen. With Mr. Donner ailing, you need me to help with the children."

Tamsen shook her head firmly. "Leanna's old enough to help. It may be that you do best by our family by leaving."

"We have enough to eat, don't we? Even if we should have to stay here till spring. If worst comes to worst, we can slaughter the mules. Captain Sutter would understand."

"All right, dear, we won't talk about it just now."

During the day, black clouds rolled up over the peaks of the Sierras and flew eastward in angry patches. A wind insinuated itself in the pines, bringing a fresh damp feel to the air.

After three days' storming, the cabins were again snowed in. Molly played games with the children until she was as restless as they. She spent hours with her hands cupped over her flat belly, happily daydreaming about how she would tell Jared the good news and what he would say. Occasionally a groan would come from George Donner when he was sleeping, sending Tamsen quickly to his corner.

One afternoon, Tamsen was reading by the light from the fireplace when Molly heard her utter a cry of dismay.

"What is it?"

"Did you read all of Mr. Hastings's book?"

"No, I meant to. . . . What does it say?"

Tamsen's voice quivered. "'The remarks here made, in reference to the mildness, and uniformity of the climate, are applicable only to the valleys and plains, for the mountains present but one eternal winter.' "

Molly's stomach pitched with fear. She struggled against it. "Lansford Hastings isn't the only one who knows about these winters," she said stoutly. "If the winters are always like this, Captain Sutter and everyone else in California knows it, too. They know we are here. They aren't just going to sit there and do nothing!"

She got up and paced in the cramped, smoky room. "I haven't heard anything outside for hours. I bet the storm is over."

"The cabin could certainly stand some fresh air," said Tamsen.

Molly and the children lifted away the boards they had used to keep the snow out. She pulled aside the cowhide flap and scooped out a handful of snow. "It's soft. Come on, let's dig." Tunneling was easy, and soon they struck through to the surface.

"The sun!" Molly cried. They all dug furiously until the burrow grew large enough to climb through. As she crawled through and stood in the snow, Molly gazed around, thunderstruck. The sun in a flawless blue sky shone down on a sparkling new world, an utterly silent world. Nothing looked the same. Their entire clearing, including the lake, was hidden under the snow.

"There's the rock by the cabin of Mr. Stanton and Mr. Elliott," Leanna pointed out.

"And there—that's the peak of the Keseberg's roof!" cried her sister, Elitha.

"Look at the big trees," cried the smallest Donner. "Now they are little trees!"

Tamsen reached the surface and gazed around with anxious eyes. "Where are the cattle? Where are Captain Sutter's mules?"

"Probably under the trees again," said Molly.

The others were coming out of their shelters, popping to the surface like inquisitive rabbits sniffing the wind. Frank Stanton, Salvador, and the other Indian guide appeared, disappeared, and came back with long poles.

Soon the air rang with exuberant cries from the children as they discovered the wonderful powder. In no time at all, they were thrashing about, and snowballs were whizzing pell-mell past everyone's ears.

"I've seen high drifts," a farmer said, "but this—this is six foot on level ground!"

Families called to their pet cows. The Indians made unfamiliar calling noises to their mules. One farmer tramped by with a shovel. Other men and women headed for the ring of trees with poles. Every once in a while they would stop and drive a pole into the snow.

"What are they doing, Molly?" Leanna asked.

"Looking for the stock and the mules."

"What if they don't find them?" piped up Elitha.

"They'll be found sooner or later," Molly comforted her.

They searched the rest of the day. Not a single horse or mule or cow was found. *This is only December,* Molly kept thinking. How could they survive until spring with no more meat than they all had on hand?

As the sun began to go behind the peak above the pass, Widow Murphy said what the rest of them were afraid to voice: "We're going to starve!" Her face puckered, and she began to cry. Her son and his wife tried to comfort the old lady.

"We best call a meeting," said Stanton. Silently the emigrants gathered in a ring around him. "Folks, we are going to have to figure out some other way to get along until they come for us. I think the best way is to put all our food together. . . ."

"No." One man stepped forward. "Some of you didn't butcher when you had the chance. I did. I got a large family. Now I'm a good Christian man, but I'll not be feeding others and taking it out of my own babes' mouths."

George Donner lay below, too sick to help in the search for the cattle. Tamsen grasped Molly's hand. "I do not believe our food will quite be enough, Mr. Stanton. I believe we shall need help."

Molly looked to the pass beyond the lake. Its glistening slope hung between two majestic peaks that soared thousands of feet above the pass itself. She met Stanton's gaze squarely.

"Some of us will have a go at the pass again," Stanton said. "The snow will form a crust in a day or two. You'll have to make up your own minds if you want to go." He paused before adding, "With food running out, it'll be just as bad staying as going."

"We'll stay," said the farmer who had butchered all his beef.

The rest of them looked at each other with scared expressions in their eyes. No one could look at the children.

40

Across the foothills of the Sierras, the November wind rattled the dry leaves of the walnuts and elms. Down in the arroyos, the luster had faded from the scarlet and ocher leaves of the oak bushes, deceptively beautiful and still poisonous. Scattered among the poison oak, waist-high patches of dying ferns struggled for life among green black clumps of berry brambles.

Che-Muc-Tah pulled his sheepskin coat closer about his neck and knelt over the saddle. A bad winter coming. Already the deer herds were grazing at lower elevations. The Chumash would be moving soon, too.

Che-Muc-Tah frowned as he considered this. It had been on his mind for several months to leave the Chumash. In Monterey he had learned that what Salvador said was true. But Salvador had gleaned only a few leaves of the truth. Micheltorena was gone, the cholos were gone. But so was the Mexican governor who had replaced Micheltorena. California was in the throes of an almost bloodless civil war.

The Chumash, the Luisenos, and the other California tribes went about their lives as if these things were not happening. They hunted, gathered, married, bore children, and generally lived peaceable lives, caring little what happened even to other tribes. In the years when the relentless Catholic priests had conceived it their duty to imprison the guileless Indians at the missions, a few strong tribal leaders had risen and struggled to understand what was happening and how to stop it. These leaders were hunted down.

In his youth, Che-Muc-Tah's mother had tried to teach him what his father had died trying to achieve. Unity of the tribes. An equal voice in the nation overtaking the land. He had failed. Leader of thousands of the fiercest warriors ever known, Tecumseh the Shawnee had failed.

What had Che-Muc-Tah accomplished? Leaving his American name behind with that part of his heritage, Che-Muc-Tah had sought to make himself part of the great Indian race whose nations were scattered so sparsely across the land. His brothers wanted no more and no less than what his father's people had wanted.

But it was too simple. White men did not understand simplicity. Matters must be complicated. Agreements must be talked to death and committed to paper in order to be violated. An endless cycle, like the seasons. The Luisenos had taught him to never fight for the land, the land belongs to God. Fight for revenge. But the Mexicans and the Americans fought for the land. The Americans would win, he knew. Frémont had known it, too, years earlier, when Daniel was learning to reason for himself the impossibility of owning land.

Where then for himself and Lark and little Hannah Grasshopper? After he had seen and heard all that he needed to know in Monterey, he had ridden far down into the narrow valley settled by the whites. He had passed two missions that had been abandoned, their priests dead or gone away. Venturing into one chapel, he had felt a surprising pang of sadness to find its walls and altar stripped, the furniture gone or broken. Indians still lived in some of the tule shacks and tended the gardens. "Everyone left," one old Indian had told him. Then, singly or in families, many had come back. They were farmers. They understood the land, but not the white foreigners or their tongues or customs. They came back to what they knew.

The Chumash would go on living as they had for thousands of years. They would not want him to try to change that. It was time to move on. Che-Muc-Tah though of Lark and Hannah Grasshopper, snug and warm in their hogan two hours away. He smiled. What would Lark say when he told her that, in the spring, he was taking her to visit his people?

41

The U-shaped wooden bows that had once yoked oxen were carefully sawed through lengthwise and soaked until they were pliant enough to pull into a snowshoe shape. Strips of hide were laced over the frames. While fifteen pairs of snowshoes were being fashioned, all the pet dogs were slaughtered and their stringy meat hung over fires and smoked.

As each pair of shoes was finished, "Try them out," said Stanton. "Get used to them."

Everyone except the Indians wanted a turn on the clumsy shoes. Off they would clump, churning the snow in showers, puffing and collapsing with laughter on the powder pack.

Early the next morning, a band of seventeen gathered in the clearing, eleven men and six women. Stanton's red mackinaw stood out in their midst. Around them stood those who were staying behind. Salvador and the other guide were coming with Stanton but had refused snowshoes. Each person carried a blanket, a knife, all the clothing he or she could wear, and food for six days, consisting of a little coffee and loaf sugar and strips of jerked meat about three inches long and two fingers wide, three for each day.

"Six days should do it," said Stanton between draws on his pipe. "In summer a man on horseback can make it from here to Bear Valley in a day."

"About thirty miles, you said?"

"About that. Bear Valley is quite a bit lower. Mightn't be any snow there at all. From that point on we should have no trouble finding game, and by another week we should reach Sutter's Fort."

Molly was in tears as she gazed at the Donners. She could not shake the feeling that she would never see them again. They had said their good-byes in the cabin. George stood unsteadily at Tamsen's side. His arm was wrapped close to his body. His eyes were bright with fever. Coming just to her husband's shoulder, Tamsen stood straight and unafraid at his side. One arm was around Elitha's shoulder.

Stumbling in the awkward snowshoes, Molly went back to embrace her once more. "I love you. We'll find help. We'll bring them back for you."

"I have complete faith in God," Tamsen answered. "Spring will be here soon, and George will be well again."

"Let's be off!" called Stanton. He turned his back on the settlement and motioned Salvador and the other guide to go ahead.

Molly fell in behind Stanton and the others behind her. She was surprised to realize that the Widow Murphy, with her son and his wife, had joined the party. They reached the northwest side of the lake and started the first steep climb. Molly bent forward and grasped her thighs with both hands to help hoist herself up the trail. Her skirts kept snagging in the snowshoes.

"Do you really believe we can make five miles a day in these contraptions?" she called with a laugh.

When Stanton called a brief rest halt, she was surprised to see the Widow Murphy reaching into her food sack. "Better not eat anything until Mr. Stanton tells us to," Molly said lightly.

The widow glared at her. "I'll eat what I want."

As the sun rose higher, the glare on the snowpack became blinding. Hour after hour they toiled, with only a short lunch break and rest stops. Still the summit loomed above them. Molly was so tired her muscles were screaming. Behind her she could see Mr. Murphy helping his mother. *She is going to slow us down,* she thought and then immediately felt guilty at such a disloyal thought.

At last Stanton called the final halt.

Molly blew out a weary breath and contemplated the pass. She pointed at it with an arm made of lead. "We can't stop yet, Mr. Stanton."

"That's all right, girl. We made five miles. We did well."

She looked back. Truckee Lake looked no bigger than a rosy copper penny. They gathered firewood and soon had a cheery blaze going on the snow. Beds of pine branches kept the melting snow from penetrating their clothing and blankets. There was a good feeling of accomplishment as the travelers settled in a circle, their feet toward the fire. Unhurriedly they ate their tiny rations of jerky and sugar, chewing it long and well, unspeaking. Afterward they sipped their coffee.

As Molly settled in her blankets, she fixed her mind on Jared and on their coming baby. Then she said her prayers. One by one she called the members of her family into mind, thinking of her mother, Hannah, her sister, Alissa. Alissa and Stephen would be married. She was so happy that she and Jared were married. . . . And she slept.

They had been underway for only an hour the next day when Stanton's voice rang out, "We're at the summit, folks!"

"The summit! The summit!" the cry rang back along the trail.

Molly forgot her hunger and her aching legs as she saw for the first time the blue green forests of California, trees iced with plump layers of snow against the purest blue sky. The mountains seemed different on the western side of the summit, spreading out more broadly and becoming less steep. She looked back. Black shadows of the pines and ridges behind them shot forward in the early sunlight, pointing the way downhill.

Families embraced each other. "We'll make it!" cried tear-ragged voices. Prairies and mountains and deserts, dust and heat and snow, hunger and thirst and lost stock, and months and months, and now—California!

"It feels different!" said Molly. "I could run the rest of the way."

Stanton grinned back at her. "In that case, let's go!"

The third morning Molly woke up to realize she was thinking about the jerky and sugar in her pack. She raised on one elbow. Everyone else was asleep. No one would see if she nibbled a bit of today's ration early. *Molly*, she chided herself. She scrambled out of her blankets, only to be hit by a wave of dizziness. She stood still, and it passed.

The Indians were both standing across the clearing under some pines. She had noticed that they never helped build fires or cut boughs. They never seemed to be tired or cold or even hungry. They didn't act human!

That day the Widow Murphy began to complain. "I don't feel so good," her voice quavered as they plodded single file behind Stanton.

Molly glanced back. The old lady's face was white and glistening with perspiration. Her son dropped back to help her.

At the rest stop, Molly noticed Stanton squeezing his fingers against his eyes. She walked over to his log.

"Molly?"

"Yes. Is something the matter?"

"Tired, girl. And I can't see. Too much staring at the snow. I'll have to stop for a while."

Molly's stomach mushroomed in fear. "I'll wait with you."

"No. It won't do for any of us to stop. You go with the Indians. Salvador speaks English."

"He does!"

"He doesn't cotton much to whites. Couple years ago some dratted hothead shot up his camp and killed some of his friends. Stay close to Salvador. I think he's the best judge of the route to follow. He'll be more certain as soon as we get out of the snow. Go now. I'll catch up."

"Oh, Mr. Stanton!"

His tearing eyes lifted bleakly to her face.

That night, the emigrants had eaten and the fire burned to coals before Stanton straggled in. He was his usual cheery self.

The next day, Stanton lagged behind soon after they started. Molly had a terrible feeling that the Indians were unsure of the direction they should take. Rather than wreck the tenuous confidence of the rest of the party, she put aside these feelings and behaved as though she had perfect trust in their guides.

The morning of the sixth day Stanton sat smoking his pipe, a cup of coffee crooked in his fingers. The rest of the party was ready to start. Molly trudged over to him.

"Are you ready, Mr. Stanton?"

"Yes, I am coming soon. Good-bye, Molly."

Tears blurred her vision as Molly turned away to follow Salvador and his companion. She looked back once. Stanton was sitting on his blanket, arms resting on drawn up legs, staring ahead. It was the last she ever saw of him.

Almost immediately the snowshoe party ran into trouble. Without Stanton, the Indians themselves appeared frightened. Stanton had told them they would be in Bear Valley by nightfall. Nightfall was fast approaching, and still it was only pines, rocks, snow, and more snow.

"Salvador!" Molly said in a voice sharpened by fear.

The Indian turned. His dark eyes were carefully blank.

"Is this Bear Valley?"

"Not Bear Valley."

"Tomorrow?"

"Maybe."

"He speaks English!" said an astonished farmer. "If this ain't Bear Valley, where in tarnation are we?"

"Stanton had no business dropping out!" said Murphy. "Our eyes are sore, too. I don't believe he went blind. He probably had some extra food and was going to go back as soon as we were out of the way. It's murder, that's what it is, leading us up here to die!"

"Nobody begged you to come," said another.

Murphy's mother began to whimper.

"What are we going to do now?" said Murphy. He turned his pack upside down on his blanket and shook it. "No more food!"

"We'll hunt," said one of the other men. For an hour before night fell, several foraged nearby. Nothing, not even a jackrabbit.

Huddled in her blanket after eating the last of the jerky and sugar, Molly tried not to think ahead. She had pictured in her mind that once over the summit, the way would be downhill. Instead it was like all the other mountains they had crossed, only worse. Each slope they hiked down gave way to another slope rising. Sometimes the rises were so dangerously steep the exhausted party circled for miles before finding a way through.

On the seventh morning everyone lingered in camp longer than usual, their faces etched with dread. They were out of food. It was beginning to snow. They scanned the trail, watching for a familiar red-jacketed figure. If Stanton would only come!

Finally they set out. Heavy, dark clouds hid the sun. It seemed to be getting colder. Molly lost all sense of direction as they plodded through snow-clogged twists and cutbacks. Suddenly the storm broke. They struggled forward until midday. Cold and hungry, white and Indian huddled together under massed blankets.

"I wish Mr. Stanton would come," ventured the younger Mrs. Murphy.

The storm raged over their heads for two days. Molly ate snow and dreamed of food and slept as if she were drugged.

During the next two days they struggled onward. Ravenous with hunger, they gnawed the leather on their snowshoes. That night one of the younger men said, "We got to face it. Without food we'll all die. I think we should draw lots. Whoever loses. . . ."

Molly waited, dreading the man's next words.

"Whoever loses, we kill quick. Food."

She gasped with horror. "Never! I'd sooner die."

The young man gazed at her. A slow smile spread on his face.

"I'll not have the blood of another on my hands," stated an old farmer.

The next morning, Molly read her own fear in the uneasy glances of her companions. Weak and ill though she felt, she dared not stumble or fall asleep. . . . Salvador and his friend were chewing pine needles. Molly picked some. She put the softer ends in her mouth and chewed. The acrid taste made her jaws ache. She ate snow and chewed the pine needles. One step following another. Was it morning, or was it evening? How long had they been walking? Someone called a halt.

Another day. She could sense the lightening of day without opening her eyes. She could stay in her blankets. She could sleep. Yes. Sleep. Molly stroked her abdomen. Suddenly her eyes snapped open. Life. She had felt the baby move. Tears burned her eyes. Praise God, a new life. O God, God, she must live! She must find a way!

"Mother?"

Molly looked around. Murphy was trying to arouse his mother.

"Mother?"

"She's dead," said the younger Mrs. Murphy. She burst into tears.

Molly struggled to her feet. One by one she shook the others awake. "The Widow Murphy has died," she said. "The Widow Murphy has died." Glances met hers. Knowledge. Understanding.

She trudged weakly over to the grieving couple. "Your mother's spirit is with God. Her shell is like all things on earth; it is born and it dies and becomes one with the earth again. Come. Come away. We will pray together." Molly threw a glance over her shoulder and shuddered.

She led them out of sight of the camp.

42

For three days they remained in this camp of death. Two others had also perished. The meat was stripped and roasted and packed in their rucksacks. The fourth morning the storm fled, leaving a shining world, as if to reassure them that God's grace was still with them. It was time to go on. Molly laced her snowshoes over her ragged boots and painfully hauled herself to her feet. Her feet were swollen. She winced with pain as she walked.

The days jumbled together as they struggled across broken, untamed mountains, up sheer rock faces, down snowy slopes, across meadows deep in slush.

One afternoon a week later their packs were again empty. They squatted around their fire like Stone Age creatures. The young man who had first suggested eating human flesh had been behaving strangely all morning, his glance flicking from one to another. At last he sidled up to Molly.

"We are out of meat. If you get me a gun, I'll get us meat."

"How?" asked Molly.

The man jerked his head toward the Indians. "Them. They ain't but half human anyway. Notice how they ain't had nothing to do with us since—since you know when. If they didn't eat like the rest of us, what they been living on?"

Molly stared at him as he crabbed off to whisper to someone else. Painfully she got to her feet and hobbled over to the Indians.

"Salvador," she croaked.

He stared at her.

"Go away. Both of you. Run for your lives. Try to find Captain Sutter's. Tell them. . . . Tell them."

Salvador stood perfectly still as if he could not comprehend. Finally his head swiveled in the direction of the young man.

"Go, and God bless you. Thank you . . . for trying. . . ."

Salvador's glance returned to her. "You come."

For a moment Molly was tempted. Something bound her to the fate of the others. She shook her head. "Good-bye."

"Pretty red hair. Good-bye, too."

"Cooper!" Alissa could not believe her eyes as Larkin's servant admitted the army officer. "How did you find me?"

Cooper was wearing a khaki uniform, much creased and stained, and over this a sheepskin coat. "Didn't you send a message to the army headquarters here?"

"Yes, last week, but—"

He smiled. "We mopped up everythng down south pretty speedily. A few detachments are still there; Colonel Frémont wanted to be in Monterey, where the action was."

"There is no action here."

"Political, not war."

"Oh. When did you arrive?"

Cooper squinted at the pale winter sun outside the window. "I'd say an hour ago." He continued to drink her in. At last he shook his head and chuckled. "I never in all my born days had so much trouble concentrating on business."

Alissa burst into laughter. "Me, too."

A sudden shyness enveloped them both.

"Don't you want to ask me about Daniel?" he said.

"Yes, but that may have to wait."

"No foolin'!"

"My parents arrived just after you left, and my sister Molly is on a wagon train that should have been here long ago. They were camped on the east side of the Sierras three months ago."

"Maybe they decided to winter there."

She shook her head. "They sent ahead to Sutter's Fort for provisions and haven't been heard from again."

Cooper's bluff expression sobered. "Not good. Let me think on that."

"What did you find out about my brother?"

"The Luisenos say he left them three years ago to come and live with a northern tribe of Chumash about seven days away."

Alissa gave a cry of dismay. "That could be anywhere."

"Yes, but it isn't. We got the tribes pretty well mapped. There's a big Chumash camp somewhere to the south of Sacramento, not a day's ride. Add to that it's in the foothills, and it shouldn't be too hard to find. I was thinking I could get leave to take some of the men and ride up there."

"Come with me to find Molly first."

Cooper looked surprised. Slowly he said, "All right." Then he added, "Why don't you stay here? Winter's mean as all get out in those hills."

She shook her head. "I can ride as well as anybody. I've the constitution of an ox."

Baylor Cooper grinned. "If you pardon my saying so, ma'am, it don't show." He opened his big hands. "Come here."

The Chumash camp lay under a light blanket of snow. Smoke curled from the hogans. Outside several of them were strings of fish smoking over slow fires. Cylindrical granaries about as thick as a man's body, made of tightly woven grasses, stood on legs a foot off the ground.

Into the camp staggered two men, crying weakly for help. The hogans emptied as men and women rushed outside. Che-Muc-Tah reached them first.

"Salvador! What happened? Sutter throw you in prison to starve?"

Salvador was too weak to answer. He fell into Che-Muc-Tah's arms. Quickly he carried the man into his hogan. Lark began to heat a gruel of venison and buckwheat.

Salvador wept. "Can't go back, don't take me back, he will kill me."

Che-Muc-Tah squatted anxiously by his side while Lark fed him. Perhaps this Sutter would have to be dealt with after all. What right did he have to treat a man like this? "What happened?" he repeated.

Salvador shook his head. He closed his eyes. "He will kill me," he said clearly. "I lost his mules. You must protect me."

"What mules?" said Lark.

Little by little, the story came out. Salvador was so overwhelmed by the thought of facing Sutter with news of his lost mules that he could not concentrate on telling his tale coherently. Only as they pieced it together did they comprehend its full horror.

"Salvador—Salvador, did you say they are eating each other?—*Americans?*" insisted Che-Muc-Tah.

"Yes! Yes!"

Lark and Che-Muc-Tah exchanged shocked glances.

"The red-haired girl saved me. 'Run,' she said. 'Run.' They were going to kill us next. . . . We have been running for five days. . . ."

Che-Muc-Tah stared at the exhausted man. His flesh had wasted to a ghastly gray. His collarbones protruded like two knobbed sticks. He tried to imagine what had happened. Sutter had sent Salvador with provisions. What kinds of fools were these Americans, to try to cross the Sierras in midwinter?

Leaving Salvador in Lark's hands, he ducked out of the hogan to explain to the waiting circle of men and women what had happened.

"How can you talk of saving them?" his lieutenant demanded. "This is an unspeakable crime. They must be possessed of the devil. I would not go a step to save one of them."

One after another, his Luisenos and the Chumash nodded their heads in agreement. The doomed must be left to their fates. He could see it in their eyes.

"I must go."

"You are only half Indian," said his lieutenant.

If his brethren would not help, he had no choice but to go to this Sutter himself and persuade him to lend men, animals, and more food. Even then, much of the Sierras would remain impassable for another three months. He could only pray that those trapped by hunger were within reach.

43

"All I'm asking is two pack animals and two horses," Jared pleaded. "They're a month overdue. Something's wrong."

Jared had climbed into the guard tower at the southwest corner of the fort wall determined to confront Sutter and wrest what he wanted. Lately Sutter had been spending hours each day in his tower.

"Nothing's wrong," Sutter retorted. "And don't you try anything, like you did before." His blue eyes glinted coldly.

As soon as he had gotten back his strength from the fever, Jared had tried to get Sutter to form up a second relief party. Sutter had refused. Jared had stolen a horse and headed out, only to have the horse spooked by a grizzly. His fall had broken a couple ribs and laid him up for another two weeks.

"They got plenty of provision, even if they are snowed in. Trappers winter in the Sierras from fall till spring."

"They ain't trappers, Sutter. It's women and children."

"You don't send good money after bad," Sutter's voice rose, as if that ended it. "You want horses, fine. Show me your money first." He turned his back on Jared and continued to gaze out the small, high opening in the tower window.

"Men come traipsing through here, back and forth, expecting goods on the cuff because they used up everything getting out here," he said over his shoulder. "I am not a government agency—or a charity ward either."

"What do you keep coming up here for? You expecting an Indian attack?" Jared sneered.

"I'm expecting the war to end! And I don't intend my property to become spoils for the victor."

Jared gave a snort of frustration and hitched his thumbs into his belt. He stared out the tower window.

Sutter glanced at him. He still looked like a good gust would blow him over. How could a youth from frontier America understand the scope of Sutter's ambition? His plan required him to be a good friend of everybody who could matter. Mexican generals in uniforms dripping with braid and brass paraded through with mistresses and trains of toadies, to be entertained at the lavish table of their good friend Captain Sutter. Hard-pressed Americans rode out, short on gaudiness but long on gall, expecting to wheedle unilateral promises of support. British diplomats in well-cut suits, French trappers, mission padres. He entertained them all. And helped wagon trains when he could. But not unreasonably.

"You have company," said Jared. "Eight men. They look like American army. And pack mules."

Sutter followed his glance. "Good. I hope it is with news that the war is over." The men headed out of the tower.

As soon as the company was within the gates, Jared realized his mistake. One of the men was a woman dressed like a man. With a shock of surprise he realized he knew her.

"Alissa!"

"Jared!" She was off the horse and embracing her new brother-in-law. "I was so happy to hear about your marriage. Our parents are in Monterey. That's how we knew about you. Is Molly here yet?"

"No. They—"

"Miss Alissa MacGowan! The last time I saw you, you had on the most enchanting ball gown."

"Good afternoon, Captain Sutter. I have heard so much about New Helvetia."

"I shall be honored to give you a tour." Sutter turned his attention to the big blond officer at her side.

"Jared, Captain Sutter, may I present Captain Baylor C. Cooper."

Baylor threw a brief salute and shook hands with both men.

"Welcome, sir. I hope you are bringing good news about the war."

"It is all but over, sir. The Americans are victorious."

"Splendid. That is worthy of a celebration."

Baylor threw up a hand. "Not now, sir. We've come about a wagon party that's overdue."

"Long overdue," said Jared passionately.

"They are merely snugged in for the winter," Sutter said lightly.

"You are probably right," agreed Baylor Cooper. "But we are going up as far as we can and try to find them and bring them down."

"You have a horse for me?" asked Jared.

"I'll lend you a horse, my boy," said Sutter bluffly. Jared glared at him.

"Good," said Alissa. "Captain, may we impose upon your hospitality until morning?"

"Indeed you may, dear lady."

An hour later Che-Muc-Tah rode through the gates.

Sutter and his guests were at dinner. The candlelit table was laden with roast fowl, smoked beef and pork, and a succulent baked salmon, as well as dishes of boiled cabbage and potatoes. Sutter had ordered a modest wine brought out, reasoning that his guests, could probably not distinguish the difference.

"Sir, there is an Indian called Che-Muc-Tah who wishes to see you." Sutter reared to his feet. "Che-Muc-Tah. Really! Is he out back?"

"No sir. He refuses to dismount until you come to the door."

"Maybe he has news of the wagon train," said Jared, rising. Sutter headed for the door. The others followed, Alissa half running through Sutter's living quarters to the wood verandah.

There, tall and immensely dignified, was a man who looked Indian in dress and hair, whose face looked—looked— Her heart began to beat wildly, and tears sprang into her eyes.

"What is it?" said Baylor Cooper, slipping a supportive arm around her. "D-Daniel?"

The Indian stared down at her. He slid silently off the horse and trod up the steps. He searched her face. "Alissa. My sister."

"Oh, Daniel!" At once she was sobbing and clinging to him. "Praise God!"

The others stood back in embarrassment, as if the tenderness of their reunion deserved privacy.

Then Baylor Cooper came forward to clasp Daniel's hand. "Che-Muc-Tah, eh?" He grinned. "Good to see you."

"Che-Muc-Tah." Sutter began to swear softly. "I'll be a cross-eyed jackass."

Alissa reached out to Jared. "Daniel, this man is our Molly's husband. Jared McC—"

"*Red hair!*" The change on Daniel's face was frightening. "My God! Is Molly in the Sierras?"

"Yes," said Jared. "We're going after them tomorrow. Why are you here? Did you know?"

Daniel's gray eyes swept over the assemblage, fastening on Sutter. "You're Sutter."

"Yes."

"Your man Salvador stumbled into my camp this morning. The wagon party has lost their way and all their food. They are—"

"My mules, too?"

"Yes."

"They are starving, aren't they?" cried Alissa.

"Yes!"

Before dawn a party welded by a sense of urgency left Sutter's Fort. Daniel had overridden Sutter's protests by insisting on more mules and more provisions to add to the stores Cooper had collected. Salvador had tried to recall landmarks for Daniel before he left the Chumash camp.

The trail from Sutter's Fort back into the Sierras was well-worn as far as the snow level, which they reached the second day. From this point riders fanned out by pairs, seeking any sign of a trail. They were hampered by the knowledge that repeated snowstorms would have banished earlier tracks. Following Salvador's fevered recollections, Daniel guided the party toward Bear Valley. Luck was with them. The weather, though cold, remained fair. The horses and mules were able to pick a fairly good track.

The fourth day they came upon the charred remains of a campfire. They dismounted and scoured the compacted snow on foot. Jared discovered a trail leading away from it. As the others crowded in to examine the trail, Daniel hung back. He reached into the fire and picked up a long bone.

Baylor Cooper appeared at his side. "What is it?"

Daniel couldn't answer. The men's glances met.

"Great heaven preserve us!" hissed Baylor in a shocked voice.

The trail led down toward Bear Valley. It was erratic, as though those forging the trail were lost or out of their heads or both. With each step, Daniel felt a mounting sense of dread.

As the afternoon waned, the sun shone into their eyes like a remorseless orange ball. Twice when the snow grew patchy the party had had to fan out and find the trail again. Jared was in the lead when he called out, "I see something!"

Unaccountably the pace slowed as though no one was willing to face the final horror of their imaginings.

Nine bundles. No fire. No sign of life. Alissa began to pray with all her might. If they were dead, she hoped Molly was not among them.

Silently they dismounted. Alissa's courage gave way as Jared, Baylor, Daniel, and the others advanced on the blanketed forms. Alissa saw a skeletal hand flutter in the air. "This one's alive!" cried a man's glad voice.

"And this one, barely. She's a woman, got red hair."

"*Molly!*" Three people rushed to the pitiful bundle. The girl opened unseeing blue eyes.

Hardened men began to cry as they lifted the wasted bodies onto swiftly made up pallets and got a fire going. Within minutes the seven survivors of the snowshoe party felt the blessed relief of food nourishing their bodies.

Hours later, Daniel, Alissa, and Jared drew together as if compelled to honor the sun as it set over the faraway coastline. They heard a small sound.

Molly was awake. She was watching them. Jared and Alissa crunched through the snow to kneel beside her. Alissa took her sister's hand. Molly's huge blue eyes filled with tears as she stared at her sister. Her gaze shifted to Jared. Her lips moved.

Jared bent to hear. Tears coursed down his cheeks. "We're going to have a baby," he croaked. He glanced up at Daniel, bringing him into the circle.

"All my life," he said huskily, "I heard my folks and the aunts and uncles tell about Hannah Roebuck, and how she married her Indian chief. About you,

Daniel, and Tecumseh. All the stories, how she was captured for a time, how she was the first white woman to ship down the Ohio to the Mississippi and clear to New Orleans."

His gaze went from Molly to Alissa. He nodded his head. "My God, Hannah's going to be so proud of her daughters."

44

It was a rare afternoon in April in San Francisco. The fogs had vanished, driven out by a balmy breeze that reminded Alissa of San Juan Capistrano. Baylor lay with his head in her lap, his eyes closed, under an apple tree. She leaned over her husband and dangled a honey-colored lock of her hair over the end of his nose.

Baylor twitched and smiled and reached up for her. Their kiss was long and satisfying.

"Where's my apples?" called a laughing voice from the house. "We want to be ready!"

Alissa broke the embrace. "Coming, Molly!"

Baylor rolled off her lap and picked up the rush basket of small, hard apples. They strolled through the long grass toward the house.

"It's a pretty house, isn't it?" said Alissa. It belonged to a wealthy Mexican family who had leased it to the MacGowans for a year and gone back to Mexico City.

"Not as pretty as ours is going to be," answered Baylor. The Coopers and the McClouds had staked out a tract of land less than an hour's ride from the city. Baylor had spent the day felling and hauling timber for the house he and Alissa would soon be sharing.

Alissa hugged his arm and laid her head against his hard muscles.

Molly was waiting for them at the top of the steps. A huge white apron covered her front. Under the cloud of red hair, her face was beautiful and clear with the glow of impending motherhood.

"Is Jared back yet?"

Molly shook her head. "But he promised they'd be here in time." Jared had gone with his in-laws to investigate a hillside property that could become a church. A small but sound structure was already on the property.

"I think Pa made the right decision," said Alissa. "I'm glad Mother talked him into staying." Alissa went ahead into the kitchen, picked up a paring knife, and began to peel apples.

Baylor found a chair and tilted it against the wall, watching the sisters.

Molly giggled. "Pa just wanted to be talked into it, Alissa. He didn't want to go back to Saint Louis if all of us were going to be out here." A distant look came into Molly's eyes. She glanced at the mound of snowy dough on her kneading cloth. She sighed.

"What are you thinking, honey?"

"All this food. . . ."

Alissa and Baylor exchanged glances.

"Jared drove me to town this morning. We heard that they brought out some of our party from the camp by the lake."

"Were the Donners among them?" asked Baylor. Molly and Jared had recounted endless tales of their months crossing the continent.

Molly shook her bright head. "George is still too sick to travel, they said, and Tamsen would not leave him. They have plenty of food, this time. . . ."

They heard voices in the street, and soon the MacGowans and Jared came in.

Hannah kissed her daughters and Baylor. "Have they come yet?"

"Not yet, Ma," said Alissa.

"Hello, children," Micah boomed heartily, as Hannah unobtrusively pulled an apron from a drawer and bent to baste the ducks roasting in the huge oven.

"Do we have a church yet, sir?" Baylor asked.

"Not yet, but soon," predicted Micah. "Oh, and we have here some letters." He patted his pocket. "One from Stephen, something about his friends' rancho."

Alissa snatched the letter and retreated to a corner to read it. "Stephen isn't just representing the Bandini-Warners, he's representing a dozen families, Pa. Ramon is helping him. He's petitioning the United States government to honor their land grants. Do you think they will? Baylor, what do you think?"

"Dunno, honey. Out of my line of work."

"I'm proud of Stephen," decided Alissa. "He's smart, and Lord knows once he gets a bee in his bonnet he won't sit still. And Ramon, too. I used to think he never wanted to do anything but entertain himself." Alissa's eyes traveled demurely to Baylor.

"That is the kind of job that turns a boy into a man," Micah observed.

"I think I hear them!" cried Hannah.

Chairs scraped and potholders and platters were abandoned. The family streamed out the back door and rushed to the street.

Daniel, in buckskins, and Lark, in a garment trimmed with red fox, were dismounting in front of the stately house. Lark's raven hair spilled to her waist. Her eyes downcast, creating an aura of obedience, she unstrapped a cradleboard from the side of her horse.

An outreach of hands escorted them into the house. Proudly Daniel introduced his family. Lark met their glances shyly. Then she laid the cradleboard on the rug and knelt over it, unlacing it. With sure hands she plucked their child from her warm bed and stood up with a proud smile, displaying her baby in the crook of her arm.

Towering over his wife, Daniel placed one coppery arm around her and said formally, "Mother and Father, this is Hannah Grasshopper, your first grandchild."

"Oh-h." Hannah held out her arms to receive the child, her face radiant with love. "Dear Lord, my children—my children."

CHRISTIAN HERALD ASSOCIATION
AND ITS MINISTRIES

CHRISTIAN HERALD ASSOCIATION, founded in 1878, publishes The Christian Herald Magazine, one of the leading interdenominational religious monthlies in America. Through its wide circulation, it brings inspiring articles and the latest news of religious developments to many families. From the magazine's pages came the initiative for CHRISTIAN HERALD CHILDREN and THE BOWERY MISSION, two individually supported not-for-profit corporations.

CHRISTIAN HERALD CHILDREN, established in 1894, is the name for a unique and dynamic ministry to disadvantaged children, offering hope and opportunities which would not otherwise be available for reasons of poverty and neglect. The goal is to develop each child's potential and to demonstrate Christian compassion and understanding to children in need.

Mont Lawn is a permanent camp located in Bushkill, Pennsylvania. It is the focal point of a ministry which provides a healthful "vacation with a purpose" to children who without it would be confined to the streets of the city. Up to 1000 children between the age of 7 and 11 come to Mont Lawn each year.

Christian Herald Children maintains year-round contact with children by means of a *City Youth Ministry.* Central to its philosophy is the belief that only through sustained relationships and demonstrated concern can individual lives be truly enriched. Special emphasis is on individual guidance, spiritual and family counseling and tutoring. This follow-up ministry to inner-city children culminates for many in financial assistance toward higher education and career counseling.

THE BOWERY MISSION, located at 227 Bowery, New York City, has since 1879 been reaching out to the lost men on the Bowery, offering them what could be their last chance to rebuild their lives. Every man is fed, clothed and ministered to. Countless numbers have entered the 90-day residential rehabilitation program at the Bowery Mission. A concentrated ministry of counseling, medical care, nutrition therapy, Bible study and Gospel services awakens a man to spiritual renewal within himself.

These ministries are supported solely by the voluntary contributions of individuals and by legacies and bequests. Contributions are tax deductible. Checks should be made out either to CHRISTIAN HERALD CHILDREN or to THE BOWERY MISSION.

Administrative Office: 40 Overlook Drive, Chappaqua, New York 10514
Telephone: (914) 769-9000

F

Ross, Bette

Hannah's Daughters

McCoy Mem. Baptist Church
134 St. Clair Avenue
Elkhart, IN. 46516
Ph: (219) 294-1131